Energy Politics and Rural Development in Sub-Saharan Africa

Naaborle Sackeyfio

Energy Politics and Rural Development in Sub-Saharan Africa

The Case of Ghana

palgrave
macmillan

Naaborle Sackeyfio
Miami University
Oxford, Ohio, USA

ISBN 978-3-319-60121-2 ISBN 978-3-319-60122-9 (eBook)
https://doi.org/10.1007/978-3-319-60122-9

Library of Congress Control Number: 2017951591

Printed on acid-free paper

This Palgrave Macmillan imprint is published by Springer Nature
The registered company is Springer International Publishing AG
The registered company address is: Gewerbestrasse 11, 6330 Cham, Switzerland

To my mother, Rose Alice Sackeyfio

Acknowledgments

This book began with a quest to situate the puzzle of energy provision and is a culmination of efforts to reconcile an electricity quagmire with a remarkable rate of access in one of sub-Saharan Africa's most promising states. The notion of electricity delivery belies the ambiguity inherent in the notion of electricity access, which may be construed in multiple ways depending on locale, connectivity, proximity to a grid or substation, as well as the politics of interpretation. It is hoped that the book in some measure captures the social, economic (rural) and political dynamics of electricity delivery and access for what is a mere afterthought in the western hemisphere, but a battleground of electoral politics in the developing world. This book is made possible by the tremendous and unyielding support of many individuals, to whom I owe a lifetime of gratitude.

As one of my strongest advocates and reservoir of immeasurable support, "Lenny" (Irving Leonard) Markovitz was an advisor and mentor unlike any. The book is as much a culmination of his critiques of the dissertation as it is a careful reformulation of its most compelling ideas. Lenny's feedback produced a springboard of ideas and grueling edits of a book proposal that ultimately shaped this study, and I am deeply grateful. I would also like to thank Sherrie Baver, who has supported my research and offered encouragement when I needed it. I am deeply grateful to my dear friend, and confidante, Kwame Akonor, whose staunch support over the course of a decade and work as a scholar is extraordinary. My wonderful and brilliant friend, Adekeye Adebajo's knack for ingenuity is unrivaled and as a prolific scholar his work is a reminder of the challenges and necessity of a Pax Africana. I also want to thank my editor, Anca Pusca, who diligently worked on the manuscript, as well as Anne Schult for her editorial assistance.

I am grateful for the support of Ike Okonta, Lilit Petrosyan, Sophia Johnson-Tran, Laurel Harris, Sunny Jiten Singh, Grace Yali Zhang, Lauren Paremoer, John Jones, Ben Waruta, Brigitte Omane, Adenike Oke Adeyemi, Lonjezo Hamisi, Fredline McCormack, Jacky Kaba, Benjamin Goldfrank, Anne-Marie Murphy, Caroline Erb, Josephine Dawuni, Kimberly Corson, Patrick Cosby and Josephine Dawuni, Nii Nai Isaac Sackeyfio and Emmanuel Sackeyfio, Michael Orlando Sharpe, and Miho Hidaka-Sharpe.

Without the assistance of Asante Danquah, who is both a friend and a former reporter for TV One in Ghana, the interviews and connections made with pivotal players in Ghana's energy sector and research for this book would have been impossible. I am forever indebted to him for his thorough work and enthusiasm for a book of this kind to be written. In addition, I am grateful to the energy officials from the Energy Commission, Ministry of Energy and members of parliament who provided meaningful insights that framed the context for approaching Ghana's energy landscape. In addition, I wish to thank Bright Botwe and Gertrude Akuffo for their assistance with archival and newspaper articles, which were critical to the research conducted for this book.

I am forever indebted to my Mom, whose unparalleled strength, unwavering love and support matter in more ways than I can count. Single-parenthood and persistence ultimately produced a triumphant individual who remains an indelible source of inspiration. My sister, Naaborko Sackeyfio-Lenoch's perpetual support, love, generosity, positive spirit and kindness are a testament to her profound mark as one of the finest human beings I have encountered. I want to thank my husband, Tomoyuki Yabe, for his love, encouragement and optimism that I'd see this book through. His patience and ability to distract and entertain our daughter, Chiyo, on long days when I was not available greatly facilitated my writing and are thus greatly appreciated.

There are countless other friends and individuals—too many to name here—to whom, nonetheless, I offer utmost thanks for myriad ways in which they helped to bring this work to fruition. To anyone I may have inadvertently left out, your generosity, kindness, patience and support are greatly appreciated and go unforgotten.

June, 2017

Contents

List of Figures

List of Tables

CHAPTER 1

Introduction

The power of an electric bolt, circuit, and streetlight is undeniable and the myriad ways that electric currents have produced milestones in communication and connectivity are rife. The invention of the light bulb revolutionized societies and provided an impetus for economy in ways that far outpaced any expectations for modern life. The provision of electricity as a powerful fulcrum for industrialization in what are now advanced economies—the United States, Great Britain, and many more—is all the more remarkable because its impact is often overlooked. Electricity has promoted economic growth through invisible linkages that bind: without electricity power lines, lighting at home and in offices, transportation systems and even literacy as well as educational outcomes would be undermined. This functionality is also underscored by the impact of technological progress and innovation that is largely subsumed as one of thousands of nearly invisible inputs that make modern living seamless, accessible and complete. Electricity, for all its purposes, remains one of the most visible yet simultaneously invisible instruments of the twenty-first century. Across much of the developing world or the global south, however, the flick of a light switch is rarely performed with certainty. Access to an amenity largely taken for granted as one of thousands of micro-processes that construe modernity is ultimately a political one. Paradoxically, the race to combat energy poverty is faced by one of the most democratic and promising states in sub-Saharan and West Africa: Ghana—considered a model state

N. Sackeyfio, *Energy Politics and Rural Development in Sub-Saharan Africa*, https://doi.org/10.1007/978-3-319-60122-9_1

for much of the continent. As a country rich in hydropower, with its Akosombo dam and Volta River project, which ambitiously sought to produce aluminum, the promise of industrialization accompanied a competitive vision for a state whose economic growth once rivaled, but has been surpassed by, that of Malaysia. What accounts, then, for the simultaneous success of electrification initiatives in ten administrative regions (akin to states) and disparities between significant sections of the country's populace since this period?

Energy demand until the twenty-first century appears to have mattered little for much of Africa's 54 states. For comparison, electricity use for the United States is about 3340 megawatts (MW) per million inhabitants, and about 1680 MW in the European Union, while sub-Saharan Africa's generation capacity is only about 100 MW per million inhabitants as of 2009.[1] Roughly 85% of 585 million people in sub-Saharan Africa without access to electricity live in rural areas; this figure is expected to rise to some 652 million by 2030.[2] Electricity access across the continent, and in developing countries elsewhere, suffers from incongruent conceptualization of what constitutes access, because classifying a village as electrified or not is rarely straightforward. Combined with the reality of considerable variation in the intensity, concentration and levels of electricity use,[3] the choice and timing to electrify towns, communities and regions is political because governments remain the primary providers of electricity in the developing world.[4] How does political choice shape rural electrification and, ultimately, public service delivery challenges that include potable water, well-constructed roads and open sewage systems? Why are hydro-rich countries energy-poor? Uneven economic and political development after independence muted engagement between state and society. Rich in projected hydropower because of numerous dams, the continent pummeled through the latter half of the twentieth century unhindered by the need for the diversification of energy inputs required for a growing economy. The 1980s and 1990s were a test for the continent's growth amid economic malaise and political uncertainty. The story of the 1990s for many an African state was how to navigate, if not circumvent, market-oriented reforms required by external donors and international financial institutions in order to reverse the economic pitfalls and the subsequent debt the continent accrued at an unprecedented pace. It is perhaps and singularly unnoteworthy that attempts to swallow a bitter pill of austerity, which paradoxically entailed a reduced role for the state and, consequently, public expenditure, produced a gap in service delivery that required a more interventionist role. Using the lens of political economy, this book explains why energy provision has become a matter for public service delivery and, simultaneously, an important fulcrum for rural development—largely through electricity, which remains promising yet primarily uneven.

Why have African states—despite seemingly ample, if not abundant, hydropower—faltered in providing efficient, steady and affordable access to rural populations who are likely to supply important sources of future capital and growth? What are the pre-requisites for timely, effective provision, given steady population growth and heightened energy demand by domestic populations? As a model state for political and economic governance, this book recounts Ghana's experiments with energy provision through dam power. The choice to focus on the rural constituents, including the poor, stems from the simple observation that the rural poor make up a large part of Africa's populace and are thus difficult to ignore.[5] It explains why the country, notwithstanding uneven provision and generation capacity, offers a cautionary tale and yet one of the continent's best hopes for solving energy poverty. The book also explains why the political leadership in Ghana and, to a lesser extent, in Nigeria, South Africa and Zimbabwe, has circumvented market-oriented and, by extension, power (energy) sector reforms, with differing consequences for electric energy provision in each state. Utilizing the period beginning from the 1990s, a critical period owing to political transitions, fragile, if not nascent, democratic rule, pivotal shifts of power and turbulent politics, the book examines the dynamics of energy provision through the lens of hydropower, and attendant institutions through the primary focus of Ghana, while lesser treatment is given to a small number of sub-Saharan states. The larger question the book answers is how various African states have either navigated market-oriented reforms of "power" or energy sectors to provide domestic supply to key sections of society—the rural populace, where the bulk of Africa's population resides.

Firstly, this book argues that political survival, state–societal relations, and the uneven agency of civil society actors have conditioned responses to energy provision, supply and demand in Ghana and other states treated in succeeding chapters. Secondly, this book argues that governments have little choice but to circumvent market-oriented policies that, for decades, dictated how African governments manage and structure their economies, if they are to end energy poverty and supply electricity to all domestic consumers. In tandem, the laudable success of a current 80.51% electrification access rate has yielded *differential* benefits for the rural poor who comprise close to 60 percent of a population of 24 million.[6] Conversely, this work demonstrates how current electricity outcomes reflect *responsive government* and attentiveness to the rural poor, despite unevenness in provision. The contested nature of electricity delivery requires a shift in the Washington consensus regime that dictates questionable prescriptions, most notably privatization and a reduction of social expenditures that hardly treat the underlying malady still persistent despite promising economic outcomes from countries like Ghana. Consequently, the book contends that international financial actors and external donors should, ideally, incentivize energy provision for developing countries by treating electricity delivery as a public rather than private good and market transaction and thus diminish the politicization of electricity as a "have vs. have not" amenity. Developing a compliance framework within pre-existing poverty reduction strategies that tackle the who gets what, where, when and how—in other words, questions of power and political survival—can potentially enhance electric energy outcomes and stem the tide of energy poverty on a continent where almost 600 million out of a population of 1.1 billion lack energy access.[7] As the case of Ghana demonstrates, Ghana's jagged success compared with other African states emanates from its deliberately partial compliance with neo-liberal or market-driven outcomes in its energy sector. The significant political costs associated with market-driven policies that aimed to end the country's subsidy, or at least limit it, along with pro-poor tariffs designed to cushion vulnerable groups like the rural poor, were decidedly critical for electoral politics.

Case Selection and Study Design

The cases explored in this book focus primarily on Ghana, with a separate chapter/treatment that discusses in a broad overview the energy quandary facing Nigeria, South Africa and Zimbabwe. In many ways, the selection of Ghana as the focus of the book is fitting. Out of 54 states, Ghana became the first to gain its independence and the first to articulate development plans for fueling industrialization, which included the creation of the world's largest man-made lake in 1966. After the country's first president, Kwame Nkrumah, articulated ambitious, if not striking, plans for a united continent—in what amounted to a bold pan-African vision of self-sufficiency and economic independence, Ghana was propelled into the limelight. To be sure, plans to produce an aluminum smelting plant were conceived as a bid for modernity and infrastructural development.

However, as the case of Ghana demonstrates, many of these hopes were dashed as foreign industry benefitted from electricity generation while domestic consumers and ordinary Ghanaians enjoyed little to no access for several decades. Thus, the transformation of electricity access from 15% at the beginning of the 1990s to an overall access rate of 80.51% is significant. When weighed against dismal rates elsewhere on the continent, this development stands as a notable development. However, the expansion of access has not managed to reach the rural poor as we might expect. By highlighting the consequences of shifting hierarchies of power implicit in the simultaneous pursuit of political decentralization, democratization and neo-liberal institutional preferences, this work highlights the triumphs and limits of the Ghanaian state in terms of the ubiquitous paradigm and dictum that espouses "minimal government."[8] Optimal provision of electricity to all groups in society was one of several important objectives articulated since the early post-independent period and an explicit goal of succeeding governments in the post-1992 period, but the transformation of access and decentralized electricity initiatives has not resulted in more widespread access, especially for the rural poor. However, this work assumes the commitment of succeeding governments in the post-independent period to providing equitable access to electricity and fulfilling the electorate's demands for goods and services. A particularly salient issue studied in the chapter establishes how attempts to capture the rural poor paradoxically produced more responsive government, as electoral outcomes increasingly coalesced around service delivery of electricity and public goods provision. The analysis that follows deconstructs and recounts the key arguments addressed in this work. The causal relationship between domestic and international institutions can hardly be overlooked. In fact, it provides exogenous and endogenous explanations for the political phenomena observed in this work.

Chapter 2 discusses the theoretical arguments that underpin this work. It reveals that, despite the adoption of a decentralized institutional framework or devolved power when local "agency" material resources are insufficient, the inadequate financial capacity of the country's local government or district assembly system has enlarged the scope of central government authority. Subsequently, "fits and starts" of electricity initiatives aimed at reducing disparate outcomes for the marginalized rural poor are commonplace. New alignments between public, government and external actors or "trustees" of development, as the chapter establishes, have facilitated measures of co-optation through service delivery of electricity under political decentralization and democratization. Using decentralization as a subnational tool of analysis allows this work to frame public service delivery of electrification as a yardstick for successful devolution of institutional authority to district assemblies or authorities tasked with local economic and political development in Ghana. In other words, the treatment of service delivery is conceived as decentralization in motion or practice of political outcomes associated with the transfer of authority from the center (central government) to district assemblies. Ultimately, this work demonstrates how a weak district assembly system facilitated and became essential to the political capture of the rural poor by the "center". The book establishes how these developments emerged as a consequence of legitimacy and accountability challenges as a response to democratizing processes. As a member of parliament noted, "[p]eople are now demanding accountability in development: water, sanitation, electricity. They want their communities developed."

Chapter 3 deploys a historical–political lens to understand the divergence between a promising energy agenda that emerged after independence in 1957 and uneven outcomes in electricity provision for several decades, including the post-1992 period. The dichotomy in access, between projected and expected outcomes, informs the evolution of divergent energy values to their reconceptualization in the post-1992 era of political transition and regime change. The chapter examines the impetus for the pursuit of partial power sector reforms, and the subsequent lifeline tariff policy targeted at the *"rural"* poor in the early 1990s was a political calculus that aimed to avoid regime change. In an era of economic austerity and neo-liberal policies that dictated a smaller role for states in economies, the pursuit of partial, not full, reforms of energy sectors bucked conventional wisdom and practice that swept through both industrialized and developing states during the 1990s. The decision to pursue this was part of a larger phenomenon of the country's partial compliance with external conditionality agreements for economic relief,[9] but in a bid to limit the political fallout of structural adjustment policies of the 1980s, which strained state societal relations and proffered a wave of social movements that led to regime change in a number of developing states, Ghana opted for the former. These efforts paradoxically account for a success rate of 80.51% in the post-1992 period.[10] This contradiction is remarkable, given that comprehensive power sector reforms ostensibly aimed to provide wider market choices and even lower prices for domestic consumers. Instead, timing and sequenced reforms informed the political incentives of succeeding governments, which sought to capture the rural vote, including that of the poor. This development, as the chapter articulates, is a powerful explanatory variable for co-optation of a key electorate in the midst of political and economic upheaval precipitated, in part, by increasing debt burdens amid market-oriented reforms of the public sector. Hence, the pursuit of a lifeline electricity tariffs policy for the poor, and *partial* power sector reforms, are logical choices for a number of succeeding administrations bent on regime survival. The chapter also demonstrates the inherent difficulty in adopting full-scale market-oriented power sector reforms that involve deregulation, privatization, subsidy, and tariff removal for states engaged in decentralization and democratization processes.

Chapter 4 examines the relationship between the politics of rural development, central and local government capacity, and electricity provision under the umbrella of poverty reduction efforts. The chapter identifies a critical irony that documents the simultaneous pursuit of decentralization in the country's administrative regions akin to states, amidst recentralization and the subsequent usurping of domestic institutional autonomy by external actors as the actual trustees of governance. By establishing these developments, which oil the wheels of the country's political economy, the chapter demonstrates how a reduced scope of government authority, in lieu of market-oriented reforms and austerity policies advocated by the World Bank and donor partners, influenced the impetus for discretionary electricity provision—as attempts to capture the rural/peasant class. Along with a lack of ownership, the diminishing returns of domestic political autonomy combined to reinforce a project-by-project approach that yielded timed and sequenced efforts to connect rural communities to electricity grids and, in turn, access. The chapter locates these developments in the growing calls for "agency" by an increasingly discontented public that includes the rural poor, thus calling into question the nature of the state's future bargains with a key section of the electorate.

Chapter 5 details electricity provision across the country's ten administrative regions. It addresses patterns of differentiation that demonstrate the emergence of electricity provision as a politicized good in contrast to the private amenity that domestic consumers typically enjoy elsewhere in the industrialized world. The cumulative result of statistical analysis suggests that there are issues beyond demographic and economic characteristics of the regions that determine variations in electrification. Most significantly, the regions with the highest rates of electricity access between the 2000 and 2008 national elections also have had the highest numbers of swing voters, that is, voters with no particular affiliation to either of the country's two dominant political parties, the National Democratic Congress and National Patriotic Party. Although in subsequent elections remarkable progress has been shown in terms of access, with many regions exhibiting official rates well over the current rate of 80.51%. These percentages, as the chapter highlights, contribute to ongoing ambiguities associated with electricity provision. Electricity access has often meant the ability to be connected to a central grid in a local community and not actual delivery to one's home. With at least five regions slated for future assistance in the form of electricity projects to boost "access", this current state of affairs reflects the country's tenuous trajectory of public vs. private goods and service delivery debates, over which a number of administrations straddle uneasily.

Chapter 5 also contextualizes the scope of successful and yet uneven provision with the significant discovery that a "politics of interpretation" accounts for the dichotomy in perceptions of successful outcomes by the Ministry of Energy—a key institution of Ghana's central government. After mapping electoral outcomes since the first effective and successful transition to a democratically elected government, quantitative results unmistakably chronicle a striking pattern. That is, previously marginalized regions had become "swing regions" in exhibiting the highest levels of electricity access, with the Volta and Upper Western regions acting as the largest beneficiaries. Another surprising outcome is that the variables of class and ethnicity are considerably small, which the chapter attributes to the cross-cutting nature of this politicized good and attendant cleavages—evident in the cyclical, sequenced nature and, in short, the political business cycle that also reveals uneven access despite remarkable success overall.

Chapter 6 offers a comparative lens of electricity provision in Zimbabwe and South Africa. The chapter broadly examines ongoing challenges of power sector delivery, reform, and energy poverty in what should be hydro-rich states. In spite of power generating capacity and potentially lucrative regional power sector arrangements on the continent, market-oriented policies to expand electricity access continue to reflect mixed outcomes in the countries examined. Concurrently, efforts to provide regular access to electricity remain difficult to implement, owing to infrastructural as well as political challenges associated with transmission and generation capacity. Since energy continues to define modern economies and the capacity for growth, the consequences of lingering challenges associated in each of the countries are juxtaposed with the pursuit of power sector reforms in Ghana, a model state, for international financial institutions.[11] Additionally, the implicit tension between state-led and market-oriented policies accounts for the quagmire associated with hydropower and electricity access, particularly for rural populations.

Based on the partial implementation of power sector reforms, Chap. 7 deals with the nature of optimal service delivery outcomes defined as equitable, consistent and affordable electricity provision. The political costs to governments undergoing democratization are likely to be fraught with peril and thus likely to be offset by cost–benefit calculations timed to the political business cycle associated with elections. The conditions for optimal service delivery of electricity inform the chapter's inquiry and conclusion that favorable outcomes, conceptualized as equitable, consistent, efficient and affordable access, are notably difficult to achieve under a market-oriented, neo-liberal framework. Indeed, the pursuit of these policies in a world where energy poverty is both a symptom and the root of economic malaise in urban but primarily rural areas is inappropriate for states where the assumption of self-regulating and perfectly efficient markets is the exception rather than a norm. As a consequence, the continued propagation of a market-oriented paradigm that inevitably constrains the scope of agency of state actors in nascent democracies that lack strong property rights institutions, widespread indigenous entrepreneurs, capital, or functioning tax regimes combined with a large number of rural poor and essentially captive electorate is inapt. The political costs, then, for regimes that utilize the provision of targeted service delivery of public/political goods to offset the privatization of (hydro) power agreements are exponential.

The Quandary of Institutional Reform: Which Institutions Matter?

Institutions matter and the question of who gets what, where, when and how is implicit in this work. Asking why hydro-rich countries end up energy-poor is inevitably wound up with questions about the role of institutional design, and who stands to benefit, and at what cost.

When rules and norms become established patterns of behavior, they structure actor choices, future institutional outcomes and produce path dependence, as historical institutionalists observe. Douglas North, in *Institutions, Institutional Change And Economic Performance*, observed that path dependence is a way to conceptually narrow choices and link decision-making through time. J. Mokyr, in *The Gift of Athena: Historical*

Origins of the Knowledge Economy, finds that institutional structures produce different outcomes and certain distinct factors define the trajectories of national and local institutions. Indeed, this reasoning offers a plausible explanation for the puzzle of uneven development of Ghana's power sector institutions, and distribution of and access to electricity from the early post-independent period through the 1990s, given inadequate and suboptimal planning that began with the completion of the Akosombo Dam in 1966. With unstable political rule and numerous coup d'états that began in the 1960s, with the last occurring in 1981, it is little wonder that, by 1990, only 15% of the population had access to electricity. Consequently, the logic underlying this work is rooted in an inadvertent "lock in" of choices that informs shifting priorities under a political framework of decentralization, producing a dynamic of rural preference and group "capture" beyond a populist rhetoric.

The book also reveals how the institutional capture of district assemblies by central government and pressures for political legitimacy under a democratic transition proffered new preferences and a shifting dialectic about the nature of political access, incorporation and public goods. An ever-changing political landscape shaped by external financial actors and institutions required a renegotiation of state–society relations that could only be effectively managed through careful placation. In the wake of these developments, strategic timing in provision and inception of electricity projects became key to the success, despite "mixed" outcomes for the rural poor. In virtually every election period for the years 1992, 1996, 2000, 2004 and 2008, newspaper articles and stories featuring electrification projects demonstrate patterns consistent with a political business cycle and the discretionary nature of provision (see Appendix 1).

The persistence of divergent institutions is a logical calculus for a continent of varied political culture, norms and preferences. For a continent of remarkable diversity, a monolithic lens is the predominant frame through which Africa is seen. Replete with malaise, dysfunction and poor administration, an ongoing narrative of economic and political catastrophe, perhaps only narrowly averted, inform much of contemporary institutional analysis. From compelling perspectives that view the problems of African political systems as a function of "quasi states and problematic exercise of sovereignty," as Robert Jackson establishes in *Quasi States: Sovereignty, International Relations and the Third World*, to others that focus on the forces of the market, states and private action,[12] the contributions in this regard are noteworthy.

This book departs from perspectives that suggest a perpetual conundrum for a continent often discussed in large and sweeping terms despite tangible and deeply path-dependent problems. No other continent has experienced energy poverty as much as Africa. Yet the fits and starts of electricity provision in both the twentieth and twenty-first centuries are as much a reflection of the requisites of modern governance checkered by inadequate recognition of multifaceted linkages that inform purposeful design and the constituents they serve. By portraying the institutional malaise in a model state of democracy and energy provision, this work demonstrates the double-edged sword of liberalization and market-oriented reforms.

While attaining a happy medium remains in flux for many an illiberal state among promising democracies, Ghana's political achievements under decentralization are not to be understated. The participatory locus that has afforded many Ghanaians a voice and measure of "agency" in articulating economic interests and preferences is unmistakable. Its elections have been viewed widely as free and fair since 1992. But the view of past and current administrations, who depict district assemblies as key stakeholders in producing favorable economic outcomes—but ill equipped to tackle service delivery and rural development taken in tandem—are telling admissions as the country hurtles forward in its plans to improve its lower middle income developed country status. The significance of this work consequently lies in the revelation of electricity access as a largely microscopic element of development that informs governmental capacity and the success of responsive government in an era when service delivery of public goods is increasingly paramount.

Despite a mixed record of implementation and effectiveness in developing countries, particularly in sub-Saharan Africa, Ghana's adoption of political decentralization amid the important and difficult process of democratization offers important and overlooked insights, most important of which focus on how fragile societies undergoing a political transition may unwittingly undermine democratic institutional norms in the process of striking bargains with sections of society. Significantly, it reveals how democratic governance became coterminous with service delivery in the wake of measures to capture the rural vote among the poor. This work sheds light on the nature of "limited ownership" in rural development in the context of anti-poverty measures and public service delivery of electricity, which make a neo-liberal critique of market-oriented reforms of power sectors essential. Energy research has typically focused on the resource curse, an unfortunate consequence in countries where rich mineral resources like oil, diamonds, gas, copper, and gold produce economic stagnation and negative political outcomes such as authoritarian or non-democratic regimes. But the more pressing impact, particularly in developing countries, of the relationship between decentralization—thought to produce better outcomes in rural economy—and the problem of unregulated rural development under this institutional process has not been fully addressed in political economy perspectives.

One of the most serious problems the new government hoped to address in 1992 was the nation's aging electric energy system, gaps in provision and the startlingly low rate of access of 15% of rural areas in 1990. With Ghana initially geared to attain middle-income developed country status by 2020, the country's leaders acknowledged that investment in energy was required for economic growth and expansion.[13]

During the 1990s, vast gaps in electric energy provision, blackouts and frequent power outages led to the emergence of a national electrification scheme to restructure the country's energy policy. With substantial gaps in electricity access, protracted plans for a multisectoral strategy for rural development, and a higher ratio of rural poverty levels impelled a response by succeeding administrations. Indeed, the World Bank's figures placed poverty for rural populations at 39% and at 11% for urban populations, respectively. Since more than 60% of the population lives in rural areas (World Bank Report, "Proposed Fifth Poverty Reduction Support Credit", 2007), these figures support the notion of electricity as a key driver of economic growth and development, and the ability to power the country's industrial and commercial development (Guide to Electric Power, 2001).

Electric energy sector losses, mounting technical and operational problems and external donor pressure prompted Ghana to pursue neo-liberal power sector reforms. Yet Ghana's adoption of partial power sector reforms, to reduce sector losses and widen the field of independent power production to increase access, offers a stark irony. As this study demonstrates, it is ahead of many of its neighbors and the states examined at the end of the book because of the *partial* nature of reform, not necessarily because of the reforms themselves. By utilizing a lifeline tariff policy designed to provide access to the poor, the progress of the country's electrification schemes has more to do with rural co-optation and a political business cycle where electricity provision has become synonymous with public goods.[14]

It is only in the past decade that scholars have begun to examine specific policies, management of electricity sectors in developing African nations and the costs for the rural poor in particular.[15] For example, Stephen Karekezi, in *Renewables in Africa—meeting the energy needs of the poor*, addressed the mixed impact of power sector reforms for the poor, and questioned the pragmatism of the wholesale acceptance of power sector reform by African governments. In citing the oft-ignored issues of transmission and distribution, he argued that urgent attention be paid to both. Njeri Wamukonya, in *Power sector reform in developing countries: mismatched agendas*, argued that the reform model essentially reflected a contested process that led many governments to question the wisdom of undertaking reform.

Indeed, the tremendous loss of autonomy and virtual political suicide in pricing reform and removal of subsidies would likely produce discontent and a political backlash. As Wamukonya found, many policies left countries worse off socially and economically than before reform. A.B. Sebitosi and B. Pillay, in *Energy Services in sub-Saharan Africa: how conducive is the Environment?*, contend that a multifaceted confluence of factors contributed to substantial gaps in access to electricity for the poor and attribute the "subdued role of the-would be recipients" as part of the problem. Though most of the authors mentioned consider the impact of market-oriented power sector reforms on the rural poor, none contextualizes these changes under the realm of decentralization or democratization, which makes this work all the more critical, because it calls into the question the benefits of local representation within district assemblies, political empowerment, and access to public–private goods, that are assumed to be more readily available for marginalized groups under decentralization and a minimally interventionist state than democratization accords. This omission is notable, given that access to any resource, public or private, is unequivocally political. Sebitosi and Pillay also observed that, at community levels, infrastructure and amenities like electrification are often erroneously treated as commodities. In this regard, electrification becomes an end rather than a means. In African politics, it doubles as the proverbial carrots and sticks in political parties that reward like-minded or politically aligned communities and conversely offer denials to those perceived as indifferent or, worse yet, hostile to the party's patronage.[16] Furthermore, a United States Agency and International Development report found, in 2010, in a comparative assessment of decentralized institutions, that electricity offers a politically attractive strategy for central governments that struggle with poor service provision, lack resources and are keen to hold on to the levers of power in terms of allocations or distributional systems of monetary transfers.

Democratization, Decentralization, and Public Goods

This work emerges out of the nexus between the critical processes of democratization, decentralization and neo-liberal power sector policies posed in juxtaposition to public service delivery, the energy industry and minimal state involvement that intersected to produce important consequences as the country embarked on ambitious plans to achieve middle-income developed status in the twenty-first century. Democratization involves political empowerment at the local level, limited government, and competitive elections. In short, it refers to the institutionalization of political power exercised directly or indirectly through participation, competition and liberty as critical components required to establish the foothold of democracy.[17] Because Ghana moved to end repressive dictatorship and usher in representative government at the end of the 1980s and into the 1990s, I discuss how a changing political and economic landscape created formidable challenges for J.J. Rawlings who suspended civilian rule in the 1980s. Indeed, these critical and multifaceted processes required striking bargains with sections of society that included rural people.

As a result of new political alignments between public and private actors, democratization will almost inevitably be hindered by an inability of the state to deliver public goods[18] and by ambiguous institutional spaces informed by the increasing internationalization of external financial institutions and actors.[19] How do nascent democracies navigate the inherent tension between central government hegemony and decentralization, while ensuring political legitimacy and survival? I explore this question by chronicling the tenuous politics of transition, the impact of structural adjustment policies that conditioned the political transition to democracy during the early 1990s, and efforts to recentralize important elements of decentralization and public service delivery under a mantle of "limited government."

Many studies claim that democracies do a better job than non-democracies in improving the welfare of the poor.[20] But few perspectives of democratization or approaches to decentralization address the tenuous process in countries that embark on both. Nor do any theories offer convincing ideas about how fragile states navigate public service delivery under conditions of neo-liberal engagement, a reduced scope for the government in the economy, dependency on donor aid and political decentralization. In fact, few offer meaningful analysis about the ways in which the pursuit of democratic practices and the clamor for public goods amid austerity measures coalesced to produce, paradoxically, more responsive government despite uneven outcomes of electricity provision for the poor.

The model of democratic governance that emerged in Ghana emphasized a decentralized institutional framework intended to do just that: to improve public service delivery, raise standards of living and reduce the numbers of those living in squalor and poverty, especially in rural areas using district assemblies as agents of individual community needs and transformation. And it is not accidental that policies of rural acquiescence emerged in tandem with the political framework of decentralization in the post-1992 period.[21] Some argue that rural co-optation was simply the result of the electoral business cycle, with political parties and incumbent governments using discretionary spending to secure votes.[22] But in the context of market-oriented philosophy about the role of government authority in the economy, others contend that the decentralization program ran concurrently—and, in some respects, in harmony—with ongoing liberalization measures linked to reducing the role of the state.[23] Another view suggests that systematic differences between younger and older democracies are driven by the inability of political competitors to make credible pre-electoral promises to voters.[24] Speeches by Rawlings and public news addresses at the end of the 1980s, nonetheless, embodied an interest in inculcating decentralized authority as a vehicle for service delivery. This political aim included plans to reduce regional disparities and poverty by according local institutions with administrative and, presumably, fiscal authority as vehicles for economic transformation.

If conventional wisdom is right, it is no surprise that younger democracies are likely to experience negative outcomes in this regard. It is feasible, then, that popular perceptions of patronage and political returns to the few persist in new regimes, simultaneously leading to expectations of "more of the same", despite heightened hopes for political and, in many cases, economic change.

With a range of functions that include promotion of economic development, productive infrastructure, municipal works and services, budgeting, finance and administration, an increasing number of districts should represent decentralization in practice. However, in societies that are institutionally weak and offer few incentives for civic participation besides the potential gains from clientelist networks, such benefits may become ambiguous. Political accommodation of economic classes or groups in society is certainly a regular and unsurprising feature of many, if not most, political systems. Size matters, and because the number of electoral areas depends on the size of district assemblies as established by the National Commission for Democracy, central or national government capture of local government/district assemblies' functions has been greatly facilitated. In essence, a weak district assembly system has provided a rationale for *recentralization and reformulation of public delivery of services* like electricity as the exclusive terrain of national government and hence facilitated the *targeted* public goods provision of electricity during electoral cycles. One could argue that such developments reflected neo-patrimonialism, or the award by public officials of personal favors, and typical examples include licenses, contracts and projects.[25]

On another note, this variable may account for the implicit quandary of diffuse political power as an avenue for institutionalizing mechanisms of co-optation in focus areas (e.g., education, feeder roads, transportation, healthcare facilities, etc.) that district assemblies would normally deliver. As Bratton and Van de Walle note, would-be leaders of neo-patrimonial regimes typically want to use a transition as an opportunity to include themselves in the new rules of the political game. One method is the use of populist ideology and rhetoric, as illustrated in the pre-transition military oligarchy of Rawlings, which faced popular protest and a crisis of legitimacy and subsequently had to quicken the pace of a "managed" transition.[26]

A second complementary strategy involves the inculcation of weak institutions that, on the one hand, offer accountability and a measure of transparency, while masking the unavoidable conclusion that these institutions are unlikely to constrain effectively past institutional practices.[27] In fact, the powerful incentives of such political actors within a regime—in this case, members of the Rawlings' government—were strongly directed by societal pressures and economic expectations in the quest to maintain political power. Therefore, weaknesses in the newly created district assemblies offered a legitimate and political conduit for discretionary outcomes in the post-1990 period. As an International Monetary Fund report noted, the collection of internally generated revenue in the district assemblies remains at a dismal 14%. The report also observed that only two out of ten regions generate a fifth of their total revenue accruals. More worrying are additional observations in the report that noted the "persistently weak capacities of district assemblies to generate adequate levels of internal revenue needs to be addressed through training programs on modalities for enhancing the level of internally generated revenues, effective monitoring of performance and the institution of an appropriate incentive schemes including the enforcement of appropriate penalties".[28]

Efforts to inculcate decentralized institutions signify more than perfunctory attempts to mitigate potential ethnic conflict or reshape institutional authority. They represent an effort to reduce the scope of state responsibility, while providing a legitimate institutional locus for central governments to accord political, administrative and, to an extent, fiscal authority for local development outcomes. Indeed, under a decentralized planning and administrative system, economic development was thought to begin with communities and their representatives, as well as the Assembly members who identified their communities needs.[29] By making these structures salient at the grassroots level through the involvement of local people in decision-making processes,[30] Rawlings hoped to accord greater financial responsibility and local development to communities themselves—especially in rural areas. These efforts, however, also served as an important means for political machinery of mobilization politics apparent in public service delivery of amenities like electricity for disadvantaged rural poor.

Additionally, at the beginning of the 1990s, former President Jerry Rawlings' government marked a political impetus geared towards regime survival by paradoxically reinforcing central government authority under democratization and decentralization. As Joseph Ayee, in *The Measurement of Decentralization: The Ghanaian Experience, 1988–92*, observed, consequent efforts at maintaining power required rigorous efforts to recentralize the state, despite an elaborate system of councils, subcommittees, district planning co-ordination units and a local government service act, which delineated expectations and functions of district assemblies. While recentralization has strengthened government performance and produced more effective responses to local issues in many countries, Ghana's experience reflects opposite outcomes. Consequently, it comes as little surprise that an official from the District Assembly Common Fund (where monies are allocated by the central government for use at the district levels) noted that administration of the fund has been very successful and stated that "honestly, if it had not been for the fund, a lot of the districts would be in darkness, especially senior secondary schools." Some agree that decentralization helped to redress inequities in resource allocation through the District Assembly Common Fund, which each district may use as it sees fit for development at the local level.

Social contract theories from Hobbes, Locke, Rousseau, Kant, Olson and others espouse the view that citizens give up some rights in exchange for protection and in return for provision of collective goods and other services from the state. An important observation of this study is that poorly functioning markets induce amenities like electricity to take on a public goods aspect, which require intervention by government.[31] For this reason, the provision of public or collective goods often operates in far more complex terms than we might expect. In the next section, I briefly discuss the consequences of structural adjustment policies, which set the stage for co-optation in service delivery of electricity as an effort to placate the negative outcomes associated with this economic framework.[32]

The Impact of Ghana's Economic Institutions and Landscape

As Ghana was a more or less compliant pupil of structural-adjustment policies—an institutional framework that called for limited state intervention in the market, privatization and more—the World Bank and International Monetary Fund entreated its leaders to correct severe internal and external imbalances. As a corrective to rampant inflation, overvalued exchange rates and import tariffs, Ghana's leaders were implored to liberalize trade and cut social programs during the 1980s, and the political repercussions were profuse. Though poverty reduction strategies (PRS), devised in tandem with structural adjustment policies, aim to include national governments as much as possible, autonomy of local actors and institutions has frequently been compromised. As Simon et al. note, "these PRSs are supposed to be formulated by governments through a process of wide-ranging consultation with civil society over the broad strategy and individual sector papers, to enhance local 'ownership' and acceptability. However, the key economic and political conditionalities remain intact..."[33]

In tandem with structural adjustment, the pursuit of political decentralization offered a legitimate means for meeting donor requirements of transparency, institutional accountability, and the presumable diffusion of power and authority in reformed subnational government or district structures. But, as this work demonstrates, such circumstances, along with a tenuous economic environment, also allowed for targeted and discretionary spending on public goods like electrification, which emerged as a salient issue for rural voters. Howard Stein, in "Adjustment and Development in Africa: Toward an Assessment" (1997), suggested that it is difficult to overlook the impact of adjustment on aspects such as real wages, income, nutrition and health on the rural poor, who were "net buyers" of food.

Minimal Government Under Decentralization

This work establishes that under tenuous economic circumstances and "minimal government" or a neo-liberal oriented framework, the "trusteeship" role that donor partners appear to have adopted diminished state autonomy and encouraged governments to placate negative outcomes through rural electrification (and decentralized) projects or co-optation.[34] Concomitantly, each of these elements facilitated discretionary public goods provision under the requisites of minimal government—amid dependence on donor aid. On one level, donor dependency encourages the rationalization of stops and gaps in poverty and development projects, since they depend on the pace of external actors.[35] On the other hand, democratization and the consequent participatory locus and empowerment of ordinary citizens heighten demands for public goods and services that governments attempted to fulfill through subtle measures of co-optation.

Field Research

The author carried out field research over the course of 24 months between 2007 and 2009. During a short trip during the summer of 2014, additional research was conducted. Since the work in this book reflects a primary focus on Ghana as a model state for energy provision, the research conducted for the additional case studies addressed in Chap. 6 reflects research conducted through library material. Nineteen formal interviews were conducted with an array of individuals from various institutions. They include members of parliament from the NDC and NPP, two dominant political parties in the country, and from the Ministry of Rural and Local government. An interview also took place with a district assembly member from the Greater Accra municipality. I interviewed officials from the Energy Commission, an independent observatory institution, and from the Volta River Authority, a governmental institution that focuses on the management of the Akosombo Dam. I also conducted four informal interviews over a two-year period with the former mayor of Accra, Nathaniel Amartyefio, and with the Chief Operating Officer from the Public Utilities and Regulation Commission, Mr. Kwame Pianim, Chief Operating Officer, Mr. Kweku Awotwi, and Mr. Essendoh from the Energy Commission. Interviews at both institutions revealed relevant actors, historic and contemporary reasons for disparities, and detail the process of NES and REP implementation and reform efforts in the power sector.

In-depth interviews were conducted with the Director, Deputy Director and other relevant officials at the Ministry of Energy to provide a thorough account of procedural implementation of the NES, REP, SHEP; how rural areas were designated to receive electricity; which areas were given priority, and so on. Records of debates on electricity access for various districts were also obtained from parliament. Additionally, twenty questionnaires were completed by energy officials in the above-named institutions. The questionnaire was administered with the help of a research assistant and former reporter for TV One—Mr. Asante Danquah, who covered matters of parliament. I targeted officials at the Ministry of Energy, the Electricity Company of Ghana—the most prominent institution, for the purposes of this study, for gauging perceptions of hydropower development, the National Electrification Scheme, Rural Electrification and Self-Help Electrification Programs. Some 25–30 questionnaires were placed in mailboxes or directly handed to the respondents at their offices and later collected by the research assistant. Documents were perused at the Office of Public Records and National Archives for newspaper articles and information was gathered on how the dominant political parties, the NPP and NDC, approached the scheme for national electrification as the first of three initiatives and then during accompanying phases in the post-1989 period. Moreover, I examined material from the Institute for Social, Statistical and Economic Research (ISSER) to determine how regime change guided implementation.

Notes

1. M. Welsch, M. Bazilian, M. Howells, D. Divan, D. Elzinga, G. Strbac, … A. Brew-Hammond, "Smart and Just Grids for Sub-Saharan Africa: Exploring Options," *Renewable and Sustainable Energy Reviews* 20 (2013): 337.
2. Ibid., 337. See the International Economic Agency for more on sub-Saharan electricity challenges and energy scenarios: http://www.iea.org/publications/freepublications/publication/WEO2014_AfricaEnergyOutlook.pdf.
3. Brian Min, Kwawu Mensan Gaba, Ousmane Fall Sarr, and Alassane Agalassou, "Detection of Rural Electrification in Africa Using DMSP-OLS Night Lights Imagery," *International Journal of Remote Sensing* 34, no. 22 (2013): 8121.
4. Brian Min, *Power and the Vote: Elections and Electricity in the Developing World* (Cambridge University Press, 2015), 7.
5. This is expertly noted by Brian Min, *Power and the Vote: Elections and Electricity in the Developing World* (Cambridge University Press, 2015), 9.
6. See "The Implementation of the Growth and Poverty Reduction Strategy (GPRSII) 2006–2009, Annual Progress Report (2006) Government of Ghana, 2007." Kankam and Boon, "Energy Delivery and Utilization for Rural Development: Lessons from Northern Ghana," *Energy for Sustainable Development* 13 (2009); Nygaard, "Institutional Options for Rural Energy Access: Exploring the Concept of the Multifunctional Platform in West Africa," *Energy Policy* 38 (2010); Sebitosi and R. Okou, "Re-thinking the Power Transmission Model for Sub-Saharan Africa".
7. See the International Energy Agency, 2014: http://www.iea.org.
8. Political decentralization is used here to denote the creation and maintenance of subnational elections and structures (USAID Comparative Assessment of Decentralization in Africa: Final Report and Summary of Findings, September 2010: 18).
9. For more on Ghana's tenuous compliance with economic reforms dictated by international financial institutions on the condition of monetary and financial assistance under malaise, see *Africa and IMF Conditionality: The Unevenness of Compliance, 1983–2000* (Routledge, 2012).
10. Given that electricity access remains abysmally low for much of sub-Saharan Africa, with many countries registering 20% or even 30%, 66% represents substantial success.
11. For more on the policies that landed Ghana in this categorization, see Eboe Hutchful, "The Fall and Rise of the State in Ghana," in *The African State: Reconsiderations*, ed. Samatar Abdi Ismail and Ahmed I. Samatar (Portsmouth, NH: Heinemann, 2002).

12. See Tony Killich, *Reaction Too Far: Economic Theory and the Role of the State in Developing Countries* (London: Overseas Development Institute, 1989).
13. Charles Wereko, President Kufuor's (2000–2008) former energy advisor, noted, in "if we want to make middle-income status in ten or even 20 years, we have to increase energy use by at least 20-fold."
14. Although this work uses decentralization as its primary frame for analysis of electricity delivery in rural areas, it does not examine decentralized state delivery of this resource in any particular or specific region, city, town or village. While there is great utility in studying individual or multiple districts or towns, the potential for varied outcomes increases, as does the margin of error for empirical observations, given the complex interlinkages between electricity, rural and urban economy, income generation and resource endowment within each of the country's ten regions.
15. For example, Karekezi (2002), Wamukonya (2003), Sebitosi and Pillay (2005), and Williams and Ghanadan (2006) examined reasons for continuing disparities in electricity access for the rural poor in sub-Saharan Africa.
16. See "Energy Services in Sub-Saharan Africa: How Conducive Is the Environment?" *Energy Policy* 33 (2005): 2045.
17. In Dahl (1971), a democratic system is one that is completely, or almost completely, responsive to the preferences of its citizens; for theories of democratization, see Lipset (1959), Weber and Durkheim (1964) and Rustow (1970) etc.
18. See Jean Grugel, *Democratization: A Critical Introduction* (Houndsmill; New York: Palgrave, 2002), 180.
19. Governments are treated as public actors, while the World Bank and International Monetary Fund, as international institutions, act as private actors.
20. See Boone (1996), Bueno de Mesquita et al. (2003), Dasgupta (1993), Franco et al. (2004), Lake and Baum (2001), McGuire (2001), Moon and Dixon (1985), Przeworski et al. (2000), Sen (1981, 1999), Siegle et al. (2004), and Zweifel and Navia (2000 cited in Ross 2006, p. 860).
21. Here, decentralization refers to the transfer of authority or responsibility from the center or central government (decision-making apparatuses) to local governments or semi-autonomous organizations (Bergh 2004). It is certainly not new to Ghana, with experiments with this form of governance in the early twentieth century.
22. See Oelbaum (2002).
23. David Simon, Duncan F. M. McGregor, Kwasi Nsiah-Gyabaah, and Donald A. Thompson, "Poverty Elimination, North-South Research Collaboration, and the Politics of Participatory Development," *Development in Practice* 13, no. 1 (February 2003): 46.

24. Philip Keefer, "Clientelism, Credibility, and the Policy Choices of Young Democracies," *American Journal of Political Science* 51, no. 4 (October 2007): 804.
25. See R. Joseph, *Democracy and Prebendal Politics in Nigeria: The Rise and Fall of the Second Republic* (New York: Cambridge University Press, 1987). As cited in M. Bratton and N. Van de Walle, "Neopatrimonial Regimes and Political Transitions in Africa," *World Politics* 46, no. 4 (1994): 458.
26. Indeed, Bratton and Van de Walle note that in the variant of neopatrimonial regimes like Ghana and Nigeria, efforts to shore up grassroots support are often hampered by lack of organizational ability, which means that managed transitions often start from above.
27. Erica Weinthal and Pauline Jones Luong, "Combating the Resource Curse Alternative Solution to Managing Mineral Wealth," *Perspectives on Politics* 4, no. 1 (March 2008): 35–53.
28. See Ghana: Poverty Reduction Strategy Paper, 2009, p. 31.
29. See Owusu, 2004, p. 170.
30. Ibid., 168.
31. See Afua B. Banful, *Essays on the Political Economy of Public Goods Provision in Developing Countries* (Harvard University, 2008), 4 and Do Institutions Limit Clientelism?: A Study of the District Assemblies Common Fund in Ghana? *IFPRI Discussion Papers* Issue 855 (2009).
32. The term "co-optation" is used to denote the use of political resources or goods to secure support from vulnerable or marginizalized populations.
33. David Simon, Duncan F. M. McGregor, Kwasi Nsiah-Gyabaah, and Donald A. Thompson, "Poverty Elimination, North-South Research Collaboration, and the Politics of Participatory Development," *Development in Practice* 13, no. 1 (February 2003): 42.
34. For more on the trusteeship role, see Lindsay Whitfield, "Trustees of Development from Conditionality to Governance: Poverty Reduction Strategy Papers in Ghana," *Journal of Modern African Studies* 43, no. 4 (2005): 660.
35. "Stops and gaps" in poverty refer to a "project by project" preference, which has been used along with the need for fiscal austerity and donor funding as a rationalization for "incremental" development.

CHAPTER 2

Decentralization and Public Service Delivery in Ghana's Fourth Republic

Introduction

In 2009, a minister of local government told me that "decentralization has not taken place in Ghana. The reason largely is that the bureaucracy … particularly the top management personnel, is not in favor of decentralization. Every impediment has been placed in the way of implementing the decentralization programme.… Some have deliberately confused it with an exercise in deconcentration."[1] Our subsequent exchange about the bureaucratic response to decentralized governance during the 1990s revealed the frustrations of local, municipal institutions and the enormous challenges state officials faced—and still face two decades later. The 1988 creation of a decentralized institutional framework for the country's ten regions was intended as a populist measure that would appeal to residents of the country's rural regions as Jerry Rawlings, a charismatic former flight lieutenant, heir apparent to a soon-to-be neo-liberal state, emerged as a champion of a disenchanted and previously neglected class. In the summer of 2009, a member of parliament explained how the creation of district assemblies (DAs), a key provision of the decentralization program, was intertwined with the move to improve Ghana's infrastructure:

> Rawlings had spoken of grassroots governance—governance that touched the lives of people—so there was a continuing cry for electrification, roads, and water, you know. So [decentralization] was the way of satisfying the populist aspirations and [of] ensuring development and for that matter

N. Sackeyfio, *Energy Politics and Rural Development in Sub-Saharan Africa*, https://doi.org/10.1007/978-3-319-60122-9_2

> electrification was linked to decentralization... The link between the electrification program in 1988 and decentralization program cannot be overlooked. It is very important when you appreciate the decentralization program, which had at its essence development of localities.

New democracies almost always face the challenge of how to cater for both the popular will and larger societal interests, while ensuring institutional legitimacy and effectiveness. The reemergence of decentralization (the process by which government prerogatives are moved from the center to the periphery[2]) constituted a decisive step toward reconciling this challenge in Ghana. During the late 1980s, political decentralization sought to empower communities—district towns and assemblies—by providing them with the tools needed to identify and respond to local needs and thus to give a voice to marginalized groups, such as the rural poor. Propelled by the World Bank and other international financial institutions, political decentralization became an ambitious anchor for restructuring governmental authority, not only in Ghana but in other developing countries. Ghana's embrace of civilian rule accompanied a new focus on good governance and market-oriented reforms that sought to restructure the state's role in the economy. Integral to this neo-liberal conception of good governance was the creation of a minimal, neutral, and accountable state apparatus, a goal that resulted in highly controversial structural adjustment programs, among them a reconstitution of public and private domains, privatization, elimination of trade barriers to produce more open economies, and public sector reform.[3]

This chapter explores the Ghanaian Fourth Republic from the post-1992 transition to civilian rule until 2008, focusing on the relationship between democratization and decentralization, the consequences of minimalist-oriented governance in the economy, and the contradictions of this approach for public service delivery. As my exploration of outcomes in the heavily regulated energy sector demonstrates, political decentralization reflects ambiguous results in Ghana, a finding that echoes studies of other African states.[4]

After Ghana became independent in 1957, Kwame Nkrumah showed little interest in devolving central government functions and power to local institutions. The country became a one-party state under Nkrumah's Convention People's Party, and the central government's penetration of local administrative development put an end to rationally organized, autonomous local authorities. When confronted with growing social discontent, the Nkrumah government responded by centralizing control.[5] The National Liberation Council deposed Nkrumah in 1966 and remained in power until 1969, when a civilian president, K.A. Busia, was installed. Planning committees were created in all the country's regions to oversee regional development and execute national-level development projects, including electrification. Although the National Liberation Council regime took the recommendations of the World Bank a step further by creating planning units in various ministries, the focus on planning at the national level resulted in little regard for rural communities.[6] Busia was deposed in 1972, and another military regime maintained control through to 1978, encouraging the continued centralization of national government and further limiting the scope of local governance and autonomous functions.

With stagnant growth, overdependence on agriculture, declining exports of mineral resources, inflation, and other economic problems, the government attempted to reverse Ghana's course, in spite of the absence of adequately trained local authorities. In 1967, the Mills-Odoi Commission was established to examine the merits of decentralization. The commission's 1967 report represented the first genuine step toward decentralization, finding excessive centralization of both authority and resources.[7] The report noted the heavy concentration of senior public servants in Accra, with fieldwork left to relatively junior officials elsewhere. Accountability was nonexistent, and government functions were excessively fragmented, rendering the co-ordination of related activities difficult and resulting in an ineffective local government system that was verging on collapse.[8] But efforts to fix the problems fizzled with political upheavals and economic downturn.

In 1982, the Provisional National Defence Council (PNDC) seemed ready to embrace decentralization, but not until 1987–88 did the regime take tangible steps toward reforming the local government system by creating districts. In 1987, the PNDC produced the Blue Book, which offered a blueprint for local government and the DAs, representing a crucial step toward local and participatory governance. Ghana would have a fused or mixed local government system that combined a prefectural-style rule of traditional district administration responsible to central government, with the local control, service provision, and tax-raising powers of devolved government.[9] In 1988–89, local government units and the DAs were charged with 86 functions, including planning, finance, budgeting, infrastructural development, and security.[10] Decentralization represented an attempt by the military regime to solidify its legitimacy and to demonstrate to donors that the country was moving toward more open and democratic politics;[11] however, these efforts provoked resistance from national-level bureaucrats, who objected to surrendering their power.[12] Other difficulties stemmed from plans to reorganize the ministries so that they would work properly once decentralized. State officials faced enormous challenges.

Nevertheless, as Eboe Hutchful has demonstrated, the World Bank came to regard Ghana as a "star pupil" for its extensive implementation of adjustment policies. According to Hutchful, the World Bank lauded Ghana's neo-liberal success but did not understand the political process or the PNDC's motivations. In any case, reform efforts stalled in 1993, months after Rawlings reshaped the PNDC into the National Democratic Congress (NDC) and instituted multiparty democracy. In Hutchful's view, foreign aid and prescriptions for economic recovery helped to promote reform efforts, but domestic interests were paramount in stifling further reform.[13]

The links between democratization, decentralization, and public goods are pivotal. Democratization seeks to transform domestic politicoeconomic processes and, in prevailing neo-liberal conceptions, is informed by norms of accountability, transparency, legitimacy, consensus, participation, pluralism, and so forth.[14] But as a result of new alignments between public and private actors, democratization will almost inevitably be hindered by an inability of the state to deliver public goods[15] and by ambiguous institutional spaces created by the increasing internationalization of external financial institutions and actors. Various studies recognize the multifaceted difficulties faced by states that have recently transitioned to democracy. As Peter Fuseini Haruna has found, Ghana's reform efforts are hindered by a centralized bureaucracy that has limited public services through a carrot-and-stick policy.[16] Indeed, the fiscal austerity that accompanies neo-liberal policies and democratization has complicated the fiscal independence of DAs, which remain largely reliant on central government assistance.

Though democracies are assumed to do a better job than nondemocracies in improving the welfare of the poor,[17] and ample evidence shows that democracies fund public services at a higher level than do nondemocracies,[18] it is not obvious that these infusions of money reach the poor, or that they produce better social outcomes.[19] However, Min offers a persuasive proposition that, in democracies, the political benefits of public goods provision are often highest in areas where the nonpolitical justification is least obvious. Rural areas with fewer profit-generating customers (for electricity), whom it is financially expensive to connect to services because of the large physical distances, pose an additional difficulty for what are often cash-strapped governments in the developing world, thus making interventions difficult to defend on economic grounds.[20] Min extends this premise by the convincing suggestion that, on political grounds in electoral democracies, the rural poor—who comprise the bulk of the population—are difficult to ignore, as they vote in higher levels (in developing countries) overall.[21] Addressing weak capacity in institutional governance and delivery of public goods while meeting economic expectations is critical in this regard. Indeed, Kurt Weyland observes that clientelism can lock people into structurally unequal exchange relationships.[22] Set against these notions, the populist-oriented policies that emerged in Ghana regarding the provision of potable water, schools, road repair, and electricity proved critical in securing rural political support after the country returned to democratic rule in 1992.

Various authors have acknowledged that decentralization can improve local government by producing and enhancing participatory norms and more efficient development strategies.[23] When the country formally returned to civilian rule, key features of the electoral system shifted, with far-reaching consequences for decentralization. A committee of experts recommended that the new constitution include a system of proportional representation to convert votes into parliamentary seats. However, Rawlings opted for a single-member-district, plurality-based electoral system. Members of the unicameral legislature are elected from districts, but the link between parliamentarians and subnational governments is weak.[24] Single-member districts may provide closer contact between politicians and constituents and strengthen political parties, and such districts have been a preferred choice among post-colonial states, as Jeffrey Herbst notes.[25] This type of electoral system tends to favor a two-party system, effectively crowding out smaller and weaker parties to produce remarkably resilient democracy and stable relations. Conversely, most forms of proportional representation have the opposite effect, weakening political links between representatives and constituents, because candidates are more likely to devote their time, resources, and attention to the party officials who determine their political fate rather than to individual voters.[26] In 1992, as the country's new president, Rawlings' decision to select single-member-district representation, on a continent where political platform and ideology matter less than the personalities of politicians and what they can offer to key constituencies, followed the conventional wisdom. Creating DAs enabled him to satisfy donor requirements regarding participatory norms and representation.

Neo-liberal assumptions equate decentralization practices with popular participation and subsequent empowerment of citizens. Popular participation is thought to enable citizens to articulate their preferences—for example, in terms of community development. The extent of popular participation in rural development projects, then, is critical to understanding the progress of decentralization and its link to rural electrification. The crux of the problem, as Richard C. Crook and James Manor observe, and as a member of parliament echoed, is that the self-help efforts succeeded, not because of decentralization, but because of the shortcomings of the DAs. Moreover, because villagers were funding their own projects, they became less willing to pay taxes to the DAs.[27] In addition, as assembly members had increasing success in developing self-help projects, the more they undermined the legitimacy of their role as representatives of a district-level institution. Thus, participation can enable rural people and other marginalized groups to effect change in their communities but can have additional consequences for national government power (recentralization) and the institutional capacity of DAs.

Decentralization and Electrification

An inefficient market and a heavily subsidized electric energy sector characterized service delivery in the 1990s, when Ghana embarked on numerous electrification projects. The presumed benefits of a minimal state in the midst of democratization all but obscure the push and pull of national politics, which operates uneasily with local institutions or DAs. Mahmood Mamdani's concept of the bifurcated state offers a compelling lens for viewing the challenges of infrastructural development.[28] Understood as proffering an exclusionary locus and divide, it is symptomatic of the enduring legacy of colonialism in terms of weak institutions and preference formation. The poor have uneven access to public service delivery, a situation that affects the overall success of decentralized electricity schemes. As Joseph R. Ayee and Kwame Ninsin have established, decentralization of institutional power not only bolsters rural co-optation but also constitutes a logical choice for a country. However, it produced ambiguous results in Ghana.[29] Exploring Ghana's democratizing processes, impetus for decentralization, previous experiments with political decentralization, and outcomes of the DA system provides a context for understanding the mixed results of the country's electrification initiatives for the rural poor.

Although officials at the Ministry of Energy promoted self-help electrification projects as illustrating the transformation of access and progressive decentralization, this development likely created a conflict of interest between central government authority in determining district or regional initiatives and its impetus for rural co-optation. In addition, as of 2009, some energy officials believed that rural electrification efforts had recorded only "moderate" success.[30] Yet just over two-thirds also rated the assemblies' performance highly, a puzzling contradiction given numerous reports showing that government officials believe that districts cannot be relied on to deliver potable water, public health efforts, electricity, and other services. Efforts to co-opt rural constituents are plausible, given widespread complaints in the media and newspapers about the weak performance of the DAs. A dichotomy persisted between energy officials' perceptions regarding the electrification initiatives and the high ratings of DA capacity in assisting with electrification.

Good governance involves many aspects, including accountability, legitimacy, and responsive institutions, understood as norms and actions around which actors' expectations converge. At a microlevel, accountability is said to involve enhancing government responsiveness to public pressure by strengthening local participation and NGO involvement.[31] An important component of changing governance and the development discourse is decentralization, which involves the devolution of political power and administrative functions to a more localized level that facilitates citizen participation. While J. Tyler Dickovick and James S. Wunsch assert that some of the central challenges of successful inculcation of decentralization stem from bureaucratic rather than electoral politics,[32] I find that outcomes of decentralized delivery of electricity are significantly connected to electoral politics in the form of rural patronage. Their broad argument about the paradox inherent in the discovery that decentralization has strengthened national-level actors at the expense of local governance is a compelling one—with implications for party patronage. Indeed, both of Ghana's primary political parties, the NDC and the National Patriotic Party (NPP), have sought to placate key constituent groups through service delivery. Dickovick and Wunsch acknowledge mixed incentives that may vary, depending on who holds power at the national level.[33] As a macro–micro linkage, in terms of democratic development and government responsiveness, it includes the promotion of civil society and local government, which can be held to account more easily than national government because of easier access to decision-making and participation.[34]

But these assumptions do not square with the preferences or expectations of the Ghanaian electorate. Alison J. Ayers argues that the democratization project pushed by Western powers propagates political transformation with the idea of a minimal, "neutral" state, the liberal public sphere, and the liberal "self", and that these goals interfaced ambivalently with weak institutional capacity in Ghana. The delivery of electricity thus provides an appropriate measure of success.[35]

Ghana's political decentralization sought to heal societal cleavages through patronage, co-optation, and a focus on rural areas. By exploring the precise nature and form of decentralization that emerged, as well as the structural issues of public service provision, this chapter reveals the underpinnings and evolution of rural accommodation.

In the 1970s and early 1980s, the first wave of decentralization focused on deconcentrating hierarchical government structures and bureaucracies.[36] The second wave began in the mid-1980s and broadened to include power-sharing, democratization, and market liberalization to expand private sector decision-making.[37] As a result, local government was envisioned as the focal point for all development decisions. During the 1990s, decentralization was viewed as a way of opening government to wider public participation, and Ghana was one of many countries to adopt this perspective.

Decentralization can take three forms: deconcentration, delegation, and devolution.[38] Deconcentration refers to the process by which the central government disperses responsibilities for certain services to its regional branch offices, without any transfer of authority to lower government, and is considered the weakest form of decentralization.[39] Delegation refers to the process whereby the central government transfers responsibility for decision-making and administration of public functions to local government or to semi-autonomous organizations that are not wholly controlled by the central government but are ultimately accountable to it; devolution occurs when the central government transfers authority for decision-making, financial allocations, and management to quasi-autonomous units of local government.[40] Devolution, which represents the strongest form of decentralization, occurs when the central government transfers authority for decision-making, financial allocations, and management to subnational and quasi-autonomous units of local government. As Sylvia Bergh notes, devolution constitutes the most direct link with democracy. The primary form the country undertook was devolution, as did other developing countries, with varying success.

In Ghana, decentralization involved the redrawing of district and subdistrict administrative boundaries, the establishment and empowerment of local government structures, and the promotion of advocacy and popular participation at various levels of decision-making. Other tenets of decentralization included: (1) local government officials would adopt legislative and administrative duties previously performed by central government, including service delivery and budgeting; (2) subdistrict councils and unit committees would be tasked with encouraging constituent engagement through access to political authority—this would also include efforts to restructure resource allocation; and (3) the development of mechanisms for sharing resources between central and local governments.[41] A district chief executive and district secretary would head each district, while the DAs would exercise local political and administrative authority. Membership in each DA ranged between about 50 and 100, based on the district's population. Two-thirds of assembly members were elected by universal adult suffrage and a simple majority system that represented the electoral areas within the district, while the remaining third were appointed by the PNDC in consultation with traditional authorities, local interest groups, and revolutionary organs. The district secretary wielded tremendous power as a conduit between the PNDC and the assemblies.[42] Members of parliament whom I interviewed suggested that Rawlings used his populist power to co-opt the district chief executive and ensure that important powers remained with the central government.

Ghana's Experience with Structural Adjustment

A failing economy, scarce commodities and unprecedented hardship, and the expulsion of Ghanaians from Nigeria in 1981 led to widespread discontent. Structural adjustment policies called for broad cutbacks to social programs and fiscal austerity measures. Ghana's 1982 Economic Recovery Program sought to reduce high rates of inflation and improve production capacity and, in combination with market-oriented reforms grudgingly embraced by the PNDC, was expected to yield significant improvement. In practice, however, the Economic Recovery Program did little to assuage the difficulties most Ghanaians faced. By 1986, as people clamored for political change and the political environment grew increasingly tenuous, the National Commission for Democracy began holding public forums regarding the possibilities for a new political system. By the end of the year, some 29,000 workers employed by state or quasi-state entities had been redeployed, and the civil service had shed 15,000 jobs.[43] To curb inflation, the government also adopted an extremely restrictive monetary policy and placed a credit squeeze on economic activity.[44] The regime flailed around, looking for solutions to the country's problems, and reevaluated its political and economic strategies for bolstering support.

By the early 1990s, the Rawlings regime sought to reconfigure state–society relations to create new governance structures that would both be accountable to the people and maintain political support. The new system was essentially grounded in reformed local government via regional co-ordinating councils; DAs; submetropolitan district councils; and urban, zonal, town, and area councils, with a district secretary and chief executive possessing final authority over decision-making. But confusion remained regarding who should bear responsibility for implementing or executing the decisions made by DAs, with district administrations, executive committees, and district secretaries vying with the DA for supremacy.[45]

In 1991–92, Rawlings banned political parties, on the grounds that they would prevent effective governance by polarizing the electorate and stymieing local participation and representation. However, after a referendum revealed Ghanaians' desire for a political party system, Rawlings had little recourse but to comply. As a system with new political parties reemerged, the country became polarized along old lines that reflected long-standing ideological rivalries.[46] The NPP and the NDC became the dominant contemporary political rivals, mimicking the earlier rivalry between the Nkrumaist Convention People's Party and Danquah/Busia Progress Party. This historic schism allowed these parties to penetrate rural areas through patronage and subsequently facilitated decentralization.[47]

Minimal Government Under Decentralization

Donors and international financial institutions had a major influence on the structure of Ghanaian domestic autonomy and resulted in contradictions in state provision for the poor.[48] As Lindsay Whitfield notes, "The zeal of donors to involve 'civil society' in policy discussions produced a divide between consultative processes and constitutional representative processes, between formal and informal institutions for operationalising participation."[49] Indeed, Irving Leonard Markovitz has observed that the frequent use and merits of civil society as an end-all in the African context are frequently misguided and exaggerated.[50]

Under a minimalist state-oriented purview, decentralization of power from the national government involved a transfer of political authority from the center to lower tiers of government. Local government thus became the focal point for all development decisions. Ghana issued Poverty Reduction Strategy papers in the 1990s, with the goal of bringing economic development to marginalized areas of the country, such as the northern, upper eastern, and upper western regions.[51] Studies have reached different conclusions about the relationship between poverty reduction and decentralization.[52] Gordon Crawford, for example, concludes that decentralization results in only a limited reduction in poverty levels and is a political rather than technical exercise. Furthermore, downward accountability mechanisms in terms of those tasked with delivery and related responsibilities are weak, which may contribute to this limited impact.[53]

Decentralization for Whom?

In theory, a decentralized political system places increased decision-making ability at the disposal of ordinary citizens.[54] In Ghana, however, popular understanding of local government functions appears to be steeped in the country's traditions of centralized public administration. In the early 1990s, when the state was perceived to be in crisis, rural residents became the focus of Rawlings' populism as he steered the country from a military dictatorship to civilian rule. The country thus took an incremental or project-by-project approach to development that can be seen in the three rural electrification plans, which sought to lift rural people out of poverty. With past and present governments resorting to the "conferment of divisible benefits" to satisfy private rural interests, rural development projects have become instrumental in creating a system of spoils, thereby maintaining a measure of rural political support.[55]

The planned transfer of authority to DAs appears to have created a cohesive environment and favorable state–society relations intricately linked to strategies for rural coalescence. The PNDC's apparent commitment to decentralizing power stemmed from a desire to improve efficiency, while the effectiveness of the soon-to-be-revamped national-level institutions was tied to a desire for political longevity. Conceived as a solution to the detrimental pursuit of state interventionism and poor governance, decentralization offered the promise of service delivery and a mandate of responsive government for Ghanaians. According to one member of parliament, in 1993, the Local Government Act 462 created the framework for a "local government system and [a] vehicle for rural development." Nevertheless, the DAs remained weak.

The key impetus for reform came from the regime's desire to survive, rather than from a belief in market principles.[56] As the public became increasingly resistant to the hardships caused by structural adjustment policies, the regime sought to mitigate the negative economic effects for urban workers, while finding new bases of political support. Ghana pursued extensive adjustment policies and barely avoided political catastrophe. The central government and the Ministry of Local Government and Rural Development sought to provide each district capital or small town with electricity, telephone service, hospitals, potable water, and other infrastructural services.[57]

The World Bank and other international financial institutions required a major transformation of Ghana's political system, including a rolling back of the state, while Ghana's post-transition governments recognized the political gains that public goods could bring. In fact, as several interviewees noted, the central government's devolution of financing, planning, and budgeting functions to the DAs created a situation in which projects such as electrification were carefully calculated to ensure political legitimacy and keep parties in power. A member of parliament and former minister of energy from the NDC party noted that the "government realized that energy and development was needed. It was part of national policy. Somewhere along the line it should have come naturally; government should realize that we should give opportunity to rural communities to develop."[58] But he also concluded, "People delude themselves into thinking that there is no politics in it, but what is politics after all? Whatever the nature of politics, it permeates every level, so many elections, and politics of local government. I go campaigning for people… I belong to a certain political persuasion and I kind of imbue them, go in there and do the kinds of things I suggest." In the words of another government official, "The impact [of electricity] is so much that, for instance … we go to some communities just before the elections to put up some signs, posters, or some things. And it is no good, because they see the importance of it and they think somehow it is politically, you know, tied to the assembly." And as another interviewee said, "We always mention finance as number one—blame it. If we strategize properly, we can reduce the number of areas that lack [electricity]. Finance will always be a problem. We use money as an excuse. It is a question of priority. When you have a list of development things you want to do, some have multiplier effects, ripple effects. It is a question of priority and political exigencies."

At first glance, the steady increase in the number of DAs to the current number of 216 in 2012 illustrates the progress of decentralization. However, this development is unexpectedly political. As Dickovick and Wunsch establish, in 2010, Ghana had 170 districts, up from 110 just a decade earlier. Although the 1992 constitution and Local Government Act of 1993 offer criteria for district creation (e.g., population or geographical contiguity), the need to create new patronage positions by creating new districts supersedes the legal framework.[59] Poor capacity, inadequate human resources and revenue remain a persistent strain. In the summer of 2009, Joshua Nicol, who served as a district fund administrator under President John Kufuor (2004–08), and an official in the Ministry of Local Government and Rural Development, who wishes to remain unnamed, noted the problems caused by these challenges. Nearly two decades later, the DAs continue to struggle to find institutional complementarity with central governments. In fact, this institutional dilemma is precisely what makes democratizing states fragile and prone to disorder and dysfunctional relationships.

Kwamena Ahwoi, PNDC secretary for local government, envisioned the DAs as a unique opportunity for Ghanaians to develop their own areas. Nevertheless, local government reform suffered setbacks as a consequence of the creation of new districts. Not only did local officials exhibit little interest in reforms, but the creation of new districts was approached with derision and skepticism because of the potential diversion of funds to the new areas.

Tailoring a political system to the African context required political actors to address the ethnicity question.[60] Attempts to mitigate the influence of ethnicity stemmed from a desire to avoid fractious politics, mobilize large numbers of constituents, and maintain political power. A political environment devoid of ethnic politics would ease future regimes' task of capturing support. Political success required a move away from personalism and toward subtler, less obvious forms of co-optation. Decentralization thus was fashioned as a political instrument to stabilize a political system widely agreed to be in peril and to secure some of the government's political objectives.[61]

Ninsin has framed the decentralization program as part of the PNDC's mobilization strategies.[62] Exploring agricultural development under the PNDC, Amos Anyimadu has found that the PNDC rushed reforms to meet conditionality deadlines or required reforms as instituted by the International Monetary Fund and World Bank.[63] Perhaps as a result, the 1988 Local Government Law placed 22 departments under the control of DAs. This law in effect abolished the separate identities of departments and organizations whose functions overlapped with those of the DAs and fused them together to promote the development of districts.[64] However, all of the bureaucracy remained located in Accra, while the local offices in the 10 regions and the then 110 capitals lacked the human capital and financial resources to carry out their assigned roles.[65] Political authority became further centralized, leaving many DAs bereft of the political will to carry out their functions as expected. With few effective mechanisms and resources to strengthen devolution of authority to the DAs, a fractious political environment created opportunities on which both the incumbent regime and the newly minted NDC sought to capitalize.

Moving Beyond Populism: A New Politics of Decentralization?

According to Nathaniel Amarteifio, former mayor of Accra, intermittent problems with water levels and overall management of the Akosombo Dam are related to continued gaps in efficient provision and even wastage in electricity delivery. Similarly, scholars have found that in other countries, a mismatch of sorts exists between DA-like powers and responsibilities on the one hand, and available resources on the other.[66] Bergh has shown that the benefits of participatory mechanisms may be blunted when they are used to establish a plethora of local institutions that compete with, or are a substitute for, nascent democratic processes. Because these institutions are often based on problematic notions of community, and frequently have limited downward accountability, Bergh believes that they are often captured by local elites or are manipulated by central government officials.[67]

"Ownership" and Measurement of Public Service Delivery Under Decentralization

As the social compact shifts from the state to markets (or to international power producers and exporters), government plays a critical role in public service and enterprises. The Ghanaian government values the resources NGOs bring to help meet the service delivery gap but nevertheless seeks to restrict their role to the sphere of social welfare.[68] In addition, as NGOs receive massive inflows of aid, the NGO sector has become a new arena for accumulation, especially for African elites.[69] These developments suggest a complex picture of state and NGO conflict, bolstered by attempts to co-opt not just NGOs but the poor—especially the rural poor—given the prevalence of an "aid dependent culture in Ghana."[70]

The relationship between governments and the NGO sector in Ghana hinges on service delivery, rural development, and poverty reduction. African states have sought, and at various times have succeeded in their efforts, to co-opt and control a growing NGO sector. In addition, governments have been motivated more by the desire to gain access to NGO funds and to monitor NGOs that might be political competitors than to make the NGOs accountable to the rural poor.[71]

Service delivery is a critical component of DA functions and an important objective in Ghana's decentralization objectives. However, living standards within the districts reveal uneven service provision in terms of community facilities and spending levels, as well as in many other areas.[72] Electricity represents both a functional element, for use in lighting, heating, and cooking, as well as, in some cases, an economic input—for example, in business and industrial enterprises. It is thus a multidimensional resource, to which governments have attempted to provide access through national and rural electrification programs.

In response to concerns about equality of access for the poor, the government created a "lifeline tariff" for those who had difficulty paying their utility bills. The political salience of access for the rural poor is evidenced by the fact that the government instituted the tariff despite donor criticism of the move. This tariff is a social one, priced well below the cost of supply, based on the philosophy that electricity is an essential service rather than a luxury and that people with low incomes should not be deprived of it.[73] Some scholars, however, have disputed the idea that rural electrification results in increased economic activity.[74] Poorly integrated local economic sectors, lack of access to capital for small and medium-sized enterprises, and poor vertical and horizontal co-ordination between DAs and the central government create obstacles for communities seeking to improve their welfare through electricity. As an official in the Volta River Authority and engineer for the National Electrification Scheme noted,

> Generally, [electricity] has made an impact, the primary use for lighting … but it is not used in high-growth industries, in factories. In rural electrification you hardly get factories established because of electrification. The corn mills, which have no means for diesel motors attached, they convert it, and they buy the electric power for the rural electrification. It is difficult to confine it in terms of income, but in terms of lifestyle of the person, the poverty level, it has an impact.

Despite enduring skepticism regarding the productive uses of electricity, the Trades Union Congress, a powerful voting bloc for many decades, has deemed energy critical to labor and commerce, but weak linkages between the various administrative departments of the DAs have prevented the development of a coherent strategy and of innovative solutions for generating revenue from electrification.

The District Assembly Common Fund

Created in 1994, the District Assembly Common Fund (DACF) sought to provide financial assistance to the DAs but illustrates the prevailing authority of the central government and symbolizes DA dependency under decentralization. The rationale for statutorily setting aside funds for the DAs rested on the notion that fiscal autonomy at the district level would lead to fiscal responsibility and transparency. Policymakers believed that residents' proximity to local administrators would increase interest in how funds were used and provide more effective checks against financial mismanagement and fraud.[75] The DACF was expected to help districts and, ultimately, citizens decide which local development initiatives to focus on. Article 252 of the 1992 constitution provided that 5% of *all* government revenue would be paid into the fund in quarterly installments. In practice, however, 7.5% of *tax* revenue (a much smaller pool of money) was allocated to the fund.[76] Moreover, disbursements are often delayed, both from the Ministry of Finance to the DACF and from the DACF to the DAs,[77] and although the DAs are required to impose a 5% withholding tax on employee salaries, some of the assemblies have failed to do so, not only costing themselves revenue but also reinforcing a cycle of dependency.[78] According to J.D. Mahama, a member of parliament from Bole, "With the operation of the Common Fund over the years, some districts are beginning to develop a dependency syndrome. And because they know that a certain amount of money is going to come regularly as a result of the Common Fund, they are not doing too much in terms of generating their own revenue at the local level."[79] Another member of parliament has called the DACF "an interventionist provision. It is so small and cannot really do much. Yet paradoxically, district assemblies rely on it as an exclusive source of revenue, which means that the essence of decentralization cannot be realized when most money is spent or originates at the center." According to this member of parliament, the central government retains exclusive authority to determine which communities receive electricity and when, illustrating the continued centralization that exists under a "decentralized" system. Said one DACF administrator during the Kufuor administration,

> We need to convince government that if you are really pushing decentralization, then we should push a lot more to the districts so that they can decide what to do with the funds. Also, as a formal institution, maybe we lack the capacity in the districts on the "know side." We need to focus our attention on training people to take over, but unfortunately the core functions are handled by the central government, so the districts don't take training as a core function—they think that should be done by central government.

Fiscal dependence on the national government to fund initiatives hardly promotes local agency.

In theory, DAs are responsible for the generation of income to fund development or community initiatives. However, poorly managed districts (particularly those that are newly created) do not encourage self-generating revenue or effective administrative and material functions. In addition, regional differentiation has encouraged political opportunism and co-optation of vulnerable and marginalized portions of society, resulting in a vicious cycle of overdependence on the central government. Although, on paper, adequate financial resources are available for all the districts (despite their rapidly increasing numbers), some aspects of their development plans do not qualify for DACF funding, affecting how much districts receive.[80] Substantial increases in disbursements to the DAs (for example, 49.5% during 1994–95 and 23.3% during 1995–96) may well have represented attempts to increase voters' support for the government or other political calculations.[81]

Bartholomew K. Armah, William Inaidoo, and Mawuli Feglo note that, from 1993 to 1999, Ghana's auditor general identified disturbing trends in the management of public accounts—wasteful expenditure, extravagance, poor accounting standards, and financial activities undertaken without following the applicable rules.[82] Those who tout the benefits of Ghana's decentralization tend to overlook these instances of fiscal mismanagement. In the words of a former official with the Ministry of Local and Rural Government,

> We have not been good enough in monitoring and evaluating what is happening down there [in the DAs]. No evaluation mechanisms of programs are put there. What is the effectiveness of those programs put there? What is the financial use of finance, funds, and all these things—is there duplication [of initiatives]?

The auditor general's report found that these shortcomings produced a number of negative consequences.[83] For example, at the national level, revenue shortfalls translate into increased domestic borrowing and higher inflation. For fiscal decentralization to succeed, DAs must be able to mobilize, manage, and equitably distribute internally generated revenues effectively. However, weak internal revenue and tax-collection mechanisms reflect continuing difficulties in establishing a culture of taxation, producing a perennial headache for central and local government authorities. At the same time, the central government provides few measures to support fiscal autonomy for the DAs, further limiting the ability of public service personnel to fulfill their objectives or undertake local government initiatives.

The National Electrification Scheme

At the beginning of the 1990s, only 480 communities, accounting for 15% of the country's total population and 5% of the rural population, had access to electricity.[84] In response, the NDC undertook its first interventionist public service effort since the beginning of the Fourth Republic, the National Electrification Scheme (NES), which sought to extend the electrical grid to all parts of the country by 2020. Under the control of the Ministry of Energy (MOE), the NES had six objectives: (1) reducing poverty, primarily in rural areas; (2) increasing socioeconomic development nationwide; (3) increasing the rural standard of living; (4) creating small to medium-scale industries in rural areas; (5) enhancing the country's systems in agriculture, health, education, and other areas; and (6) creating jobs in rural areas and reducing high rates of rural-to-urban migration.[85] From 1995 to 2000, the NES implemented the first two of its five phases, resulting in the electrification of 13 district capitals as well as 407 towns and villages en route to the district capitals.[86] Dissatisfied with the pace of electrification and with the target dates for their connection to the grid, many rural communities began pushing the government to develop a new program. In response, during the 1990s, the government instituted the Rural Electrification Program (later the Self-Help Electrification Program).[87]

In Ghana, as elsewhere, the early stages of rural electrification involved connecting major provincial towns, with later stages bringing remote villages and towns online.[88] Rural communities clamored for electricity as a means of development and, during the 1980s, political instability led governments (military and otherwise) to seek to provide power as a means of winning support.[89] According to the former head of the Volta River Authority, Kweku Awotwi,

> It was only when the macro-economy and currency stabilized in the mid-80s that electricity consumption began to increase. You know, liberalization and stabilization happened around the same time, because this is what the World Bank wanted. It was then that income started to grow again. Trade started to flourish, and there was trade in and out of exports to some extent. Barriers were dropped and a lot of imports came in. But this flourishing of economic activity was reflected in the consumption of electricity. You know, income got higher, households, businesses got started, and there was a spread of wealth, if you like, in rural areas.

Many officials within the MOE gave Ghana high marks for access to electricity, which is available in the country at rates that exceed those of its neighbors. As one Volta River Authority official and engineer for the NES said,

> I have had the privilege of doing a little bit of work outside Ghana, and when you do comparisons in the subregion, Ghana is way, way ahead of most other countries. Most of them, when you go to their capital and then you leave the capital, there is nothing else in terms of electrification. We have been able to cover all the regional capitals, the district capitals, all the major towns and villages have been covered, so the impact has been very, very great.

Nonetheless, donor countries such as Canada, Japan, France, and India have played critical roles in rural electrification. These countries spent decades focusing on neglected areas and jump-starting income-generating activities for small enterprises utilizing electrification. On the other hand, Ghana continues to face problems regarding utilities that waste electricity and quality of electric provision, and little attention has been devoted to the rural population's current and future energy needs. These problems are compounded by a disconnect between the perceived benefits of electrification and the multiple layers of rural development. With a panoply of domestic and international actors claiming to represent the poor,[90] and competing views on how to improve their lives through public goods and service provision, the precise relationship between electricity and poverty reduction is unclear. Given that the country's power-sector framework privileges industrial users and wealthy residential customers, equitable access to electricity may not even be possible for rural populations that largely rely on wood fuels and biomass. Energy commission predictions that biomass will continue to predominate in these areas until 2020 and possibly beyond are also troubling, given the pace of the country's economic development and quest to attain full middle-income status. Indeed, the problem of electric energy inequities is reflected in low consumption rates in rural areas and enormous disparities with urban households. For example, a survey conducted by the Ghana Living Standards Survey (GLSS), Round 6, noted that less than 50% of rural households use electricity as a main source of lighting, in comparison with 88.6% for urban households.[91] According to one interviewee, Ghanaian elites have appropriated far more than their fair share of modern energy services. In addition, the Rural Electrification Program has offered lucrative political opportunities. By making electrification "rural" and thus populist, the NDC could distinguish itself from the NPP and other political parties. This approach further strengthened Rawlings' populist appeal, counteracting the long-standing neglect of rural residents.

Under the National Electrification Scheme, which began in 1990, the Rural Electrification Program became the Self-Help Electrification Program (SHEP), during the 1990s, in response to rural areas' increasing impatience with the pace of electricity provision. Touted by MOE officials as another decentralized effort stemming from the districts themselves, the SHEP allowed certain communities that did not want to wait their turn in the Rural Electrification Program and that could afford to purchase their own electric poles to obtain connections to the grid. During SHEP's first (1990–91) and second (1992–94) phases, roughly 250 communities were connected to the national grid.[92] SHEP 3, which covered the 1994–2008 period, resulted in the electrification of 700 communities.[93] Over the past decade, SHEP 4 has continued the process, with the goal of providing electricity to thousands of communities.

My research indicates that government and electric company officials viewed SHEP as another mobilizational tool. While DAs were designed to operate on a nonpartisan basis, they have become increasingly partisan, and providing communities with electric poles has become one way that legislators at all levels can votes. Moreover, the Ghanaian people are aware that this tactic is being used: as a former official for the Ministry of Local and Rural Government observed, "On radio you hear people saying, politicians have brought us poles again, so when is the electricity coming?"

Despite electricity's status as a political bargaining chip, SHEP indeed increased the Ghanaian population's access to power. By 2006, 3200 of the country's towns were connected, with 2100 of them having gained that status via SHEP. The increase in the percentage of the population that had access to the grid from 15% in 1989 to the current rate of 80.51% is considerable.[94] Such remarkable growth reflects the success of political and administrative decentralization, since DAs have co-ordinated a pooling of communities' resources to enable them to obtain poles.

The Drawbacks of Decentralization

Particularly in the African context, "centralized decentralization" has enabled certain resources to take on a "public goods" element. Zimbabwe, Uganda, Rwanda, South Africa, and others view "decentralized governance" as a suitable mode of authority in which poverty reduction interventions can be conceived, planned, implemented, and monitored.[95]

Ghana's *Poverty Reduction Strategy* and *Vision 2020* goals refer to decentralization as a framework for outreach, rural development, and implementation in its districts. Ghana has made important strides in governance, and civil servants display a notable commitment to efficient and transparent institutional processes. But continuing aid dependence and national budgets, largely supplemented by World Bank and IMF concessionary loans, have entrenched the role and domestic involvement of international financial institutions in questionable ways, producing what Whitfield calls "trustees of development."[96] In many ways, the extent of donor or international financial institution influence on domestic policy produced a reconstitution of public and private domains.[97] Ghana's domestic autonomy is considerably circumscribed, limiting the state's ability to attend to the poor.

The political, fiscal, and administrative limitations of decentralization demonstrate the extent to which central government hegemony over fiscally derived functions has encumbered Ghana's DAs and local government—a U.S. Agency for International Development (USAID) report notes the inadequacy of funding and questionable assignment of devolved responsibilities to subnational governments.[98] The appointment of district chief executives by the president has added local-level intrigue to an already fractious political process.

Moreover, conflict has also arisen between the speakers of the DAs, who are elected by members, and district chief executives; between DAs and district-level central government ministries and departments; and between district chief executives and local chiefs.[99] These squabbles have sapped energy and political will from the DAs. In addition, although 30% of DA members are appointed by the president (a provision intended to ensure that all assemblies include technocrats), the DAs are dominated by political activists and local notables.[100]

The DACF has become a tool of central government dominance that limits subnational government capacity to undertake successful projects and development. Dickovick and Wunsch assert that bureaucrats and civil servants in sectoral as well as line ministries may be reticent to cede policy authority to local government units.[101] In effect, gaps in capacity building, and the absence of self-sustaining mechanisms that truly reflect decentralized elements require more attention than they currently receive.

Other contradictions are also evident in public opinion surveys regarding the effectiveness of decentralized institutions and the responsiveness of both local and national representatives. A 2005 Afrobarometer survey noted not only that 65% of Ghanaians were satisfied with the performance of parliament, but also that "a majority of Ghanaians felt they were able to command the attention of their elected national and local representatives. Those who expressed this view with regards to their local representatives (assembly members) were comparatively higher (63 percent) than the proportion sharing similar opinion about national representatives (MPs), 55 percent."[102] These results are at odds with other evidence, including newspaper articles, that chronicles dissatisfaction with public service delivery, including electricity provision. In 2014, for example, 75% of Ghanaians described the government as "having performed 'badly' in providing reliable electricity."[103]

Consequently, the high rate of satisfaction with the government makes sense only if Ghanaians have been politically co-opted. In 2009, Barbara Murray, a senior governance adviser for the Canadian International Development Agency–Program Support Unit in Ghana, acknowledged that government officials believe that municipal and metropolitan DAs are "not ready, do not have the capacity, or cannot be relied on to deliver proper services, a rationalization that is used to justify inaction or used to argue the merits of a project-based approach."[104]

Conclusion

In 2015, Ghanaians went for 159 days with no electricity, a phenomenon known as *dumsor*, or a period where darkness is more prevalent than light.[105] *Dumsor* has both private and public effects and short and long-term consequences for businesses, hospitals, universities, factories, shopping malls, and schools—in short, it impacts all aspects of Ghanaian life, reducing productivity and increasing uncertainty.

The pursuit of economic reform, the scaling back of government intervention in the economy, and adjustment policies have produced difficult development choices in an era of minimum-oriented government.[106] Voters appear increasingly aware of the sophisticated ploys used during the political business cycle. During the 1992 and 1996 elections, concessionary spending increased, much to the chagrin of the World Bank,[107] and in the 2008 and 2012 (arguably) elections, in a familiar ploy documented by newspapers and political observers elsewhere, the NDC government sought to buy the rural vote with the sudden appearance of potable water, electricity, roads, and other services in many regions where the party felt it needed to secure support. Voters have recognized the growing role that public service delivery plays in the domestic political environment and have demanded more from DA and parliamentary representatives, increasing the dilemmas associated with the provision of government services.

However, poor horizontal linkages between agencies and administrative departments within the DAs and inadequate communication have hindered the effectiveness of decentralization and, in some cases, have produced a duplication of effort. Inadequate vertical co-ordination has also resulted in significant challenges: as one interviewee remarked, the DAs "do not talk to each other." In addition, the DAs lack trained personnel and face other bureaucratic constraints. The increase in the number of DAs, despite their questionable capacity to function, suggests that the pursuit of suboptimal strategies of public service delivery is intentional, a point supported by some of my interviews. The profusion of project-based or targeted discretionary approaches to service provision has debilitated Ghana's capacity-building and consequently rendered the political culture of self-help inherently ineffective.

The notion that incumbent governments will tend to invest in areas that assure political returns—that is, where support is the greatest—remains compelling.[108] In this regard, timing and sequencing of electricity projects are critical. By arguing that democracy favors the delivery of public goods owing to the lucrative political externalities generated by their provision, Min (2015) suggests that political actors can influence timing, siting and modes of delivery of public goods projects, which is ultimately connected to political objectives.[109] Indirect strategies of co-optation ultimately influenced, and were a logical outcome of, reduced government in an era of neo-liberal policies. It is no accident that officials vigorously pursued the autonomous development of districts to bolster fiscal and administrative decentralization. Voters in rural Ghana adopted the rallying cry "No electricity, no power," marking a turning point in government–society relations and in the prevailing rural co-optation approach.

Ten of the 15 members of parliament I interviewed acknowledged that, since 1992, Ghanaian governments, regardless of political party, have used electrification as an implicit tool for co-optation. As a result, rural residents now resist taxation and electricity bills more intensely than ever, viewing service delivery as the exclusive responsibility of the state and something for which they should not have to pay. Moreover, public perceptions of malfeasance, corruption, and misappropriation in electricity distribution have mushroomed, as newspaper articles and public opinion surveys demonstrate.

Despite the tremendous increase in the number of Ghanaians who are connected to the electrical grid, electricity is often unavailable—one of the many paradoxes of centralized decentralization. Citizens expect quality delivery of services, such as water and electricity, yet sacrifice quality as a result. As the DAs assume greater responsibilities, their financial, material, and infrastructural capacity to carry out and implement development projects lags. And, in the most critical paradox of all, the intrinsic contradictions involved in simultaneously empowering and attempting to co-opt rural voters may yet upset the delicate balance between the Ghanaian central government and the DAs.

Appendix: Research Methodology

In the summer of 2009, I conducted fifteen interviews with members of Ghana's parliament. A year later, I distributed a questionnaire to 19 officials with the Ghanaian Ministry of Energy and the Electricity Company of Ghana, asking about their perceptions regarding the capacity of the Akosombo Dam, a primary source of hydropower; the Self-Help Electrification Program; and the capacity of DAs to promote rural electrification. Respondents were asked to answer questions 1–5, 7, and 10 with a number between 1 and 10, with 1–3 indicating "poor," 4–5 indicating "fair," 6–7 indicating "good," 8 indicating "very good," and 9–10 indicating "excellent." For questions 6, 8, and 9, they were asked to select one of three responses: high, moderate, or low. Table 2.1 shows the questions asked and the responses received.

Table 2.1 Rural electrification questionnaire results

Rural electrification questionnaire																				*Mean*
1. How has the Akosombo Dam, a significant source of hydropower and electricity, been managed since the beginning of the 1990s?	6	4	8	4	5	5	4	4	5	6	8	8	5	4	4	7	5	5	6	5.4
2. How successful has the Rural Electrification Program been since its inception in the 1990s?	7	4	5	3	8	5	4	5	3	8	10	5	6	5	3	8	10	8	7	5.7
3. How would you rate the success of Ghana's Self-Help Electrification Scheme, which emerged in the early 1990s?	6	3	7	5	3	3	m	5	5	5	10	6	6	2	4	4	8	5	8	5
4. How connected is rural electrification to income generation and rural development outcomes?	7	4	6	6	1	2	3	6	8	3	10	7	10	5	5	5	4		10	5.4
5. How would you rate the capacity of District Assemblies in assisting with rural electrification and the self-help electrification scheme?	6	2	5	3	3	4	3	6	6	6	9	6	1	6	6	9	8	7	6	5.4
6. How would you rate the effectiveness of Ghana's decentralization program and devolution of authority to district assemblies?	m	m	m	m	l	m	m	M	m	L	H	m	L	m	h	m	L	m	m	N/A
7. Has the politicization of electrification in the Fourth Republic helped advance rural electrification?	7	2	6	2	5	2	6	4	2	4	7	9	2	5	2	8	7	3	6	4.7
8. Have the WB's and IMF's policies reduced the scope of government in Ghana in terms of economic expansion and programs geared toward rural development?	m	m	m	m	m	h	L	M	M	m	M	H	L	m	m	M	H	h	m	N/A
9. How would you rate the capacity of District Assemblies in terms of financial and material capacity to address the needs of communities?	m	m	m	l	l	L	m	M	L	L	H	M	L	m	l	M	M	l	l	N/A
10. How would you rate Ghana's overall performance in terms of electrification?	6	4	7	5	5	5	6	5	5	5	7	8	6	5	6	5	7	6	7	5.8

Source: Created by the author

Three of the eight respondents from the Ministry of Energy evaluated SHEP's success (question 3) as "poor"; four chose "fair," while one did not answer the question. These responses indicate that, despite the Ministry of Energy's official statements touting the program's effectiveness, administrators do not personally share that assessment. However, 68% of the respondents had relatively high assessments of the DAs' performance regarding SHEP, a finding that supports the view that DAs do a good job in the face of numerous financial constraints that affect their ability to meet their administrative, fiscal, and development responsibilities.

For question 6, regarding the effectiveness of the devolution of authority to the DAs, 13 respondents selected "moderate," four chose "low," and two selected "high." When asked to assess the DAs' capacity to meet their communities' financial and material needs (question 9), nine respondents answered "moderate," nine said "low," and one chose "high," indicating a split in perceptions that contradicts widespread observations both in interviews and in the literature. This finding suggests a gap between expectations and standards of operation and may reflect the ambiguous results of ongoing decentralization efforts and the nature of capacity-building.

Notes

1. Unless otherwise cited, all quotations in this chapter are taken from my confidential interviews and personal communications with government officials in 2009. In "The Measurement of Decentralization: The Ghanaian Experience, 1988–92," *African Affairs* 95, no. 378 (January 1996): 31–50, Joseph Ayee notes that deconcentration was taken to mean the "authority for the discharge of specified functions to the staff of a central government ministry or department at the local level to make administrative decisions on behalf of the central government or authority" (37).
2. Diana Conyers, "Decentralization: The Latest Fashion in Development Administration?" *Public Administration & Development (Pre-1986)* 3, no. 2 (1983): 97.
3. Alison J. Ayers, "Demystifying Democratisation: The Global Constitution of (Neo)Liberal Polities in Africa," *Third World Quarterly* 27, no. 2 (2006): 329.
4. See James Tyler Dickovick and James S. Wunsch, eds., *Decentralization in Africa: The Paradox of State Strength* (Lynne Rienner Publishers, Incorporated, 2014), exploration of a rich account of over 10 states.
5. Harriet B. Schiffer, "Local Administration and National Development: Fragmentation and Centralization in Ghana," *Canadian Journal of African Studies* 4, no. 1 (1970): 74–75.

6. Leslie E. Grayson, "Decentralisation in Planning and Economic Decision-Making in Ghana," *Journal of Modern African Studies* 13, no. 1 (March 1975): 126–33.
7. Ibid., 127.
8. Kwamena Ahwoi, *Local Government and Decentralisation in Ghana* (Accra: Unimax Macmillan, 2010), 19.
9. J. Naustdalslid, *Decentralisation Policies in Ghana* (Oslo: Norwegian Institute for Urban and Regional Research, 1992); Crook and Manor, *Democracy and Decentralisation*; Stein Sundsøl Eriksen, Jon Naustdalslid, and Arild Schou, *Decentralisation from Above: A Study of Local Government in Botswana, Ghana, Tanzania, and Zimbabwe* (Oslo: Norwegian Institute for Urban and Regional Research, 1999); George Owusu, "Small Towns and Decentralised Development in Ghana: Theory and Practice," *Africa Spectrum* 39, no. 2 (2004): 167.
10. Ayee, "Measurement of Decentralization," 38.
11. See Daniel Green and E. Gyimah-Boadi, "Review of Ghana under PNDC Rule," *Africa Today* 43, no. 4 (October–December 1996): 431–34.
12. Gyimah-Boadi, *Ghana under PNDC Rule.*
13. Eboe Hutchful, "Why Regimes Adjust: The World Bank Ponders Its 'Star Pupil'," *Canadian Journal of African Studies/La Revue canadienne des études africaines* 29, no. 2 (1995): 306.
14. See Ayers, "Demystifying Democratisation," 322–23.
15. See Jean Grugel, *Democratization: A Critical Introduction* (Houndmills: Palgrave, 2002), 176, 180.
16. Peter Fuseini Haruna, "Reforming Ghana's Public Service: Issues and Experiences in Comparative Perspective," *Public Administration Review* 63, no. 3 (May 2003): 343–54.
17. See Michael Ross, "Is Democracy Good for the Poor?" *American Journal of Political Science* 50, no. 4 (October 2006): 860; See Peter Boone, "Politics and the Effectiveness of Foreign Aid," *European Economic Review* 40, no. 2 (1996): 289–329; Bruce Bueno de Mesquita, Alastair Smith, R. M. Siverson, and James D. Morrow, "Logic of Political Survival Cambridge, Mass" (2003); Partha Dasgupta, *An Inquiry into Well-Being and Destitution* (Oxford University Press on Demand, 1995); Álvaro Franco, Carlos Álvarez-Dardet, and Maria Teresa Ruiz, "Effect of Democracy on Health: Ecological Study," *BMJ* 329, no. 7480 (2004): 1421–23; David A. Lake and Matthew A. Baum, "The Invisible Hand of Democracy: Political Control and the Provision of Public Services," *Comparative Political Studies* 34, no. 6 (2001): 587–621; David A. Lake and Matthew A. Baum, "The Invisible Hand of Democracy: Political Control and the Provision of Public Services," *Comparative Political Studies* 34, no. 6 (2001): 587–621; James W. McGuire, "Social policy

and mortality decline in East Asia and Latin America," *World Development* 29, no. 10 (2001): 1673–97; Bruce E. Moon and William J. Dixon, "Politics, the State, and Basic Human Needs: A Cross-National Study," *American Journal of Political Science* (1985): 661–94; Adam Przeworski, Michael E. Alvarez, José Antonio Cheibub, and Fernando Limongi, "Democracy and Development: Political Institutions and Well-Being in the World, 1950–1990," (2001): 236; Amartya Sen, *Poverty and Famines: An Essay on Entitlement and Deprivation* (Oxford University Press, 1981); Amartya Sen, *Development as Freedom* (Oxford: Oxford University Press, 1999); Joseph T. Siegle, Michael M. Weinstein, and Morton H. Halperin, "Why Democracies Excel," *Foreign Affairs* 83 (2004): 57; Thomas D. Zweifel, and Patricio Navia, "Democracy, Dictatorship, and Infant Mortality," *Journal of Democracy* 11, no. 2 (2000): 99–114.

18. Most recently Brian Min, in *Power and the Vote: Elections and Electricity in the Developing World* (Cambridge University Press, 2015) addresses this question in compelling fashion. Also see George Avelino, David S. Brown, and Wendy Hunter. "The Effects of Capital Mobility, Trade Openness, and Democracy on Social Spending in Latin America, 1980–1999," *American Journal of Political Science* 49, no. 3 (2005): 625–41; David S. Brown and Wendy Hunter, "Democracy and Human Capital Formation: Education Spending in Latin America, 1980 to 1997," *Comparative Political Studies* 37, no. 7 (2004): 842–64.; John Gerring, Strom C. Thacker, and Rodrigo Alfaro. "Democracy and Human Development," *The Journal of Politics* 74, no. 1 (2012): 1–17; Robert R. Kaufman and Alex Segura-Ubiergo, "Globalization, Domestic Politics, and Social Spending in Latin America: A Time-Series Cross-Section Analysis, 1973–97," *World Politics* 53, no. 4 (2001): 553–87; James W. McGuire, "Social Policy and Mortality Decline in East Asia and Latin America," *World Development* 29, no. 10 (2001): 1673–97; Stasavage, David, "The Role of Democracy in Uganda's Move to Universal Primary Education," *The Journal of Modern African Studies* 43, no. 1 (2005): 53–73; Jose Tavares and Romain Wacziarg, "How Democracy Affects Growth," *European Economic Review* 45, no. 8 (2001): 1341–78.
19. Ross, "Is Democracy Good for the Poor?" 860.
20. Brian Min, *Power and the Vote: Elections and Electricity in the Developing World* (Cambridge University Press, 2015), 8–9.
21. Ibid., 27. Min offers fascinating perspective on the notion that rural poor vote on higher levels in developing countries, with India as an example, than in the developed world.
22. Kurt Weyland, *Democracy without Equity: Failures of Reform in Brazil* (Pittsburgh: University of Pittsburgh Press, 1996).
23. See Dennis A. Rondinelli, G. Shabbir Cheema, and John R. Nellis, *Decentralization in Developing Countries: A Review of Recent Experience*

(Washington, DC: World Bank, 1983); James S. Wunsch and Dele Olowu, eds., *The Failure of the Centralized State: Institutions and Self-Governance in Africa* (Boulder, CO: Westview, 1990); Richard Crook and James Manor, *Enhancing Participation and Institutional Performance: Democratic Decentralisation in South Asia and West Africa: Report to ESCOR, the Overseas Development Administration, on Phase Two of a Two Phase Research Project* (London: Economic and Social Committee on Overseas Research, 1994).

24. Dickovick and Wunsch, *Decentralization in Africa*, 92.
25. Jeffrey Herbst, *The Politics of Reform in Ghana, 1982–1991* (Berkeley: University of California Press, 1993).
26. See Jennifer A. Widner, ed., *Economic Change and Political Liberalization in Sub-Saharan Africa* (Baltimore: Johns Hopkins University Press, 1994).
27. Richard C. Crook and James Manor, *Democracy and Decentralisation in South Asia and West Africa: Participation, Accountability, and Performance* (Cambridge: Cambridge University Press, 1998), 222.
28. Mamdani, Mahmood. *Citizen and Subject: Contemporary Africa and the Legacy of Late Colonialism* (Princeton University Press, 1996).
29. See Ayee, "Measurement of Decentralization"; Joseph R. A. Ayee, *Towards Effective and Accountable Local Government in Ghana* (Legon-Accra: Ghana Center for Democratic Development, 2003); Kwame Ninsin, *Ghana's Political Transition* (Accra: Ghana Freedom, 1996).
30. These responses came from a questionnaire that I administered in 2009. For details on the questionnaire, see the appendix to this chapter.
31. See Ayers, "Demystifying Democratisation," 329.
32. J. Tyler Dickovick and James S. Wunsch, eds., *Decentralization in Africa: The Paradox of State Strength* (Boulder, CO: Rienner, 2014).
33. Ibid., 91.
34. Ayers, "Demystifying Democratisation," 329.
35. Samuel, P. "*Huntington, Political Order in Changing Societies* (New Haven, 1968)." argues that the slow development of political institutions coupled with rapid social change could lead to political decay, instability, and even violence in developing societies because of the incongruence between resources and infrastructure and the mobilization of new societal groups. This argument is instructive here because the process of decentralization attempted to localize development initiatives and create political structures directly accountable to the people, thereby heightening rural residents' expectations.
36. See World Bank, *Somalia: Country Re-Engagement Note* (Washington, DC: World Bank, April 2003), 1. Available at http://documents.worldbank.org/curated/en/830051468781503521/Somalia-Country-re-engagement-note.

37. G. Shabbir Cheema and Dennis A. Rondinelli, eds., *Decentralizing Governance: Emerging Concepts and Practices* (Cambridge, MA: Ash Institute for Democratic Governance and Innovation, John F. Kennedy School of Government, Harvard University; Washington, DC: Brookings Institution Press, 2007), 2–4.
38. See Dennis Rondinelli, "What Is Decentralization?" in *Decentralization Briefing Notes*, ed. Jennie Litvack and Jessica Seddon (Washington, DC: World Bank Institute, 1999), 2–5. See also Andrew N. Parker, *Decentralization: The Way Forward for Rural Development?* (Washington, DC: World Bank, 1995).
39. Jennie Litvack, Ahmad Junaid, and Richard Bird, *Rethinking Decentralization in Developing Countries* (Washington, DC: World Bank, 1998), 4. Available at http://www1.worldbank.org/publicsector/decentralization/Rethinking%20Decentralization.pdf; Sylvia Bergh, "Democratic Decentralisation and Local Participation: A Review of Recent Research," *Development in Practice* 14, no. 6 (November 2004): 780–90.
40. Ibid., 781.
41. Kwamena Ahwoi, *Enhancing the Decentralization Programme: District Assemblies and Sub-Structures as Partners in Governance* (Accra: Institute of Economic Affairs, 2000), 2.
42. Mike Oquaye, *Politics in Ghana, 1982–1992: Rawlings, Revolution, and Populist Democracy* (Accra: Tornado 2004), 265.
43. Kodwo Ewusi, *Trends in the Economy of Ghana, 1986–1988* (Legon: Institute of Statistical, Social, and Economic Research, University of Ghana, 1988), 46.
44. World Bank, 1987, 4.
45. Oquaye, *Politics in Ghana*, 265.
46. For more on historical and ideological rivalries between political parties in the 1992, 1996, and 2000 elections, see Minion K. C. Morrison, "Political Parties in Ghana through Four Republics: A Path to Democratic Consolidation," *Comparative Politics* (2004): 421–42.
47. Green, "Ghana's Adjusted Democracy"; M. Bawumia, "Understanding Rural–Urban Voting Patterns in the 1992 Ghanaian Election," *Journal of Modern African* Studies 36, no. 1 (1997): 47–70; Michael Bratton, Philip Alderfer, and Neo R. Simutanyi, *Political Participation in Zambia, 1991–1996: Trends, Determinants, and USAID Program Implications* (Zambia Democratic Governance Project, 1997).
48. See Lindsay Whitfield, "Trustees of Development from Conditionality to Governance: Poverty Reduction Strategy Papers in Ghana," *Journal of Modern African Studies* 43, no. 4 (December 2005): 641–64; Ayers, "Demystifying Democratisation."

49. Whitfield, "Trustees of Development," 653.
50. Irving Leonard Markovitz, "Uncivil Society, Capitalism and the State in Africa," *Commonwealth & Comparative Politics* 36, no. 2 (1998): 21–53.
51. These regions have high percentages of agriculture, low percentages of industry, and lower median incomes and electrification rates than the country's other seven regions. According to the Ministry of Energy, only about 30% of the nearly two million residents of the Upper East have access to electricity.
52. See Richard C. Crook and Alan Sturla Sverrisson. "IDS Working paper 130." *Brighton: Institute of* (2001); Richard C. Crook, "Decentralisation and Poverty Reduction in Africa: The Politics of Local–Central Relations," *Public Administration and Development* 23, no. 1 (2003): 77–88; Paul Smoke, "Decentralisation in Africa: Goals, Dimensions, Myths and Challenges," *Public Administration and Development* 23, no. 1 (2003): 7–16; Gordon Crawford, "Decentralization and the Limits to Poverty Reduction: Findings from Ghana," *Oxford Development Studies* 36, no. 2 (2008): 235–258; Crawford (2008).
53. Gordon Crawford, "Decentralisation and Struggles for Basic Rights in Ghana: Opportunities and Constraints," *The International Journal of Human Rights* 14, no. 1 (2010): 134, 135.
54. Oquaye, Mike. *Politics in Ghana, 1982–1992: Rawlings, Revolution, and Populist Democracy* (Tornado Publications, 2004).
55. Konings, Piet. *The State and Rural Class Formation in Ghana: A Comparative Analysis* (KPI, 1986), 2.
56. Hutchful, "Fall and Rise."
57. Ghana Statistical Service, (GSS) 1995 cited from Owusu, George, "Small Towns and Decentralised Development in Ghana: Theory and Practice," *Africa Spectrum* (2004): 165–95. L.
58. Post-independence political and economic upheavals contributed to the limited attention to domestic energy provision.
59. James Tyler Dickovick and James S. Wunsch, eds., *Decentralization in Africa: The Paradox of State Strength* (Lynne Rienner Publishers, Incorporated, 2014), 105.
60. See Oquaye, *Politics in Ghana*, 265.
61. Ayee, "Measurement of Decentralization."
62. Ninsin, *Ghana's Political Transition.*
63. See Amos Anyimadu, "Some Institutional Aspects of Agricultural Development Policy under the PDNC," in *Ghana under PNDC Rule*, ed. E. Gyimah-Boadi (Dakar: CODESRIA, 1993).
64. Ayee, "Measurement of Decentralization."
65. The substantial increase reflected in the current number of districts reflects few changes or the circumstances noted above.

66. See David Simon, Duncan McGregor, Kwasi Nsiah-Gyabaah, and Donald A. Thompson, "Poverty Elimination, North-South Research Collaboration, and the Politics of Participatory Development," *Development in Practice* 13, no. 1 (February 2003): 46.
67. Cited in Anne M. Larson and Jesse C. Ribot, "Democratic Decentralisation through a Natural Resource Lens: An Introduction," *European Journal of Development Research* 16, no. 1 (2004): 1–25.
68. Dubash, Navroz K. "Revisiting Electricity Reform: The Case for a Sustainable Development Approach," *Utilities Policy* 11, no. 3 (2003): 143–54.
69. Gary, Ian. "Confrontation, Co-operation or Co-optation: NGOs and the Ghanaian State during Structural Adjustment," *Review of African Political Economy* 23, no. 68 (1996): 163.
70. On the difficulties of delineating the differences between local/indigenous and foreign/international NGOs and their activities, see Joel D. Barkan, "I. Elections in Agrarian Societies," *Journal of Democracy* 6, no. 4 (1995): 106–16. Ian Gary, "Confrontation, Co-operation or Co-optation: NGOs and the Ghanaian State during Structural Adjustment," *Review of African Political Economy* 23, no. 68 (1996). For discussions of the typology of NGOs, which include community-based organizations, service or intermediary NGOs, and international and relief organizations (which tend to be foreign), see Michael Bratton, "Beyond the State: Civil Society and Associational Life in Africa," *World Politics* 41, no. 3 (1989): 407–30; Alan Fowler, "Distant Obligations: Speculations on NGO Funding and the Global Market," *Review of African Political Economy* 19, no. 55 (1992): 9–29.
71. A. Bebbington and J. Farrington, "Governments, NGOs, and Agricultural Development: Perspectives on Changing Inter-Organisational Relationships," *Journal of Development Studies* 29, no. 2 (1993): 25.
72. Xiao Ye and Sudharshan Canagarajah, *Efficiency of Public Expenditure Distribution and Beyond: A Report on Ghana's 2000 Public Expenditure Tracking Survey in the Sectors of Primary Health and Education* (Washington, DC: World Bank, 2002). Available at http://documents.worldbank.org/curated/en/711501468774879785/Efficiency-of-public-expenditure-distribution-and-beyond-a-report-on-Ghanas-2000-public-expenditure-tracking-survey-in-the-sectors-of-primary-health-and-education.
73. World Bank, *Ghana: Sector Reform and the Pattern of the Poor—Energy Use and Supply* (Washington, DC: World Bank, 2006). Available at http://documents.worldbank.org/curated/en/421071468252576846/Ghana-sector-reform-and-the-pattern-of-the-poor-energy-use-and-supply.
74. See Gerald Foley, *Electricity for Rural People* (London: Panos, 1990).
75. Institute of Economic Affairs, Ghana (2002) Monograph series, No. 3.
76. Ibid., 4.

77. Bartholomew Armah, "Public Sector Corruption and Macro-Stability: Evidence from the Auditor-General's Reports: from *A Review of the Auditor General's Reports* 1993–1999 *The Institute of Economic Affairs*, 2003.
78. Ibid.
79. Parliamentary Debates, (Ghana) Fourth Series, Official Report (2003), 730.
80. IEA Report Number 3, 2002.
81. See, for example, Ayee, "Measurement of Decentralization."
82. Bartholomew K. Armah, William Inaidoo, and Mawuli Feglo, *The Ghana Poverty Reduction Strategy and Its Link to the 2003 Budget* (Accra: Institute of Economic Affairs, 2003).
83. Ibid.
84. Ministry of Energy document, 2006.
85. Ministry of Energy document, 2008.
86. Ministry of Energy document, 2008.
87. Information provided by two engineers who noted extensive lobbying by chiefs and opinion leaders.
88. Foley, *Electricity for Rural People*, 9.
89. Ibid., 11.
90. See Lindsay Whitfield, *The Politics of Aid: African Strategies for Dealing with Donors* (Oxford: Oxford University Press, 2008).
91. Ghana Living Standards Survey (GLSS), Round 6: "Poverty Profile in Ghana.
92. National Electrification Scheme, Ministry of Energy, 2008.
93. Ibid.
94. These figures come from Ministry of Energy report, 2016.
95. John-Mary Kauzya, *Local Governance Capacity-Building for Full Range Participation: Concepts, Frameworks, and Experience in African Countries* (New York: United Nations, 2003).
96. Whitfield, "Trustees of Development," 660.
97. See ibid.; Ayers, "Demystifying Democratisation."
98. USAID Comparative Assessment of Decentralization in Africa: Final Report and Summary of Findings, September 2010, http://pdf.usaid.gov/pdf_docs/PNADX211.pdf.
99. Emmanuel Gyimah-Boadi, Political Decentralization: Achievements and Challenges in "Reflections on Ghana's Decentralization Program: Progress, Stagnation or Retrogression," Decentralization Symposium, Center for Democracy and Development, (CDD-Ghana) 2009: 7.
100. Ibid., 6–7.
101. Dickovick and Wunsch, *Decentralization in Africa*, 92.
102. Afrobarometer Briefing Paper No. 20, 2005, www.afrobarometer.org.

103. http://afrobarometer.org/countries/ghana-1.
104. Reflections on Ghana's Decentralization Program: Progress, Stagnation or Retrogression," Decentralization Symposium, Center for Democracy and Development, (CDD-Ghana) 2009.
105. Caterina Clerici, Marisa Schwartz Taylor, and Kevin Taylor, "Dumsor: The Electricity Outages Leaving Ghana in the Dark," *Al-Jazeera*, 2016. Available at http://interactive.aljazeera.com/aje/2016/ghana-electricity-outage-dumsor/.
106. See Owusu, "Small Towns and Decentralised Development," 165–95.
107. See Kwame Akonor, *Africa and IMF Conditionality: The Unevenness of Compliance* (New York: Routledge, 2012).
108. Gary W. Cox and Mathew D. McCubbins, "Electoral Politics as a Redistributive Game," *Journal of Politics* 48, no. 2 (May 1986): 370–89.
109. Brian Min, *Power and the Vote: Elections and Electricity in the Developing World* (Cambridge University Press, 2015), 15.

CHAPTER 3

The Historical-Institutional Context for Electrification and Power Sector Reform in Ghana: 1992–2008

When asked about the circumstances and impetus for rural electrification schemes, a prominent member of the NDC party noted how the political will was not in place until 1992.[1] In the analysis that follows, I determine the extent to which power sector reforms successfully reduced electric energy gaps, particularly in rural areas. I argue that the intersection between historically uneven policies in Ghana's energy sector and the politics of the post-1992 period, during which a clamor for economic change, accountability, and public goods delivery emerged to counter an urban bias, produced a political will to address inequities in electricity provision. I contend that the resulting *partial implementation* of power sector reforms paradoxically produced an overall success in electricity access for the country and, at the same time, differential benefits for the rural poor. This chapter advances the view that the decision of subsequent governments in the post-1992 period to circumvent comprehensive power sector reforms accounts for the success of state-led decentralized electrification initiatives and schemes.[2] These policies arguably, and perhaps ironically, represent a triumph of democratic governance for the rural populace, because concerns about this segment of society reflect more responsive governance. The chapter also finds that implicit concerns about social equity or access for the poor explain the resistance of subsequent governments to adopting full-scale market-oriented reforms of the electric energy sector. I concur with Edjekumhene et al. (2003), who point to a lifeline rate policy that keeps the price of electricity well below market value as

N. Sackeyfio, *Energy Politics and Rural Development in Sub-Saharan Africa*, https://doi.org/10.1007/978-3-319-60122-9_3

evidence of measures to placate a resistant public.[3] Indeed, I maintain that the partial nature of power sector reforms represents a *logical choice* for a shifting economy marked by the increasing salience of service delivery. Most remarkably, it allowed governments to reap political gains and support from the rural populace.

This chapter explores the nature of institutional relationships within Ghana's energy sector, market-oriented reforms of the power sector, and the consequences of targeted rural electrification programs that aimed to reduce the electric energy gap. By contextualizing the historical development of Ghana's energy institutions, the chapter examines the manner in which particular groups, like the rural poor, have benefited from electricity delivery. As a central public service issue, electric energy provision is often identified by members of parliament as critical to poverty reduction efforts and economic development in terms of income-generating activities. In this regard, a former minister of energy, Honorable Joseph Kofi Adda, remarked a decade ago, "The nation's future in the energy sector is driven by a policy that is rooted in the overall development agenda of reducing poverty and becoming a middle income nation by 2015."[4] It is unfortunate that, in spite of a burnished status as one of the fastest-growing economies on the continent, an endemic mismatch between heavy investments in hydropower, thermal plants, and the use of offshore oil to power the country and the results they have achieved is apparent. Although efforts have been made to move beyond electricity provision through grids, Ghanaians do not always enjoy regular or more efficient provision of electricity in urban or, more importantly, rural areas, despite a remarkable nationwide access rate of 80.51%. The notion of electricity access conceals what are essentially stark differences between actual connectivity, quantity and supply. In fact, as an Afrobarometer survey finds for 2014–2015, though many Africans sampled across 36 states that include Ghana note the problem of electricity provision, only 31% rank it as a challenge. The tables below from Afrobarometer are illustrative. In the second chart, 30% of Ghanaians are connected to the grid, but access is only occasional or never, while only 37% are connected and have electricity all the time. Although the problems of collective action and malaise are well known, they offer a puzzle, nonetheless. However, it is worth noting that it is unclear if generator use for electricity access is included within the figures for those connected (Figs. 3.1 and 3.2).

A prevailing view among policymakers and energy officials is that electricity is a key indicator of a minimum standard of living and an economic

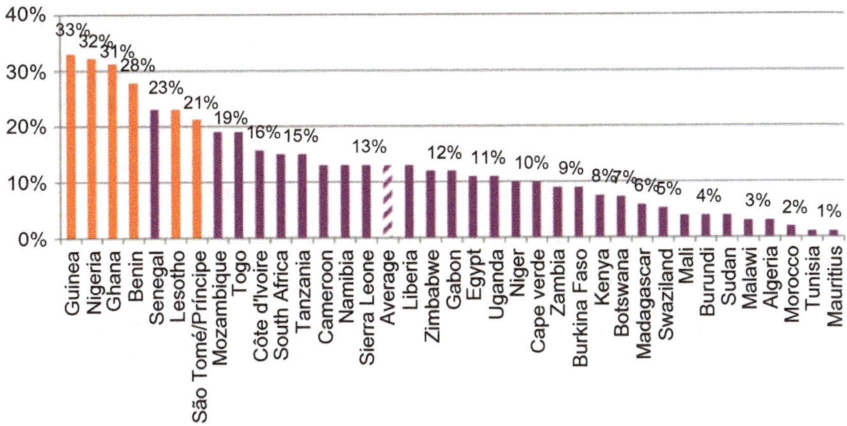

Fig. 3.1 Afrobarometer survey of 36 African countries
Source: Afrobarometer Round 6 New data from 36 African countries, Dispatch No. 75, 14 March 2016

input for income generation and rural development. However, measures to restructure the power sector to improve access and rescue underperforming energy institutions demonstrate an inherent tension between neo-liberal or market-oriented expectations for performance and efforts to provide public service delivery for the bulk of the country's mostly rural population. Consequently, I examine the structural underpinning of Ghana's energy institutions and the relationships between them in the context of closing the electric energy gap in what should be a hydro-rich economy.

History Matters: Energy Generation in Ghana, the Akosombo Dam, and the Volta River Project

Though electric energy provision within a decentralized political framework has produced small triumphs for the rural populace owing to populist measures—exercises in political electoral politics via timed and deliberately sequenced electricity projects since the 1990s—the performance of key energy institutions cannot be overlooked. Despite an uneven history of hydropower generation, beginning with the Akosombo Dam from the mid-1960s to the early 1980s, the country was well poised to provide electricity to all ten of its regions, according to the data analysis

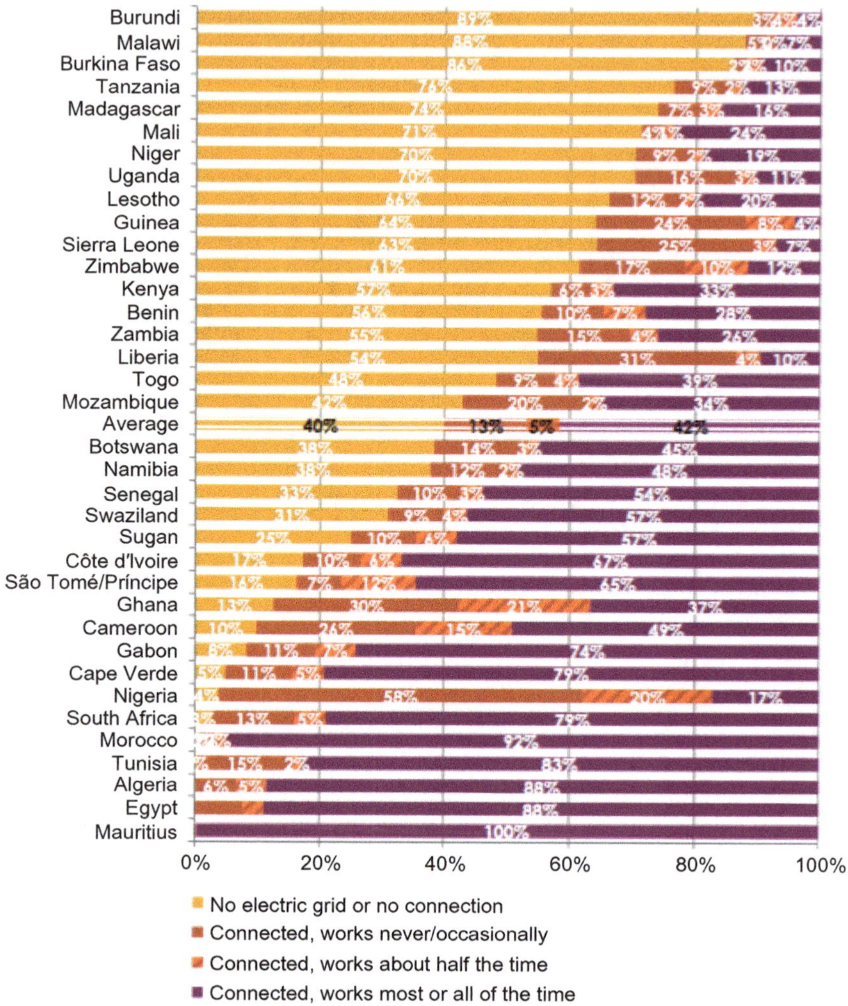

Fig. 3.2 Afrobarometer table of grid quality and connectivity
Source: Afrobarometer Round 6 New data from 36 African countries, Dispatch No. 75, 14 March 2016

conducted in this study. After the overthrows of Nkrumah and Busia, political instability, frequent regime change, and deteriorating economic conditions prompted a decline in the performance of Ghana's energy institutions. Disruptions in quality and quantity became the norm, with priority reserved for urban areas and a few industrial users. By 2000, indigenous sources of energy comprised 90–95%, with only 5–10% generated by hydropower, according to the Energy Commission's July 2006 report.[5] Electrification was identified as a key input for industrial and agricultural development, starting with the Second Development Plan (1959–1964). The political vision of modernization and industrialization, largely through the aluminum smelting that the dam promised, failed to materialize, owing to partisanship, political instability, and frequent regime change. Prior to independence, colonial administrations did little to electrify the country, except in key areas like parts of the Cape Coast and Accra, where significant commercial or economic activity was centered. However, efforts to develop the country's first hydroelectric project were first promoted by Sir Kitson, who noticed the potential for electrification while on a voyage down the Volta River.[6]

In 1955, the Volta River Preparatory Commission found hydropower essential for the development of the aluminum industry, with the secondary aims of providing electricity to as much of the country as possible and providing an abundance of cheap electricity to other industries as well. As a newly independent country that hoped to encourage development through self-sufficiency and reliance on its own natural resources and manpower, the importance of the dam as a symbol of independence and economic hope can hardly be overstated. The optimism of this period was largely inspired by the nationalist fervor and hopes for economic development that Kwame Nkrumah and other key nationalist figures spurred in pro-independence movements. But the ensuing realities of inadequate economic planning, infrastructural deficits including financial and administrative resources, and weak institutional configuration complicated the emergence of coherent development strategies capable of complementing vital economic inputs like electricity.

The history of generation is divided into three periods, with the first characterized by isolated generation facilities and low rates of electrification. The second period comprises the "hydro years" (1966–1980s), when the Akosombo Dam was built in 1966 and the Volta Lake constructed.

During this period, demand for electricity increased dramatically and, in fact, exceeded the capacity of the Akosombo Dam with the construction of the Kpong hydroelectric power plants, completed in 1982. In the mid-1980s, efforts to increase generating capacity emerged. In the third phase of energy development, the Takoradi thermal power plant was built to lessen the vulnerability of the power system caused by insufficient rainfall and resulting low inflows into the Volta Lake. While thermal plants helped to meet the shortfall in supply, halts nevertheless continued.[7] In the statement to parliament in 2007, the former minister of energy, Honorable Kofi Adda, noted, "the revolutionary rhetoric in play did not facilitate the use or generation of funding needed to secure extra generation capacity… following droughts during this period" (Hon. Joseph Kofi Adda, Statement to Parliament, June 6, 2007).

To supplement current generation, the Bui hydro project was commissioned a little over a decade ago and finally completed in 2013. Located on the Black Volta, on the border between the Northern and Brong Ahafo regions, approximately 150 km upstream of the Volta, it is expected to provide 10% of the country's present energy requirements of 1700 megawatts (MW). Unlike the Akosombo Dam, which primarily supports hydropower generation, the Bui project includes an irrigation component for up to 30,000 hectares of land.[8]

Uneven gaps in distribution over the past few decades reflect the maladies of provision for predominantly domestic consumers. Though consumers in the distribution system are typically categorized as industrial, commercial, or residential customers, the first group represents the primary recipients of electricity. The distribution system comprises poles and wires in neighborhoods, underground circuits, and electricity substations, which are fenced yards with switches, transformers, and other electrical equipment. These substations connect the district capital (town) with surrounding areas that are usually rural. From conversations with MOE officials and from official reports citing the achievements of the NES, one gets the impression that the connection process from district capitals to surrounding towns has been more or less seamless since the energy crises of the late 1990s. However, periodic electric energy shortfalls over the course of several years, in spite of the MOE's efforts to allow independent power producers (IPPs) to develop and operate power plants, offer further evidence of continuing gaps.[9]

Ghana boasts of several public and 11 private institutions, which include the MOE, the Energy Commission (EC), the Public Utility Regulatory Commission (PURC), the Volta River Authority (VRA), the Electric

Company of Ghana (ECG), the Ghana Grid Company (GRIDCO), and the Northern Electricity Distribution Company (NEDCO), formerly the Northern Electricity Department, a subsidiary of the VRA. As part of the power sector reforms initiated in 2005, the VRA relinquished its transmission authority to GRIDCO, which is government-owned but an independent transmission utility whose primary customers are ECG and NEDCO. The MOE essentially formulates energy policy, while the EC constructs energy policy and is totally involved in planning, technical regulation, and monitoring. The PURC regulates electric rates and the VRA has the sole responsibility for electricity generation and transmission. The PURC is noteworthy for its autonomous, self-regulating status. It regulates the whole energy sector, in addition to the water and telecommunication sectors, and has ensured expanded electrification through the application of a performance-based rate adjustment mechanism.[10] In this formulation, the performance of the utility is partially based on the assessment of its technical performance and the number of new connections. According to some observers, efforts of the PURC, along with other government initiatives, may have contributed to higher rates of electrification.[11] The MOE is a critical actor in the electric energy complex of the country in setting target dates for the country's electrification schemes and the construction of grids. Additionally, it acts to promote efficient energy practices, encourage productive use of electric power, and the direction, co-ordination, and development of hydroelectric prospects for major river basins within the country.[12] Despite its well-defined responsibilities, the MOE's status as a regulator has not always been apparent. A former VRA official noted, in 2009, that the MOE is not only poorly run, but lacks staff with appropriate expertise and knowledge, and thus offers few incentives for high performance.[13]

In short, a panoply of energy institutions in West Africa's premier state, albeit a model one, are nonetheless plagued by weaknesses and, in some cases, disjointed policies, which are reflected in the fits and starts of electrification that remain ongoing.

For example, the VRA is noted for its technical and financial performance, but the ECG is prone to high system losses (20%) and poor service quality.[14] Wastage has also plagued the industry, as Mr. Nathaniel Amarteyfio, the former mayor of Accra, noted in our informal interview. Additionally, many rural customers are increasingly reluctant to pay for an erratic supply of electricity. The Centre for Policy Analysis (CEPA) notes that these problems contribute to further deterioration in performance by the industry. When ISSER's *Guide to Electric Power in Ghana* was published in 2005, the authors noted that no significant investments had been made in the company's distribution network over the past ten years, resulting in unreliable supply and periodic extended outages. A 2001 management audit of the operations of the ECG supports these contentions, noting that although "the company had a sound record in system planning, the company [sic] represented an electric utility in crisis."[15] In the absence of consistent and stable collection rates, it is little wonder that the ECG and NED operations experienced losses of 26% and 30% per annum, respectively.[16] A decade and a half later, the ECG's successor, the GRIDCO, still has a substantial distance to go in reversing the declining trust of domestic consumers.

Issues of Transmission Versus Generation Capacity

The relationship between generation capacity and transmission illustrates how energy sector policies have privileged urban and industrial consumers. Though generation capacity was assumed to be ample after the completion of the Akosombo Dam in 1966 and resultant electrification schemes, a 15% access rate for the entire country in 1990 suggested wide disparities between generation and transmission capacity. However, the former head of the VRA found that the transmission system was sufficient to sustain the country's energy needs, and he contends that gaps in electrification were the result of low demand. As he notes, the transmission system was adequate, but full utilization was absent until the late 1980s, when the Economic Recovery Program and injection of capital and donor funds helped to strengthen the economy.[17]

Power plants are typically located at one point, while electricity must be moved from that point to the consumer. Ghana's transmission system is composed of an interconnected system of lines, distribution centers, control plants, and substations that connect the district capital to nearby towns. In December 2003, the existing transmission system comprised 36 substations and approximately 4000 circuit kilometers of 161 kV (a kilovolt is a unit of power in an electric circuit or substation that powers a town or district capital) and 69 kV lines including 129 km of double-circuit 161 kV lines connecting to Togo and Benin.[18] With plans for continued expansion buoyed by the construction of the Bui Dam in 2013, 2831 MW were available for grid power supply as at the end of 2014, and the generation was 12,963 gigawatt hours (GWh), consisting of 64.7%

hydro, 34.75% thermal, and 0.05% solar power. According to an Energy Commission Report, grid electricity available for supply in 2015, based on the planned expansion of generation capacity, would be 15,000–15,200 GWh. As it stands, planned increases in capacity, which were accompanied by power barges from countries like Turkey to supplement power crises almost a year and a half ago, have yet to exhibit a dramatic shift in generation and, ultimately, provision. Popular refrains from Ghanaians lament the seemingly short-term fixes as opposed to long-term solutions. These concerns are inevitably bound up with electoral politics and with the nature of the country's uneven energy policies, as well as the problematic nature of how energy access for residential use is defined. Being on the grid, for example, is not synonymous with electricity flow, given that informal, illegal connectivity or sharing access with neighbors is prevalent.

Though the Akosombo Dam has six power-generating turbines and thermal plants, generation and distribution remain critical challenges that are reflected in residential electricity arrangements. As ISSER reported in 2006, "The major characteristic of residential electricity arrangements are [sic] a 'compound house' phenomenon, which essentially entails a number of households living in a compound and sharing basic amenities like a single electric metering system."[19] Unfortunately, infrastructural development—that is, the necessary inputs for development of commercial and industrial areas—has not borne out as envisioned. Some observers in the electricity industry argue that limitations in electricity service delivery to consumers are both technical and infrastructural in nature.[20] As one former energy official argued, while electrification in itself did not move the country any closer to the economic development envisioned in the Nkrumah era, it remained a vital input in complementary strategies that took off in the 1980s. Consequently, it comes as little surprise that later efforts to reduce the electricity gap, particularly in rural areas, included a focus on developing productive uses, for example, income-generating activities.

The transmission infrastructure built to supply electricity to the entire country was neglected until 1988. A prominent official from the VRA informed me that this had little, if any, bearing on rural expectations from the government and more to do with growing incomes.[21] Nevertheless, almost ten years later, it was all but inevitable that network problems and inadequate access would spur pressures to reform the transmission system. According to an industry insider, partial power sector reform measures involved setting up an office to monitor transmission, and introducing competition to drive down costs, improve efficiency and quality of service, and facilitate open access. Yet reportedly, as late as 2008, implementation of comprehensive power sector reforms remained absent. In 2006, the VRA was set to implement other mechanisms that would improve supply and lower costs. As I was informed by a prominent official from the VRA over a decade ago:

> The fact of the matter was that VRA had built these 500 megawatts of thermal and we were only getting 50% of this. How are we going to fix this? What are we going to do to get this fixed? I probably spent two months on this, coming up with a plan. When I got there, they had a measure called partial availability, just sitting there. But how much of it is running every day? You want it to be around 90 percent. When I got there it was around 40 percent. The year after I left [2006] it had dropped... we made some operational fixes. It was a combination of partial fixes and operational fixes. We had to figure out ... Again, because I am an outsider, I could make some decisions without [politics getting in the way]. (Personal communication, 2008)

Other measures included the unbundling of the sector with public–private partnerships, a single transmission utility to be publicly owned, creation of distribution zones, and the establishment of a transparent regulatory regime. To this end, two regulatory bodies were established in 1997 to supervise electricity service provision. The PURC, established under Act 538, was to be responsible for rate determination and monitoring quality. The second regulatory body, the EC, was established under Act 541 as the licensing authority for electricity utilities, with further statutory responsibilities for technical standards and indicative planning.[22] As an important body, the EC is tasked with ensuring a sustainable energy supply, and the efficient development as well as utilization of energy resources, along with developing uniform mechanisms that ensure effective production, transmission, distribution, and sale of both electricity and natural gas.[23] Both institutions emerged because of rising inequities in provision, intermittent shortages, and the mounting frustration of domestic consumers in both urban and rural areas.

Ghana represents the second-largest producer of electric energy in West Africa after Nigeria, in terms of generation capacity and consumption. But consumer access, especially for the rural poor, is uneven, despite significant headway and a price-distorting program of electricity subsidization sold to residential consumers, which is paid for with higher rates for industrial consumers. What is more, increasing rates have not necessarily coincided with more optimal outcomes in terms of generating revenue and reversing utility losses. What explains this anomaly? In both formal and informal interviews, energy officials noted that utilities failed to improve their operational capacity adequately in terms of efficiency. Other perspectives evince the view that utilities need to improve their efficiency in order to be financially sound and lower their rates for consumers of electricity,[24] which would heighten the risk of dwindling support from rural areas. More importantly, though, the pressure on the PURC to keep rates low prevails amid efforts to attract IPPs.

The Impact of Privatization and Power Distribution and Generation

Market-oriented reforms of power sectors for developing states in sub-Saharan Africa show only partial success in countries that have chosen to adopt them. As I demonstrate in this section, prevailing assumptions of thriving markets, private investment, deregulation to spur competitive energy sectors, and greater efficiency have not resulted in significant revenue or boosted commercialization in terms of a range of independent power producers. Instead, by ignoring the political lessons of structural adjustment policies, tenuous circumstances for state–society relations, and the widespread view of electricity as a "public good"—given consumer reluctance and in some cases refusal to pay for irregular access—these reforms facilitated co-optation by a government unwilling to bear a heavy political price. In effect, privatization of energy institutions aimed to produce a scenario in which the state would retain only a regulatory role.[25] As P.O. Pineau explains it, a "country ownership syndrome," or donor imperatives, plagued efforts to reform the country's electric-energy paradigm, which I maintain helped to structure discretionary provision and provide a rationale for the slow or halting progress on donor assistance.[26]

In the industrialized world, the promise of a public, vertically integrated, centralized power system is a reality: people have reliable and affordable power, and the problems facing these countries are those of a mature system.[27] The USA, for instance, allowed independent power producers to sell electricity to investor-owned utilities—a significant shift that demonstrated how independent generators could be integrated into a grid system and unraveled the notion that the utility sector was a natural monopoly.[28] Consequently, a number of other countries, like Chile and the United Kingdom, began to promote private competition in the energy market, while others followed suit from the 1980s and beyond.

However, developing countries faced a different set of problems. In the 2000 census, for instance, only 17% of Ghana's rural population had access to electricity.[29] Rural access has since shown a remarkable improvement—48.6%, versus 88.5% for urban areas, when the Ghana Statistical Service surveyed households between 2005 and 2013.[30] For many decades, the electric utility industry in sub-Saharan Africa was state-owned. Prior to 1997, the government of Ghana and state-owned electricity utility organizations combined operational responsibilities with policy and regulatory issues. However, during the 1990s, the United Nations Industrial Development Organization (UNIDO) found that power sector reform emerged in developing countries as part of externally driven, macro-economic structural adjustment policies that called for the elimination of state-led development paradigms, in favor of open and free competitive market economies.[31] These ideas took root as a consensus in development thinking, and co-operation broadened. The objectives included poverty reduction as a primary objective of development, the idea that economic growth was best achieved through the private sector, a role for government in helping the private sector flourish, and so forth.[32]

After a series of energy crises and intermittent power outages during the mid to late 1990s prompted discussion of reform to streamline processes within the power sector, the Ghanaian government sought to overcome the limitations of the previous institutional blueprint. Indeed, the MOE indicated, in a 2006 policy report, that power sector restructuring would attempt to make utility companies more efficient in their operational capacities, and aim for greater transparency and independence in utility companies—especially with regard to rate-setting. Likewise, macroeconomic and fiscal crises led to efforts to implement a wide range of structural adjustment programs, with the goal of reducing public spending and increasing private capital flows into economies.[33] Consequently, in 1994, the government of Ghana issued a Statement of Power Sector Reform to indicate that electricity reform would take place.

As Dubash notes, these trends represented a broader political framework of reform during the 1980s and 1990s that included an expanded role for private corporations and a renegotiation of the appropriate role of the state in economic activity, which led developing countries towards markets and away from state-led activity.[34] The prevailing wisdom held that the injection of private capital would rehabilitate existing installations and lead to the creation of new power plants.[35] As a result, major international lending banks and development agencies promoted a policy prescription for developing countries that included privatization of state-owned enterprises. African states like Ghana, South Africa, Mozambique, and Zimbabwe subsequently sought to capitalize on the promise of sizable profits from privatization and commercialization of their power sectors. However, Sharon Beder asserts that these policies benefitted international financial institutions, often at the expense of local business and, undoubtedly, the poor, since the incentives to construct and operate energy infrastructure in developing countries favored foreign investors rather than third-world governments.[36]

As a consequence, the newly minted NDC government began electricity reform in 1993, the same year that the World Bank announced its plans to encourage (or push) countries to liberalize their electric energy sectors. This impetus emerged as a result of donor fatigue from a decade and a half of concessionary financial support and interest in reallocation of funds to other sectors. It was thought that governments would mobilize large amounts of capital necessary to develop and sustain the power sector.[37] One area of reform initiated at this time was epitomized by the introduction of competition in supply and the encouragement of private-sector investment via independent power producers, which necessitated transparency in regulation, leading to the development of a sustainable electricity industry.[38] In a 1999 policy statement, the government outlined plans "to shift emphasis from the country's traditional reliance on multilateral organizations to finance existing power utilities, with the aim to encourage nontraditional sources including direct investment by private investors to participate in power sector development."[39]

In 1997, a restructuring plan was approved, which opened power generation to competition, and introduced concessions to end market segmentation by retaining rate regulation for small consumers, while allowing large customers to be served directly by generators. However, this reform plan was never implemented, because of opposition from a subsidiary of Kaiser Aluminum, which sought to maintain a sweetheart deal with the VRA. In fact, the VRA argued that the unbundling of the power sector would weaken the VRA as a competitor in the proposed West Africa Power Pool, a regional arrangement to increase electricity access.[40] The breakup of the country's monopoly, as noted earlier, resulted in little substantive action, and although the PURC and EC were created as part of efforts to examine industry practices, ensure equitable rates, and establish effective pricing mechanisms, little came of efforts to privatize the VRA fully, which remains government controlled and subject to politicization.

Other analyses found that western multinational corporations sought investment in developing countries as a source of new markets, because profit opportunities declined in affluent countries, especially in traditional areas such as primary industries and manufacturing. This development, combined with the Asian Development Bank's recommendation in the mid-1990s that electricity industries be restructured to introduce competition and reorganized into corporate, commercial entities, prompted interest in a number of states. For instance, South Africa's efforts to attract foreign investment by privatizing its national utility in the 1990s resulted in unemployment for large numbers of people. In preparation for partial privatization of Eskom, the national electricity provider in the country eliminated subsidies, and household bills in the poorest areas increased by up to 4%. At the same time, bills for industrial consumers fell by 15%.[41] One could argue, as John Stern does, that the sustainability of a "commercialized, unbundled utility depends on the establishment of effective and autonomous regulatory institutions, whose success depends on possessing and developing a regulatory memory".[42]

Power sector loans, too, were contingent on government commitments to introduce competition and private participation.[43] These measures were triggered by a supply crunch, due to a drought that reduced the output of Ghana's predominantly hydro system (more than 90% of net generation) in a context of rapidly rising demand.[44]

In any case, subsequent rate increases and the partial removal of subsidies to make utilities more competitive produced huge financial losses, in part the result of subsidies left in place to avoid a political backlash from the electorate. Indeed, stalled reforms and the inability of the regulator and, by extension, the government, to make critical decisions that would impact harshly on the general populace are to blame.[45] Essentially, in the view of a largely rural populace, the domestic tax, or tariff (a term used by the PURC, not meant to imply a tax on imports) is too high, while utilities and investors seeking to recover costs believe they are not high enough. In a climate of economic uncertainty, a profit model for electricity sectors where poverty is rife can prove intractable.[46] In spite of suggestions to establish "fixed rates or charges" for the poor, along with private-sector participation, it is unlikely that electrification in rural areas would significantly improve, given the profit motive.[47] A political culture of patronage remains endemic in twenty-first-century politics and provides an important contextual landscape for both rural and national politics.

Following concerns about making power accessible for the poor, a lifeline philosophy emerged, and external actors, such as a Canadian consulting firm, suggested that it was politically expedient for governments to do so. According to this philosophy, electricity is an essential service rather than a luxury, therefore people of low income should not be deprived of it, and 50 kilowatt hours (kWh) is deemed adequate to serve rural customers and the urban poor.[48] These developments, and the largely stalled process of electricity reforms, support the notion of rural co-optation; after all, rate increases would unduly affect the rural poor, who comprise the bulk of the population.[49] By all accounts, a "project by project" political culture emerged to produce political instrumentalism and development projects, conditioning the rural populace to associate the political power of the state and its officials with the provision of public goods,[50] which speaks for the ability of the incumbency to use resources for this purpose. Whether owing to a credit squeeze or the continuing impact of adjustment policies, Nugent notes that "observers of the political scene commented on the fact that there were relatively few development projects to point to by comparison with 1996."[51]

In any case, according to the government of Ghana, the rate of electrification more than doubled from 1988 to 2003, from 23% to 50%. In pointed remarks, a high-ranking NDC member of parliament noted in the summer of 2009 that "the political will to undertake electrification was not in place until 1992." Without the introduction of industrial and commercial rates, most of the 180,000–200,000 "lifeline" customers would, indeed, have lost the use of electricity because of an inability to pay.[52] Other structural changes endeavored to create competition in supply, transparency in the regulation of sector operations, effective commercialization of operations of electrical utilities, and encouragement of private investment in the development of the electricity sector.[53]

In many democratic governments, emerging liberal business elites who replaced former military rulers and party bureaucrats tended to see market reform as a decisive break from the statism of the old guard. Significantly, many governments felt compelled to accept that the rewards of tapping into the expanding flow of international investment outweighed the risk of abandoning the old state-utility model.[54] Noted members of the old guard (Rawlings' PNDC military regime) used the very same model they previously criticized to reap the gains in private-sector contracts and lucrative deals that accorded them power and status, much to the chagrin of casual observers.[55]

The consequences of these developments are hard to miss, especially when viewed through the lens of globalization.[56] In a new age of convergence, economic outcomes are shaped by regulation and, in turn, the energy sector. Since the 1990s, many countries liberalized their power sectors and opened them to private competition. However, Anil Hira concluded in 2003 that the benefits of privatization of electric and gas markets are not as clear-cut as pro-privatization adherents assert. He argued that the benefits of privatization are likely to be extremely inequitable, for instance along the lines of producing versus nonproducing countries and poorer versus wealthier populations.[57] This observation is quite relevant for countries with large numbers of rural and economically underprivileged residents who might fall prey to exploitation by the few private producers and utility companies that exist. When processes of restructuring and privatization transfer control of vital resources and services to transnational corporations, new burdens for the poor are generated in unanticipated ways.[58]

For example, a West African Power Pool (WAPP) regional electricity power agreement created almost two decades ago may increase energy trade and promote foreign investment in electricity and gas sectors. If lucrative, this arrangement could save the region $3.5 billion over 20 years.[59] Indeed, the EC notes that "to ameliorate the overall power supply shortage prevailing in the country, emanating out of inadequate fuel supply for power generation, investments in liquefied natural gas (LNG) as an alternative gas supply to augment the limited local and unreliable gas from the West Africa Gas Pipeline from Nigeria should be pursued."[60] However, electricity markets in West Africa remain weak, despite the fact that this planned regional power pool project includes Nigeria, Ghana, Benin, Togo, Cote d'Ivoire, Burkina Faso, and Niger. Since these states are not currently equipped to create strong institutional frameworks like those of the Southern Cone countries, which have managed to secure a measure of autonomy from both international and domestic forces through regulatory policies in their energy sectors, the benefits for the former are questionable—especially since it is not possible, at this juncture, to create similar environments. For instance, Argentina created ultra-competitive conditions for foreign investors in electricity while maintaining close ties to the gas market, and Brazil has attempted to create a competitive domestic market, in which its own state companies are favored.[61] Despite the increasing expansion of electricity markets in these states, and the noticeable privatization of power sectors, issues of equity are essential to the welfare of rural residents who stand to be further marginalized, in terms of cost concerns and social safety nets. It is unclear how residential customers would benefit from such schemes, particularly in regard to rural electrification initiatives. Accessibility of information is key and, despite a public freedom of information act that readily makes it so, an overall literacy rate of 56.3% is a critical gap to overcome.[62]

Configuring the impact of market liberalization on electric energy policies may enable us to unpack the processes of state regulation and autonomy in national electrification schemes and the accompanying infrastructure, but understanding the changing dynamic of political actors and institutional change is equally important. While Jeffrey Herbst, in his 1993 study, focuses primarily on the politics of reform in Ghana, his discussion of the antagonistic and problematic relationship between the government and private sector as a central difficulty for the state is persuasive for approaches to the energy sector, deregulation, and economic growth.[63]

Electrification, Infrastructure, and Performance of Industry

The relationships between electrification, infrastructure, the performance of industry, and small and medium enterprises are significant, with the potential to improve the livelihoods of the rural poor. Electricity is a critical component of infrastructure and is vital for structural growth and performance of firms across sub-Saharan Africa. Physical infrastructure, including water, energy, telecommunications, and transport systems, affects economic processes in myriad ways. The technical attributes of infrastructure, according to Banji Oyelaran-Oyeyinka, include "scale, indivisibility, multiple use and general functions," as separated from other forms of capital. However, frequent power outages typically mean that industries must acquire standby generators to support their operations. In most African countries, agricultural and industrial production is constrained by inadequate backward linkages to exploit agricultural raw materials, often located within inaccessible but rich rural communities. This remains a challenge for Ghana, a country that draws substantial revenue from agricultural output. More importantly, Oyelaran-Oyeyinka recognizes that such processes make up a complex of backward and forward linkages that are taken for granted in dynamic industrial environments. Infrastructure affects three broad groups: firms, industrial systems, and consumers. Spatial or geographic concentration by firms or businesses is critical, since the provision of public utilities like transportation and communication induces strong externalities and directly impacts factor prices, as well as growth and revenue. Uneven or inefficient energy access produces barriers for enterprise: (1) when its absence compels firms to generate their own power, which can place a financial burden on them and place major impediments on new investments; and (2) when high transaction costs, poor telecommunications, and/or frequent power outages impede networking among firms.[64]

A cogent question to consider is how firms or businesses respond to fluctuations in infrastructural deficiencies. If firms invest extensively in the acquisition and maintenance of private infrastructural services in urban locales, then what of marginalized populations in rural areas? Viewed this way, the severity of spillover effects belies an 80.51% electrification rate, and it comes as little surprise that inefficient electric energy provision produces lower yields and higher costs for both industrial users and, more importantly, domestic consumers.

There is a direct correlation between energy intensity and productivity, with the former defined as energy consumption per unit of production output. Though the precise nature of electricity linkages to productive uses is spurious for some, energy officials identify it as critical. Noting that electricity gaps have produced onerous circumstances for populations elsewhere, Mr. Emmanuel Asafo, an engineer and official for the VRA, noted, in 2009, that "countries like Burkina Faso and Cote D'Ivoire do not have the electrical infrastructure that Ghana has, and there is a correlation" (Personal Communication).

As Douglas Barnes has observed, many African countries have not successfully implemented rural electrification because of inadequate national development models, which can be attributed to nascent infrastructure. For small and medium enterprises, functioning as income-generating vehicles that rely on electricity as an infrastructural input, the challenges are acute.[65]

Constraints and Continuing Challenges

Although levels of electrification in rural Ghana far outpace those of neighboring countries like Cote d'Ivoire, Benin, and Togo, full electrification remains elusive for the bulk of rural society, who are poor. Most households that can afford to pay for electricity are located in densely populated urban areas and, according to a VRA official whom I interviewed in 2009, "Sometimes one half of a house has access and the other does not."[66] Widely recognized challenges currently facing Ghana's energy sector include: (1) rapidly growing demand for energy by all sectors of the economy and a growing population; (2) the risk of a fundamental imbalance between energy production and indigenous resources, evident for all major energy forms; (3) high levels of end-use inefficiency, culminating in waste of final energy forms; (4) inefficient pricing of energy services; (5) operational inefficiencies of the utilities, leading to high losses and consequent increases in costs of supply and distribution; (6) overreliance on wood fuels, which could threaten the forest cover; (7) failure to exploit solar energy, which is relatively abundant; and (8) inadequate investment due to lack of capital.[67] Despite these constraints, energy officials remain optimistic about the prospect of electrification for the entire population and have noted that efforts are underway to utilize solar energy in the coming decade.

Though other power supply alternatives, like wind and solar energy, are likely to materialize in the future, rural residents will probably continue their reliance on wood fuels for cooking and lighting.[68] According to a 2006 Energy Report by the EC, 90–95% of indigenous power use stems from wood fuels or biomass, 5–10% comes from hydroelectric power, and less than 1% from solar energy. These patterns are expected to continue, raising further questions about access and the ostensible benefits that electrification is said to afford for the rural poor.

Disruptions in access for the commercial sector and electricity crises since the late 1990s offer additional insights into continuing gaps that are widely overlooked in recognition of the country's overall success in electrification. As output fell significantly in the manufacturing industry, profoundly affecting small-scale enterprises and services, Ghana's industrial and commercial sectors bore the brunt of the 1998 power crisis. Production costs rose as many companies procured power generators to fill the electricity gap.[69] In the decade since then, subsequent governments following the Rawlings administration have announced plans for a power supply increase, but higher electricity rates and ineffectual management of the crisis confounded efforts to avoid energy crises, which occurred intermittently until 2007. The Association of Ghana Industries and Trades Union Congress made two observations in a 2000 workshop that provided first-hand evidence of the impact of electric energy on their industries and operations. Firstly, despite the Volta River's capacity and efforts to increase generation and transmission, power supply to end-users continued to be characterized by low reliability and poor quality. Troubled electricity provision also affected small-scale enterprises, a critical source of income for the rural poor, and the steel industry, among others. The result is that labor and production were negatively affected, lending further support to the notion of electricity as a key economic driver.

What Have Market Reforms and Liberalization of Power Sectors Meant for the Rural Poor?

Adequate and sustained transmission of electricity to rural communities depends on autonomous regulatory institutions, under a framework of decentralization, that can offer independent and objective assessment, tying electricity provision to economic livelihoods that can support the rural poor. Despite the merits of liberalization of power sectors and decentralized rural electrification projects, these initiatives have not worked as expected, becoming, instead, as Karekezi and Kimani put it, an "avenue for the collection of additional revenue for utilities and the Treasury with little to show for in terms of expansion of electrification."[70] One can argue that the provision and expansion of decentralized electricity initiatives simultaneously empower constituents, while limiting the scope of central government mechanisms that are primed for patronage during electoral cycles. Their analysis suggests that a closer look at the consequences of reform is sorely needed. Other analyses suggest that, "despite fundamental differences in conditions and motivation for reform, non-OECD reform policies were largely based on the theoretical analyses and policy recommendations of economists concerned principally with deregulation in the US and Europe, with a high degree of uniformity in expectations about reform goals and processes."[71] Unsurprisingly, developing countries within sub-Saharan Africa chose to adopt piecemeal reforms, preferring unsustainable subsidies and low rates to protect economically vulnerable populations.

While Ghana is at the forefront of transparent processes in terms of pricing reform, it does not appear that a balance has been achieved between cost recovery for power utilities and protection of customer interests, despite rate increases and adjustments. To be sure, the decision to reform the electricity sector in Ghana with World Bank assistance and conditionalities resulted in the government of Ghana assuming primary control of the process and preferring to implement its own prescriptions.[72] Ostensibly, these measures were taken to allow for domestic autonomy. Yet pricing reform and a lifeline or "social" rate targeted at poor and low-income households have not noticeably reduced the energy gap. It is quite possible that "gradualism", or incremental efforts to stretch the co-optative impetus that electrification affords, accounts for this outcome. In any case, future outcomes remain far from clear, but it is likely that, in the years to come, electricity affordability will depend on the extent to which economic growth and stability accrue to the bulk of the population, as well as on how many independent power producers emerge alongside their pricing systems.

Additionally, the so-called "socialization of loss" is significant. In effect, governments make considerable concessions that allow IPPs to distribute and transmit electricity to industrial and, more importantly, domestic populations. The controversy surrounding this development is embodied in the idea of rigid take-or-pay contracts that reduce the scope of autonomy, while ensuring high costs for governments.[73] With Ghana and over 20 other countries at various stages of initiating or implementing reform of their power sectors, Karekezi and Kimani, writing in 2002, questioned the seemingly blanket acceptance of power sector reforms as inherently beneficial. In this view, the benefits of IPP distribution are weighted against issues of equity, particularly for the rural poor, given the logical removal—or at least substantial reduction—in electricity subsidies to garner more profits. These pricing systems appear to downgrade the quality, capacity, and reliability of electric energy systems and thus require reassessment in the current models proffered particularly in sub-Saharan Africa.[74] Though Ghana has only partially implemented them, succeeding administrations and energy officials I interviewed mentioned the government's plans to pursue further power sector reforms, which is not only puzzling, but also ambiguous, given the protracted and uneven nature of the implementation to date.

Conclusion

For a country that should be thriving, based on several energy sources that include the Akosombo, Kpong, and Bui Dams, the relationships between generation, transmission, and distribution of electric energy and the primary institutions that govern the power sector in Ghana remain uneven. Indeed, the weak autonomy of the VRA and lack of adequate manpower, skills, and incentives to perform within the MOE have resulted in a lackluster response to the country's electrification gap, in tandem with frequent regime change and political instability. These developments were partially reversed in the 1990s, as the Rawlings NDC government attempted to implement the National Electrification Scheme and later the Rural Electrification Program. The consequences for growth and the gross domestic product (GDP) are considerable. In a report two years ago, the EC reported a decline in GDP growth from 7.1% in 2013 to 4.2% in 2014, with a further projected decrease to 3.5% in 2015 in the context of a power crisis they noted had worsened.[75]

This chapter has found that the irony of Ghana's much-lauded progress in its rate of access lies in the partial nature of market-oriented power sector reforms (in place as of 2008) and the unevenness of energy policies, in terms of timing and sequencing, that have inadvertently promoted a political business cycle of access. The limited scope of implementation should give pause to the much-heralded market-driven power sector reforms presumed to generate profits, rescue ailing energy and utility sectors, and drive down prices through competitive policies. This finding is significant for two reasons. Firstly, the commendable rate that Ghana has managed to achieve, relative to its neighbors and other states in sub-Saharan Africa, calls into question the merits of a pro-privatization approach, given the absence of truly competitive markets for other goods and services and large numbers of African populations unable to link themselves productively to the economic arena. Borrowing from successful models from countries like Chile and Australia, privatization was expected to introduce competition to challenge ailing government monopolies. Yet experts remain skeptical. For these reasons, energy values and how states define them potentially shape the future of energy sector relationships, as well as external actor or private power production that links national energy objectives to decentralized initiatives to assist rural people in the process. Secondly, a one-size-fits-all policy, implicit in the structure of market-oriented power sectors, remains problematic, since African states face a different set of problems from the mature, developed power sectors of the West. As long as local perceptions of an energy or electricity "social compact" persist, governments are likely to disavow liberalization of electric energy regimes and perhaps limit the ability of independent power producers to operate.

In 1988, the World Bank noted that governments in developing countries aimed to use electricity as part of a broader "social compact," with the implicit understanding that subsidies would make electric power more affordable and accessible—which, in turn, was presumed to propel key sectors of the economy forward. Although the problems inherent in the utility sectors of developing countries have more to do with the failure to implement the public-utility approach practiced in the global North, myriad quandaries facing these countries make comparisons difficult in terms of the current realities in Ghana and sub-Saharan Africa.[76] As the social compact shifts from the state to markets (or to international power producers and exporters), the role of government in public service and other enterprises in the twenty-first century will be a critical dynamic to consider. The strength of Ghana's two regulatory bodies in the electricity sector—the Energy Commission, a technical regulator, and the Public Utilities Regulatory Commission, a rate setter—is remarkable, which makes it unfortunate that the intersection of electric energy generation, transmission, and delivery in tandem with thermal plants, gas supplies, and IPPs remains uneven.

While a number of scholars urge caution in the wholesale adoption of market-oriented reforms of electric energy sectors, and argue that it is not yet clear that the poor in particular benefit, others argue for a sustainable development approach to combating ailing power sectors and lack of competition. Recent studies suggest that corruption in private utility production is an emerging, serious, and poorly understood problem in light of the elite capture of energy benefits, which is alarmingly common.[77] If these trends are any indication, they portend grave consequences for programs like rural electrification and local private investment in utilities.

It is safe to conclude that any additional reforms undertaken will require careful scrutiny and a delicate balancing act among decentralized institutional structures, market-oriented power sector policies, specific measures underpinning these processes, and group interests, which remain paramount in nascent democracies. On the other hand, the clash between the lagging capacity of energy institutions, the marginal status of the Northern region, and the donor-driven initiatives requires new solutions, particularly from subnational governments. With an entire institution devoted to electric energy provision in the Northern region, the continued marginalization, development challenges, and uneven access speak volumes about the treatment of the rural poor, of whom the region is largely comprised.[78] Significantly, the trusteeship role that the donor and development community is increasingly playing calls into question the future of power sector reforms, given that external actors are providing public goods, such as water, roads, food security, and electricity, to a considerable extent. What this means for public and private spaces is anyone's guess. But it is clear that greater inclusion of the rural poor under electricity provision faces further hurdles, given the murky role of independent power producers. Most importantly, the inadequacy of the dialogue between the district assemblies and the rural populace on the question of equity, pricing reform, and agency in determining optimal outcomes for their communities under a political decentralized framework requires urgent and renewed attention.

Notes

1. A noted energy insider remarked, in an interview, that the partial nature of the power sector remained in place as late as 2008.
2. The National Electrification Scheme, Rural Electrification Program, and Self-Help Electrification Program are the primary initiatives referred to throughout the chapter.
3. Ishmael Edjekumhene, Martin Bawa Amadu, and Abeeku Brew-Hammond, *Power Sector Reform in Ghana in the 1990's: The Untold Story of a Divided Country versus a Divided Bank* (Kumasi, Ghana: Kumasi Institute of Technology and Environment [KITE], 2003).
4. Hon. Joseph Kofi Adda, Statement to Parliament, June 6, 2007.
5. Energy Commission, *Strategic National Energy Plan, 2006–2020, Main Report*, August 2006.
6. Total electricity demand before the construction of the Akosombo Dam cannot be determined because of the dispersed nature of the supply resources and constrained nature of electricity supply during this period. See the Institute of Statistical, Social and Economic Research (ISSER), *Guide to Electric Power in Ghana* (Legon: University of Ghana, 2005), 17.
7. Ibid., 16–17, 20.
8. *Daily Graphic*, April 20, 2007.
9. ISSER, *Guide to Electric Power*, 12–13.Apart from residential consumers, who are considered small users, other consumers include nonresidential

and small industrial users, known as special load tariff customers (SLTs), such as offices, banks, and other small businesses (Ibid., 1).The IPP initiative emerged in the past decade and represents part of the country's efforts to privatize the power sector as part of power sector reform and improvement of access. Some of these IPPs include Cen Power, a local Ghanaian IPP, the Shenzhen Group from China, the Ranhill Consortium from India, and the Brazilian Consortium (Ibid., 13).

10. See Stephen Karekezi and John Kimani, "Status of Power Sector Reform in Africa: Impact on the Poor," *Energy Policy* 30, no. 11 (2002): 935.
11. See W. Gboney, "Power Sector Reform in Ghana," *AFREPREN Occasional Paper No. 5: Power Sector Reform in Africa—Proceedings of a Regional Policy Seminar*, ed. Stephen Karekezi, John Kimani, and Jennifer Wangeci (Nairobi, Kenya: African Energy Policy Research Network, 2001), 26–34.
12. Ibid., 6.
13. Personal Communication, 2009.
14. James H. Williams and Rebecca Ghanadan, "Electricity Reform in Developing and Transition Countries: A Reappraisal," *Energy* 31, no. 6 (2006): 815–44.
15. ECG Management Support Services, 2004.
16. ISSER, *Guide to Electric Power*, 40.
17. Personal communication, 2008.
18. ISSER, *Guide to Electric Power*, 4.
19. ISSER, *Guide to Electric Power*, 1.
20. See ISSER Guide to Electric Power: 2005 and 2006.
21. Personal communication, VRA official, 2008.
22. ISSER, *Guide to Electric Power*, 28, 34.
23. Energy Commission, *Ghana: 2015 Energy (Supply and Demand) Outlook*, April 2015, viii.
24. Ibid., 7.
25. Jacques Girod and Jacques Percebois, "Reforms in Sub-Saharan Africa's Power Industries," *Energy Policy* 26, no.1 (1998): 21–32.
26. Pierre-Olivier Pineau, "How Sustainable Is Policy Incoherence? A Rationalist Policy Analysis of the Cameroonian Electricity Reform," *Journal of Cleaner Production* 15, no. 2 (2007): 166–77.
27. See Navroz K. Dubash, "Revisiting Electricity Reform: The Case for a Sustainable Development Approach," *Utilities Policy: Strategy, Performance, Regulation* 11, no. 3 (2003): 144.
28. Raymond F. Hirsh, *Power Loss: The Origins of Deregulation and Restructuring in the American Electric Utilities System* (Cambridge, MA: MIT Press, 1999).
29. Ishmael Edjekumhene, Akosua B. K. Amaka-Otchere, and Harriette Amissah-Arthur, *Ghana: Sector Reform and the Pattern of the Poor—Energy*

Use and Supply, ESMAP Technical Paper 097/06 (Washington, DC: World Bank/Energy Sector Management Assistance Program, 2006), 9.
30. Ghana Living Standards Survey (GLSS), Round 6: "Poverty Profile in Ghana, 2005–2013" (2014), 32.
31. For more, see *Industry and Trade in a Global Economy, with Special Reference to Sub-Saharan Africa* (United Nations Industrial Development Organization, 2000).
32. Lau Schulpen and Peter Gibbon, "Private Sector Development: Policies, Practices and Problems," *World Development* 30, no. 1 (January 2002): 1–15.
33. Williams and Ghanadan, "Electricity Reform."
34. Dubash, "Revisiting Electricity Reform."
35. *Power Sector Reform in Sub-Saharan Africa*, ed. John Turkson (New York: Macmillan, 2000), cited in John Turkson and Norbert Wohlgemuth, "Power Sector Reform and Distributed Generation in Sub-Saharan Africa," *Energy Policy* 29: 135–45.
36. Sharon Beder, *Power Play: The Fight for Control of the World's Electricity* (Victoria, Australia: Scribe Publications, 2003), 275.
37. Ibid., 144.
38. See Dubash, "Revisiting Electricity Reform."
39. *Statement of Power Sector Development Policy* (Accra: Government of Ghana, 1999).
40. Williams and Ghanadan, "Electricity Reform," 828.
41. Karekezi and Kimana, "Status of Power Sector Reform," 287.
42. John Stern, "Electricity and Telecommunications Regulatory Institutions in Small and Developing Countries," *Utilities Policy* 9, no. 3 (September 2000): 148.
43. ISSER, *Guide to Electric Power*, 25.
44. See Williams and Ghanadan, "Electricity Reform."
45. Edjekumhene, Amaka-Otchere, and Amissah-Arthur, *Ghana: Sector Reform*.
46. See Ishmael Edjekumhene and Navroz K. Dubash, "Achieving Public Benefits by Default," in *Power Politics: Equity and Environment in Electricity Reform*, ed. Navroz K. Dubash (Washington, DC: World Resources Institute, 2002), 117–37.
47. Karekezi and Kimani establish as much in "Status of Power Sector Reform," 935.
48. Edjekumhene, Amaka-Otchere, and Amissah-Arthur, *Ghana: Sector Reform*, 26.
49. Karekezi and Kimani, however, note that, "on closer scrutiny, it appears that the majority of the poor may be adversely affected by hikes in electricity tariffs, if and only if, the country's electrification levels are relatively

high—possibly implying that both the poor and non poor are electrified." "Status of Power Sector Reform," 932.

50. Karl Quaye Botchway, "Paradox of Empowerment: Reflections on a Case Study from Northern Ghana," *World Development* 29, no. 1 (January 2001): 135–53.
51. See Dr. A. Afrifa, "Inside the Mind of the Ghanaian Voter (III)," *The Chronicle*, August 16–17, 2000.
52. *Statement of Power Sector Development Policy*, 11.
53. ISSER, *Guide to Electric Power*, 34.
54. Williams and Ghanadan, "Electricity Reform," 836.
55. See Paul Nugent. "Living in the Past: Urban, Rural and Ethnic Themes in the 1992 and 1996 Elections in Ghana," *The Journal of Modern African Studies* 37, no. 2 (June 1996): 287–319. See also Paul Nugent, "Winners, Losers and Also Rans: Money, Moral Authority, and Voting Patterns in the Ghana 2000 Election," *African Affairs* 100, no. 400 (2001): 405–28.
56. Defined as the closer integration of economies and elimination of rules and regulations in many developing countries to stabilize the flows of volatile money in and out of countries, as well as convergence in finance, labor, technology, etc. Joseph E. Stiglitz, *Globalization and Its Discontents* (New York: W.W. Norton, 2002).
57. Anil Hira, *Political Economy of Energy in the Southern Cone* (Westport, CT: Praeger, 2003).
58. See Mary E. Hawkesworth, *Globalization and Feminist Activism* (Lanham, MD: Rowman & Littlefield, 2006); Stiglitz, *Globalization and Its Discontents.*
59. ISSER, Guide to Electric Power, 2006, 8.
60. Energy Commission, *Ghana: 2015 Energy (Supply and Demand) Outlook*, April 2015, vi.
61. See Hira, *Political Economy of Energy*, 69.
62. For more on this survey, see Ghana Living Standards Survey, Round 6 (GLSS 6) 2016, 17. http://www.statsghana.gov.gh/docfiles/glss6/GLSS6_Main%20Report.pdf.
63. Jeffrey Herbst, *The Politics of Reform in Ghana, 1982–1991* (Berkeley and Los Angeles, CA: University of California Press, 1993).
64. Banji Oyelaran-Oyeyinka, *Learning to Compete in African Industry: Institutions and Technology in Development* (Burlington, VT: Ashgate Publishing, 2006), 113–14.
65. Douglas Barnes, *Electric Power for Rural Growth: How Electricity Affects Rural Life in Developing Countries* (Boulder, CO: Westview Press, 1988).
66. Confidential interview, with a former Volta River Authority engineer, July 2009.
67. *Strategic National Energy Plan*, 2006–2020, 23.
68. Ibid.

69. Edjekumhene, Amaka-Otchere, and Amissah-Arthur, *Ghana: Sector Reform*, 8.
70. Karekezi and Kimani, "Status of Power Sector Reform."
71. Williams and Ghanadan, "Electricity Reform," 821.
72. Edjekumhene, Amaka-Otchere, and Amissah-Arthur, *Ghana: Sector Reform*, 19, 24, 31; Edjekumhene and Dubash, "Achieving Public Benefits by Default." Edjekumhene and Dubash note that power sector reform in Ghana helped to usher in a transparent governance system for the power utilities, with the PURC incorporating several principles of good governance in its structure and functions.
73. Dubash, "Revisiting Electricity Reform," 147.
74. Karekezi and Kimani, "Status of Power Sector Reform."
75. Energy Commission, *Ghana: 2015 Energy (Supply and Demand) Outlook*, April 2015, xiv.
76. Dubash, "Revisiting Electricity Reform," 144.
77. Emmanuelle Auriol and Aymeric Blanc, "Capture and Corruption in Public Utilities: The Cases of Water and Electricity in Sub-Saharan Africa," *Utilities Policy* 17, no. 2 (June 2009): 203–16.
78. The Northern region, incidentally, has one of the third lowest rates of electricity access at some 43% (source, MOE).

CHAPTER 4

The Unfolding Nature of the Rural Poor, Rural Development and Public Service Delivery of Electricity in Ghana's Fourth Republic

Introduction

Statistical evidence suggests that electricity consumption is strongly correlated with wealth, while gaps in electricity strongly correlate with extreme poverty and those living below $2 per day.[1] While the fastest growing economy in sub-Saharan Africa is one of the continent's most hydro-rich, successful rates of electricity provision to large swathes have not managed to trickle down to the rural poor as targets of a number of "access" initiatives. During the 1990s—and amid Ghana's ambiguous embrace of structural adjustment policies—rural development approaches largely supported by the World Bank, International Monetary Fund and donor governments received renewed attention. These efforts aimed to support and create, when appropriate, income-generating enterprises and activities in rural areas. An implicit focus, however, included critical inputs like electricity provision as an indirect index of higher living standards and impetus for rural development.

The focus on rural development and tacit emergence of electricity provision at the dawn of the Fourth Republic is hardly surprising. Rural preference, populist initiatives, glaring gaps in electricity access, and a charismatic military ruler-turned-civilian president produced a new discourse on the country's economic development. As the country embarked on a new trajectory of political governance—in the form of decentralization, which aimed to devolve political power to local government and ordinary citizens—rural development and, more significantly, rural electrification assumed center stage, as a critical progenitor of growth (however imprecise

N. Sackeyfio, *Energy Politics and Rural Development in Sub-Saharan Africa*, https://doi.org/10.1007/978-3-319-60122-9_4

the linkages). Indeed, national policy frameworks noted poor rates of electricity access as a primary, if not central, culprit of economic stagnancy in the pre-1992 period for the rural population—which constitutes some 56.1%, of which 80% are poor. Thus, as this chapter demonstrates, the remarkable and widespread success of electricity provision of 80% is not matched by acute challenges for the rural poor. In spite of a public service delivery framework that developed during the late 1990s, and recognition of a symbiotic relationship between rural development outcomes, infrastructural/livelihood approaches and electricity access for the rural poor, an apparent disjuncture is unmistakably evident.[2] As a consequence, I argue that external conditionality requirements and an "ownership" syndrome over rural development approaches have limited domestic autonomy and enhanced incongruent patterns of electricity delivery for the rural poor since the post-1992 period. Conversely, the circumvention of donor authority and increasing reliance on the nongovernmental organization (NGO) sector reflects an ongoing and contentious struggle to retain a locus of autonomy that supports uneven outcomes. What is more, the dependence on intergovernmental transfers (District Assembly Common Fund) limits the autonomy of district assemblies, since transfers tend to be conditional, or directed by the center, and public service provision is inhibited at the local levels.[3] Governmental autonomy, as used here, denotes the ability of the state to make decisions independently of external actors—that is, donors. It is evaluated in the context of rural development outcomes and, to a small extent, poverty reduction strategies that attend to the poor. Ownership is a closely related concept and refers to actual capacity and implementation of policy directives.[4] By linking the evolution of rural development approaches to public service delivery, this chapter demonstrates how ambiguous service delivery outcomes and a lack of "ownership", especially by local institutional actors,[5] potentially debilitate and limit more favorable outcomes for the rural poor in the Ghanaian economy. Appropriately, this chapter examines the relationship between rural development and poverty alleviation efforts to uncover potential synergies in service delivery of electricity as a "livelihood" component. Though the chapter offers a cursory treatment of the productive uses of electricity in rural development, for example, in income-generating activities, it nonetheless places public service delivery of electrification squarely within a politics of poverty reduction and rural development frameworks that emerged in the mid-1990s with donor support.

Rural Development Perspectives and Approaches

Rural development, as treated here, denotes national and subnational interventions to raise living standards, generate employment, and utilize resources in ways that produce and sustain thriving communities where farming and an informal sector are primary modes of subsistence. With frequent regime change and political instability spanning several decades, rural development lagged considerably in virtually all ten regions. However, in the post-independent period, successive governments attempted to tackle the objective of rural development by launching programs for rural employment and initiatives to support food production, such as Operation Feed Yourself. Rural development concerns also emerged in lieu of efforts to transform Ghana from a low-income to a middle-income country by 2020, and these plans were articulated in the National Development Policy Framework and the National Development Planning Commission in 1994.[6] Approximately 56% of Ghanaians reside in rural settlements and of this number roughly 80% are classified as poor. The Ghana Institute for Economic Affairs (IEA-Ghana) attributes this to significantly inferior living standards in contrast to urban areas. During the 1990s, rural development schemes took center stage in donor-initiated efforts to combat endemic poverty and regional disparities in the country's ten regions. Accordingly, a focus on development of regional economies and renewed interest in agricultural productivity emerged, along with a concentration on linkage effects. For example, policymakers viewed the transfer of resources from agricultural to nonagricultural sectors—in the form of food, raw materials, capital, labor—as critical to marketing, storage, processing, transport and other goods and services.[7] As a result, the post-1992 period reflected new interest in addressing rural development gaps through the provision of electricity as an infrastructural input in urban and rural areas as well. By identifying gaps in particular services, it was hoped that newly created district assemblies, as new vehicles for institutional decentralization, could tackle these burgeoning problems. Consequently, adequate availability of, and access to, relevant rural goods and services became a critical component of rural development.[8]

An early model for rural development, which emerged during the 1950s, aimed to correct regional and rural disparities arising from the pursuit of growth-pole strategies in developing countries.[9] Introduced by John Friedman and M. Douglass in the 1950s, it called for the pursuit of planning that "must be decentralized, participatory, and deeply immersed in the particulars of local setting", which was a departure from top-down, centralized approaches that positioned the state at the center. After moving away from centralized to decentralized institutions in the post-1992 period, governments sought to promote self-help initiatives like electrification, but since political elites were reluctant to cede much control to the lower tiers of government, significant reorientation in a top-down approach occurred only incrementally. As Robert Price found, kinship, individual identity and expectations worked to disrupt modern bureaucratic norms and values.[10]

Robert Bates, however, offered intriguing explanations for the ability of African governments to pursue interests detrimental to the rural majorities.[11] He noted that because the individual costs of collective action were usually too high, owing to repressive tactics such as fueling factional conflicts, few were inclined to participate in joint action. With past and present governments resorting to a "conferment of divisible benefits" to satisfy private rural interests, rural development projects became instrumental in creating a system of spoils, thereby maintaining a measure of rural political support. Bates' characterization is largely valid, because his descriptions of African agricultural policies, class formation and the problematic nature of state development remain applicable to many African countries.

Perspectives on Poverty and Adjustment

The problems associated with uneven development reflect a plethora of work on poverty.[12] However, approaches to combat the predicament of the rural poor were also recognized by African governments, donors, international financial institutions and NGOs. The latter, in particular, sought to address the plight of the rural poor within a neo-liberal framework that called for a reduced scope for the state. For example, during the 1990s, the World Bank brought the problem of poverty into closer focus in a document entitled *1990 World Development Report: Poverty*, where it pledged commitment to reducing the scourge of poverty.[13] As a consequence, the Millennium Development Goals (MDGs) emerged as part of a global framework, premised on the belief that poverty could be eradicated. In short, the MDGs aimed to promote "participatory" projects that would give agency to local voices, amid a process of decentralization that a number of countries embarked on.

As the MDGs emerged to counter extreme poverty—that is, the numbers of people living below a dollar per day as well as those living below two dollars a day—the privatization of basic services like water and electricity produced deleterious circumstances for the poor and needy.[14] In the wake of structural adjustment and neo-liberal policies, Bryceson argues that poverty reduction efforts took a "backseat" in developing countries, as competing solutions for the agrarian poor produced a quandary over implementation.

The potential connections between poverty reduction, rural development and electrification are noted in a MOE report in 2008. In it, the MOE offered the view that electricity provision was critical in rural areas, through productive uses such as improvement in economic livelihoods. However, weakly functioning rural markets, and inadequate backward, forward, labor, horizontal, vertical, and institutional linkages between national and local decentralized structures limit favorable outcomes for poverty reduction and economic livelihoods expansion. Faced with urban sprawl and growth in deagrarianization,[15] many of the country's regional governments do not have the resources, the differentiated frameworks, or adequate proper capacity to provide public services for markets to thrive. Indeed, Yaro Awetori concludes, in his study of livelihood activities in rural Northern Ghana, that homogenizing rural strategies that fail to pay attention to differentiation in socioeconomic terms not only neglects the reality of rural societies, but misinforms policy.[16] Additionally, inadequate resource flows—like network redistribution from the nonpoor to the poor and destitute—portend negative repercussions for both groups, further destroying the economic base of the area and encouraging more out-migration.[17] In the realm of adjustment, for instance, power can be used to deprive people of the rights of access to productive resources. During the 1990s, this dynamic became evident after Ghana's renewed experiment with decentralization. While Sally Burrows (1992) depicted the fairly rapid growth of rural towns, which remarkably outpaced growth projections, this success was largely attributable to NGO support.

Despite a recurring trade in balance, which produced severe deterioration, donors nonetheless rewarded Ghana for being what Eboe Hutchful terms a "star pupil of adjustment." In the midst of periodic noncompliance, the debt level more than tripled to $4.6 billion, with crucial debt to export levels quadrupling to 4.36 billion in the period 1980–1993.[18] Significant inconsistencies between adjustment and poverty reduction encouraged an anti-orthodoxy approach, which sought to explain market failures that extended beyond the public and private goods distinctions.[19]

In the latter decades of the twentieth century, much of the literature on rural development was framed through the lens of dependency, liberal, neo-classical and neo-liberal tenets. In the wake of case studies that documented declines in peasant commodity, agricultural production and diversification of nonfarm or agricultural activities, deagrarianization[20] and "depeasantization" are terms that came to characterize this process. Consequently, agricultural labor displacement and an eroding rural agricultural base caused policymakers to reexamine the terms under which structural adjustment and neo-liberal policies affected the rural poor. However, Yaro Awetori argues against perspectives that suggest an "invariable move from agricultural to non agricultural activities." Perhaps this accounts for why rural development officials in the Ministry of Rural and Local Government offer ambiguous conceptions of spatial and infrastructural components for district-level development, preferring to leave those to the District Chief Executives in attendant areas that exhibit mixed success in adjustment and neo-liberal policies.

As African peasant farmers elsewhere began to experience the constricting effects of structural adjustment on their commodity production, a pressing need for coping strategies emerged. Hence, a rural livelihood approach developed with the recognition that farming households were increasingly resorting to income diversification to secure economic needs (Ellis, 2000).[21] But even though donors joined the chorus and moved to operationalize what they understood as the livelihood strategies concept,[22] few connections were made between resource endowments and the vulnerability of rural people by African governments. Thus, ongoing criticisms of district assembly capacity, and regional and district differentiation in factor and resource endowments make such identification of backward and forward, horizontal, vertical or institutional linkages to mitigate their circumstances all the more critical.

For more wealthy households, an accumulation strategy is likely to yield positive outcomes, but vulnerability to market fluctuations and the agrarian calendar push poor households to pursue nonagrarian income-earning activities in already saturated markets. Over time income diversification may exacerbate rather than improve interhousehold economic differentiation.[23] Nonetheless, a "sustainable rural livelihood" approach that supports the drive of African rural dwellers for income diversification stresses the importance of reducing poor household vulnerability, although long-term strategies are virtually ignored.[24] Ultimately, this perspective does not capture the "nitty-gritty" of such processes in terms of local spatial, social and institutional linkages that, in many cases, obscure the pursuit of nonfarm livelihood approaches. Bryceson cogently observes that the sustainable rural livelihood approach's ahistorical, nonsectoral approach sidesteps the implications of fundamental changes in rural dwellers' agricultural commodity production and social dynamics within rural communities and households.[25] Arguably, electricity is one vital component, which calls into question the sustainability of rural livelihoods for broad sections of today's African rural population, especially under decentralized rural development, largely monitored by the donor and development community (NGO). Even the innovations of cane and rattan weavers in rural Ghana—as "creative adaptations to market opportunities, innovation and entrepreneurship are a miniscule part of rural development."[26] Unfortunately, this approach may not account for the sometimes discontinuous, disequilibrating circumstances that face the rural dweller, especially when taken in lieu of rural flight and urban overcrowding.

Nevertheless, George J. Sefa Dei observed how peasant communities utilized an "exit" option to minimize their participation in the national economy.[27] In this view, rural dwellers are depicted as remarkably resilient in their ability to navigate changing national and rural economies. What remains less well known and difficult to capture is the dynamic relationship between rural and national political economies and the structural articulation of policies[28] especially relevant to Ghana's ongoing decentralization efforts. His conclusion that Ayirebi farmers likely viewed state adjustment as uncertain and changeable explains their desire to cling to old alliances. Emergent from Dei's explanation are how regime interests and political co-optation evolved, along with Rawlings' ability to maintain popular support.

The anchors of rural development are not easily identifiable, given the plethora of NGOs and indomitable donor presence for several decades now. There are approximately 1168 NGOs registered in Ghana.[29] The country's relative stability, openness to foreigners and comfortable living conditions have attracted aid-oriented organizations, whose target population includes the rural poor, with the aim of providing public goods like clinics, education, running water and, in some cases, electricity.[30] The activities of donors and aid organizations are typically viewed as positive elements in developing countries. Predictably, generous aid and various development projects are enthusiastically welcomed in recipient countries and Ghana is no exception. However, a long-term institutional presence has worked to limit domestic ownership of important decisional processes, most visibly in district assembly autonomy. A number of studies, for example, demonstrate how rural-development outcomes often work suboptimally in countries marked by lengthy donor presence. At the time of Helleiner's writing in 2001, foreign assistance accounted for approximately 50% of the national budget in Ghana.[31] That has since changed, with an (foreign) aid threshold that is estimated to be 40.7% of GDP.[32]

However, this level of extensive donor assistance, which is accompanied by neo-liberal oriented poverty reduction strategies, raises the troubling question of "national ownership" and by extension rural development.[33] Indeed, these policies call into question the efficacy of good governance and appropriate scope of government in relation to external interests or donor power. Even when rural dwellers possess key economic inputs like land ownership and capital—all potential catalysts for rural development—absent infrastructure and unpredictable market forces can produce negative outcomes.

Some perspectives reflect the view that centralization and weak devolution prevent a viable bottom-up approach that could facilitate regional development from small towns in lieu of top-down power dynamics.[34] Perhaps critically, devolved power has not effectively empowered district assemblies in fiscal and material terms and the pursuit of effectual service delivery of electricity as part of the larger goals of rural development appears all the more tenuous.

The self-help, self-reliant values approach that Rawlings promoted with the inception of district assemblies in the late 1980s facilitated a participatory element in a number of respects. In early 1992, Ghanaian newspapers were replete with stories about how citizens served as partial architects for transformation of their communities. In the Eastern region, for example, citizens in Apeguso, a rural town in the Asuogyaman district, endeavored to raise funds for a power project. Likewise, residents embarked on a power project in Achinakwim in the Ejisu-Juabeng district of the Ashanti region. Moreover, Tetrem citizens in the Ashanti region initiated and took part in development projects. In short, a plethora of newspaper articles document how some rural communities are providing materials for power projects, such as power poles. Yet from these remarkable efforts a much-needed "snowball" effect has largely failed to materialize, which is why the gains associated with such efforts quickly dissipated. Indeed, the capacity to generate regional resources and the politically messy process of nominating metropolitan, municipal and district chief executives underscores the gap between ideals and practice.[35] This observation, was in fact, noted by most, if not all, participants in a symposium on the progress of Ghana's decentralization program. Filling positions and locating individuals willing to relocate to the "hinterland" or rural areas remains a continuing challenge—well into the twenty-first century.[36] Collectively, these constraints demonstrate the limits of a "minimal" state that espouses a participatory element on the local level without adequate resources that build self-sustaining communities that clamor for public services/goods like electricity.

Participation and Rural Development

On another note, Paul Streeten questions the assumption that participation for the poor is key, particularly where the operations of NGOs are concerned.[37] He called for a rethinking of participation and argued that closer attention should be paid to who takes decisions at what level, as well as sequencing in terms of the links between governments, NGOs and affected communities. In the quest to empower the poor and marginalized, to become agents rather than spectators or even passive recipients of benefits, the objectives of participation, though vital, are not always clear, as Streeten notes. For donor partners and NGOs, the dilemma over whether to focus on service delivery or encourage participation is a matter that requires greater scrutiny and further clarification. Since participation can take many forms, determining the appropriate model for any developing country is essential.

The Duplicity of Decentralization: A State-Centric Model

As Lawrence D. Smith notes, "since latching onto the concept of decentralization in the 1980s, donor agencies and many countries have been struggling to make it work…the deception lies in the term's simplicity… when the questions of what and how are raised, the issue becomes quite a vexing one."[38] In lieu of numerous services and development gaps that district assemblies continue to face, development partners or donors and, increasingly, NGOs have moved in critical ways to fill this gap. The demand for services, marginalization, and neglect of remote—often rural—areas prompted many to channel their resources in a bid to fulfill this aim. As a result, the interventions of development partners or donors often reflect the use of budgetary support mechanisms, which have inadvertently structured political capture by leaders, while providing a legitimate rationale for incremental efforts. Smith's observations are explained by the contention of Mary Galvin and Adam Habib that "although donors claim to support community oriented decentralization, in practice they promote state-centric decentralization. Not only does this reinforce the institutional bias of government, it undermines the original motivation and rationale for decentralization."[39] It is little wonder that decentralized public service delivery took on a state-centric focus that is inimical to the delegation of authority.

Poverty reduction strategy papers suffer a number of constraints that, most notably, include the need to accord more ownership to national governments, and more participatory results-oriented strategies to help governments adopt more pro-poor policies.[40] It is especially revealing that Ethiopia, Rwanda, Kenya, Mali and Zambia have all taken steps to broaden the scope for participation of various stakeholders,[41] while Ghana, surprisingly, has not. For instance, this became apparent with the revelation that the involvement of sectoral ministries, legislators, decentralized administration, and civil society groups in the Poverty Reduction Strategy Paper (PRSP) formulation process was demonstrated to be less than satisfactory. For example, Ghana and other governments accelerated the process in order to reap the maximum benefit from debt relief under the enhanced Highly Indebted Poor Country (HIPC) Initiative.[42] A key official formerly with the Ministry of Rural and Local Government identified inconsistencies in policy monitoring and, more significantly, the dangers of duplication in promoting rural development efforts. To this end, Cheru (2006) observed that

> Ghana, as one of the best managed economies in Africa, illustrates the problem. Centrally and in the ministries, government lacks in-house capacity for policy analysis and monitoring. This is a paradox since Ghana is one of the few African countries endowed with numerous research institutions, think tanks, local consultancy agencies, and policy-oriented NGOs. Yet no efforts are made by government to utilize existing knowledge and capacity outside government.[43]

With questions concerning the efficacy of donor and NGO-led budget support programs, Tim Unwin argues that such approaches obscure social equity issues in dispersal. Aided by an erroneous model of development, neo-liberal budget support programs adhere to the notion that "absolute" poverty can be eliminated through economic growth.[44] The financial and accountability risks are well known.[45] Allocating large sums of money as part of a long-term strategy to combat poverty and encourage economic growth contributes to political co-optation—particularly when political elites in home countries use "development projects" to enhance their political capital: it reifies donor dependency. Akwasi P. Osei, for example, found that the enduring legacy of economic dependency is connected to the failure to adopt far-reaching policies that would effectively restructure society.[46] In framing these circumstances through the lens of the colonial period, he demonstrates how institutions inherited from the British colonial power stymied development. But Gocking (1999) criticized this notion, suggesting that Nkrumah's efforts to industrialize the country through the Volta River Project and attempts to build infrastructure and public services offer evidence of a "radical" departure from colonial policies.[47] Unfortunately, Nkrumah's efforts did not go far enough and were ultimately derailed by political turmoil and disjointed policies. Moreover, the consequent donor dependency that began in the 1980s and culminated in the 1990s is akin to a "trusteeship" role that Whitfield (2006) contends further marginalized the plight of the rural poor.

The proliferation of NGOs in Ghana and in many states across sub-Saharan Africa is indicative of a neo-liberal agenda and reflective of the rollback of the state.[48] The comparative advantage of NGOs should make them ideal institutions to assist in this endeavor,[49] but key processes are evident in the relationship between governments and NGO sector in Ghana, which hinge on service delivery, rural development and poverty reduction. Conversely, the Ghana has successfully co-opted a growing NGO sector. Governments appeared more often than not motivated by the desire to gain access to NGO funds, rather than by a desire to make NGOs monitor NGOs they fear as political competitors and thus be accountable the rural poor.[50]

NGOs and Rural Development

During the 1980s, NGOs faced a skeptical Provisional National Defence Council or military regime. But in the 1990s, the ability to soften the blow of adjustment in the public sector produced a more favorable view. As Aloysius Denkabe observes, the advent of a reduced public sector produced expectations that NGOs would support development by according priority to regional and district administrations initiatives.[51] In keeping with this observation, the then director of NGO affairs at the Ministry of Employment and Social Welfare, Bridget Katsriku, noted that "the government values the resources NGOs bring to help meet the 'service delivery gap' but at the same time wants to circumscribe their role to the sphere of social welfare."

Ian Gary (1996: 63) notes that as an arena for considerable inflows of aid, the NGO sector represents new ground for accumulation, especially for African elites. Although beyond the scope of focus here, these developments suggest a complex picture of state and NGO conflict, an "aid dependent culture, along with attempts to co-opt the latter as well as the rural poor."[52]

The political co-optation of NGOs is evident in the various ways that the Ghanaian state, according to Ian Gary, sought direct and indirect ways of controlling the sector and throughout the creation of government-organized nongovernmental organizations (GONGOs). As a creation of national governments, nominally independent but operating under government control, Ghana is one of many countries that utilizes GONGOs to divert resources meant for "legitimate NGOs". This has involved the adoption of various means to counter and appropriate some of the funds flowing to NGOs.[53] In short, an extensive NGO and donor presence in Ghana limits the extent to which district assemblies exercise a meaningful locus of budgetary control, authority over rural development, and poverty reduction goals that are part and parcel of domestic "ownership" of these elements. The result is a glaring gap between quixotic prerogatives of decentralization and district assemblies as conduits of self-reliant, self-help development initiatives that Rawlings once espoused in the prelude to democratization and return to civilian rule in 1992.

Rural Electrification

Rural electrification and its attendant benefits for use in cottage and rural industry are considered promising for rural development.[54] Grid electricity, however, remains the preferred method for providing rural electrification, since it allows people to use standard electrical equipment and appliances without any practical constraint on the quantity of electricity consumed. But in remote, rural areas this approach is difficult to use.[55] Others scholars argue that electrification is indispensable, but not instrumental for development in rural areas.[56] However, from the industrial revolution in Europe and America, to the ongoing and rapid industrialization of countries like China and India, and the multibillion-dollar electronic industry of the western world, electric power transformed society in innumerable ways.[57] Tsai (1989) considers it nearly ubiquitous and essential in terms of economic growth and development, while others contend that access to electricity is a basic human right, along with access to clean air, water, shelter and food. The ways it can improve the livelihoods of the rural poor are numerous: carpenters enjoy bandsaws and mechanized equipment, power looms replace hand looms, and electric motors take the place of oil-powered machines. It has also availed blacksmiths with power hammers and metal workers with power pressing machines (United Nations, 2006).

The role of energy values is likewise important. Understanding how a particular country defines them can shed light on local conflicts, distributional policies, and political processes. To understand the role of energy values, one need only explore the course of electrification as an important resource and symbol of development in the history of Ghana. Built in 1966 to supply hydropower for aluminum smelting and domestic use, the Akosombo Dam emerged as a powerful symbol of progress and industrialization. A tenuous political process almost derailed the completion of the dam—owing to financial constraints and disputes between the Nkrumah administration and Busia's Progress Party over the dam's utility. But according to an EC official, the promise of hydropower subsequently resonated as a political tool and unfulfilled legacy.[58] Yet, the Volta River Project and the Akosombo Dam offered few returns or benefits for rural electrification (and for development in general) but caused political infighting and internal disillusionment.[59]

Synergies and Dissonance in Rural Development Outcomes and Electrification in the Post-Independence Period

In the first half of the twentieth century, British colonial administrations accorded little priority to rural development. Rural areas were mostly relegated to agricultural production and extraction of natural resources. Urban areas, on the other hand, were significantly developed because of a colonial preference for comfort and convenience. It was only in the independence period and thereafter that rural development emerged on the national agenda of Nkrumah, Busia and subsequent leaders in the contemporary period.

The first statement linking economic development to electrification was formulated during discussions of the proposed construction of Lake Volta. Before Nkrumah's tenure as head of state, the Convention People's Party (CPP) envisaged Lake Volta not only as an impetus for industrialization but as a transport link between the northern and southern regions of the country. Ultimately, Nkrumah's social policies were guided by several aims: universal free education and health facilities; quality water and sanitation; affordable housing for all; and wide access to electricity. Armed with these basic human rights, there would be no limit to the development of Ghana.[60] Yet Nkrumah liquidated the cocoa co-operative societies, groups of relatively wealthy and stable farmers, because he sought to centralize control of cocoa marketing and to use rural resources to industrialize and create a coherent economy.[61]

Under a Second Development Plan (1959–1964), large sums were allocated for rural housing, electricity, education, health, sanitation and water supplies, but these were subsequently neglected as urban areas received priority.[62] Given an unstable political climate and unclear energy goals, little was done in these years to expand Nkrumah's electrification goals, which in any case focused on urban areas. Moreover, the provincial interests of chiefs, as well as linkages between transnational corporations, party functionaries, law-enforcement agents, local businessmen and state bureaucrats fueled corruption and a loss of legitimacy for the Nkrumah regime. For example, the pursuit of import-substitution policies encouraged rent seeking through control of import licensing and rationing of foreign exchange, which invited corruption and inefficient allocation of resources.[63] In a succession of oustings by the military regime, following the coup that toppled Nkrumah's government in 1966, cocoa prices fluctuated and rural conditions deteriorated in the 1970s.[64]

The Second Republic began with K.A. Busia's tenure (1969–1972) and, in a bid to ensure political survival, Busia sought to appease the poor through a "social justice" program that included rural development and, consequently, rural electrification. For example, approximately 100 communities were linked to the grid during this period. On matters of rural electrification, Busia proved adept, as a politician, using the Progress Party (PP), an opposition group that had broken from the ranks of the CPP to emphasize the supply of electricity in its manifesto during the political business cycle.[65] Through the Ghana Water and Sewerage Corporation, excess power and water were gleaned and Busia's home region of Brong-Ahafo saw more rural electricity projects undertaken than any other region. Other projects, including transport, communication, and health care, were implemented and the communities in which they were undertaken developed a strong sense of identification with the PP. Though Busia appeared to adopt some liberal tenets like minimal government,[66] he merely modified Nkrumaist socialist-style policies, like the provision of electricity, roads, water, intended to preserve the bureaucratic core.

Subsequent governments made few attempts to elicit local views on development, or on electricity provision, except for Acheampong's Operation Feed Yourself (OFY), which nevertheless failed to produce significant results.[67] Growing discontent with the Busia administration and mounting economic problems resulted in a second coup d'état by the military government of General Acheampong (1973–1978). As a result, little progress was made to expand Busia's electrification program. Indeed, Acheampong's Supreme Military Council was marked by endemic corruption, despite promising policies for the agricultural sector (Lumsden, 1980; Jeffries, 1982).[68] Curiously, few if any electrification plans emerged for rural areas in the succeeding governments of Lt. Gen Frederick W. K. Akuffo, or in the brief return to democratic government during Hilla Limann's (1979–1981) tenure. A precarious economy prodded the country into further instability with the resulting coup in December 1981 when Jerry Rawlings deposed Limann.

The next two years proved economically disastrous, and the military oligarchy of Rawlings, and economic deterioration of the economy combined with fiscal austerity left little room for rural development or attendant economic inputs like electrification. For example, in the mid to late 1980s, politically active Ghanaians withdrew from political life in what would come to be known as the "culture of silence" or politically repressive period.[69] In a second coup, orchestrated by Rawlings via the PNDC, a populist agenda and radical nationalist economic program targeted elites. A presumably progressive period appeared to offer opportunities for rural voices to emerge and demand synergistic policies that would link rural development outcomes to electrification as a "soft infrastructural input." With Rawlings' creation of revolutionary grassroots organizations and attempts to stabilize the economy through administrative controls and mass mobilization, such action was possible.[70] But the Rawlings regime later resorted to authoritarian measures to curb "excessive" mobilization, to avoid "an unstable" political environment. In a bid to reverse what he termed "excessive" mobilization and restore monetary and fiscal control to a spiraling economy, Rawlings utilized repressive tactics to silence opposition. Consequently, the resultant "culture of silence" helped to mute opposition to Rawlings' structural adjustment policies, which entailed heavy liberalization of the economy and privatization of state industries.

An Economic Recovery Program (ERP), created in the 1980s, sought to provide basic services, alleviate the economic crisis, and in turn dent internal opposition. Initially, cocoa farmers were pleased with the emphasis on rural empowerment, since it appeared that rural actors and social systems would take center stage in Rawlings' economic objectives. Indeed, the success of these policies became apparent in higher agricultural yields and subsequent rural mobilization (Mikell, 1989). But market-oriented policies and neo-liberal reform efforts shifted the emphasis from rural producers to rural organizations that were structured, not surprisingly, in ways that lent support to the government.[71] Unfortunately, history has not borne out Mikell's prediction that the PNDC's need for political support and heightened rural production would help youthful, educated and elite groups gain control of economic and political decision-making in rural areas.

In many accounts, external pressures by donors and international financial institutions (IFIs) on a weakened regime, as well as some internal opposition to structural adjustment policies, pushed Rawlings to begin political reforms, with local elections used as a first step to shore up his legitimacy, beginning in 1988. This period has been interpreted as one in which Rawlings drew on the strength of his popular appeal, a fragile economy and a belief in his sole ability to steer the country on the right course. Kwame Boafo-Arthur asserts that Rawlings drove the NDC to ensure his succession as head of state and indirectly perpetuate his rule under the guise of a democratic constitution.[72] The decision to hold local elections did not reduce criticism of Rawlings' regime or attract much urban support as it was intended to do. Instead, by subjecting his regime to the type of scrutiny he had imposed on his predecessors through his orchestration of coups d'états, he encouraged demands for more formal political liberalization.[73] Thus, the dominant mood among Ghanaians at the end of the 1980s reflected a hunger for the substance of democracy, rather than piecemeal measures.[74]

Shifting Dynamics of an Urban–Rural Dichotomy and Patterns of Electric Energy Use

What explains persistent disparities between the urban and rural populace? The reward system in Ghanaian society offers big dividends to those who are close to the "center" or supply system, usually located in urban locales or the capital, for instance. Additionally, highly specialized service providers, such as lawyers, doctors, bankers, and teachers, have a variety of economic, cultural and social reasons for wishing to work in major towns.

There are also political reasons for previous urban bias. Because political power is concentrated among the professional classes in the country's major towns, the possibilities for political pressure by rural populations were considerably weaker in the pre-1990 period.[75] Subsequently, as Ayeetey-Attoh notes, "development planners were concerned with disparities, resulting inequalities in and between, regions because the persistence of poverty in specific areas is . . . one of the most critical problems facing planners and policy makers in the developing world."[76]

On another note, patterns of energy use offer insight into spatial urban and rural differentiation as well as the gap between both classes. Both the urban and rural poor are affected by energy pricing and electricity tariffs, which are also unfavorable to small and medium enterprises.[77] While nearly all African countries seek to restrict urban growth rates, few have succeeded. But the bulk of domestic usage is concentrated in urban areas.[78] The Accra–Tema and Sekondi–Takoradi regions, for example, account for the bulk of electricity available and in use in Ghana, for both domestic and industrial consumers.[79] Similarly, Randolph Quaye argues that taking the term "development" for granted obscures the actual process of development as an arena of negation and struggle, which has produced unintended outcomes that greatly affect structural and institutional disparities.[80] Using the example of the Northern Region Rural Integrated Programme (NORRIP), he attributes incongruent development to these circumstances. For Gyampo, two chief causes of gross disparities between urban and rural areas are attendant. First is the privileging of urban or industrial districts like Accra, Tema, Koforidua, Cape Coast, and Kpando during the 1970s. In later years, areas such as Kumasi, Sunyani, Sekondi–Takoradi, Winneba, Kibi and Keta received similar treatment. All these districts are located in the southern region, the more developed area of the country. Second, production-related structural inequalities between rural districts influenced the persistence of disparities. However, these are not as clear-cut as the north/south and rural/urban boundaries. Because rural districts are primarily tied to subsistence agricultural production, they are at a disadvantage in terms of export commodity production and as recipients of services/goods like electricity are understandably targets for political opportunism.

Several members of parliament alluded to "capacity" to describe the pressures of migration from rural and to urban areas, difficult economic prospects, and a yearning for the trappings of city life, including access to electrification and education. For example, one MP remarked that:

> There are regional and spatial disparities. Poverty, for instance, is still high in the Northern, Upper East and Upper West regions. Whereas relative poverty in the other seven regions of Ghana declined, the same cannot be said of the three aforementioned regions in the north of Ghana. Urban incomes continued to lead, thus sustaining the tide of rural–urban migration . . . [As long as] the wide rural–urban dichotomy remains, rural–urban drift will continue. An emerging feature, however, is that a greater part of Accra, which is considered to be metropolitan, registered a high level of poverty. The urban dynamics and pressures on the lives of rural immigrants cannot be ruled out. Given the foregoing, it is not difficult to say that the development-policy strategy is not working and for that matter it would be difficult to meet the rural development goals. Rather, the policies are spurring on more and more rural-urban drift.[81]

An interview with the former head of the rural policy unit for the Ministry of Rural and Local Government revealed that no comprehensive rural development policy exists to police Ghana's growth and poverty reduction—a startling disclosure in light of the passing of the local government Act 462, which was designed to promote rural development. It is no surprise then that a project-by-project culture emerged—for example, in electrification.

The limited capacity of DAs and the duplicitous nature of the district assembly system has been so glaring that another member of parliament remarked that:

> Both Rawlings and Kufuor placed a high premium on energy, in terms of rural electrification, thermal power generation, and the politics of petrol. But in terms of commitment and foresight for bigger power capacity expansion, Kufuor's administration had a little edge over Rawlings. He [Kufuor] went in for the second major hydroelectric dam [the Bui Dam] in Ghana. Because of their heavy dependence on central government finances, the districts are unable to take policy decisions that will bring growth. Until the assemblies are able to generate their own incomes, the decision to take radical reforms in prevailing rural development in Ghana will remain a mirage.[82]

Governments, Electricity and the Rural Vote: "No Electricity, No Power"

More than ten years ago, the donor community and critics within Ghana worried about the politicization of adjustment and missed financial targets.[83] With the consequential rural bias that emerged in the 1980s rural producers became the beneficiaries and locus for political support.

Consequently, the PNDC shifted its focus from urban to rural areas and institutionalized this impetus through decentralization. In a survey of voters who participated in the 1988 elections for district assemblies, Kojo Busia found that 64% were rural and 36% were urban.[84] This represented the first time that any regime in post-colonial Ghana commanded such extensive support from the rural classes.

While rural bias is certainly not new (it dates back to early 1980s),[85] newspapers like the *Daily Graphic*, *Daily Guide*, and many others frequently feature stories about electrification, and this indicates the extent to which electricity remains salient. As an EC official associated with the NES and SHEP informed me in July of 2009, "in the last 10 to 15 years a lot of attention has been given to rural communities to make an improvement in living standards. The government (NDC) tried to stop the rural to urban flow by creating rural electrification policies." After a decade of tenuous economic and political conditions, rural areas became a key win for the NDC party, which was not expected to do well. This same official noted that the NDC government came to be known as the "electrification government" and that "electrification had become a political tool that no government could afford to take for granted; if not, they wouldn't be around" (anonymous, personal communication, July 2009). Should the rural class become more politicized, it will be interesting to view the course of mobilization, collective action and linkages they make, if any, with the urban poor. Table 4.1 that follows below demonstrates the pace with which electricity and rural development projects took center stage in 1992—the year in which Ghana returned to civilian rule and of its first election in over a decade.

Green (1996) observes that "of ten agreements signed with the World Bank since 1993, many were directly or indirectly usable for rural development purposes: including national livestock services, national electrification, education, etc." Rawlings' immense political capital and donor-support explains his ability to satisfy various classes in society like the agrarian poor, which had enormous implications for Rawlings' ability to appease a previously ignored rural constituency in the country. In fact, succeeding governments appeared more willing to invest funds and resources in areas that ensured political and most likely economic returns.[86] Consequently, Rawlings and the NDC were pioneers of a rural-based approach that, for the first time, reversed an urban bias that had been part and parcel of

Table 4.1 Table of newspaper articles

Reference	*Date*	*Page*	*Headline description*
NP. 1/162	01/03/1992	Back	Kusa near Fomena in the Adansi West District embarks on Dev. program
"	01/04/1992	6	Nkonya South branch of JFM Inaugurated.
"	"	7	Development through mobilization
"	"	8	Osenase Power Project
"	"	"	Mehame Electrification Project
"	"	8–9	Trede citizens raise funds for project
"	01/09/1992	7	New power transformer for Aboso
"	"	8	Akyem—Apapam power project
"	"	"	Drobo to enjoy electricity
"	01/20/1992	8	Maase electrification project
"	01/21/1992	Back	Nsutam completes first phase of power project
"	01/31/1992	Back	19 villages in Amansie East undertake power project
"	02/04/1992	Back	Wasa Nkran undertakes Dev. Projects
"	02/05/1992	Back	10 communities receive PAMSCAD assistance
"	02/06/1992	"	Four areas to benefit from power project
"	02/07/1992	"	Self-help remains vital element in Dev.
"	02/12/1992	"	Botoku starts Dev. Project
"	02/15/1992	"	Set up funds to finance small scale project
"	"	"	8 communities to tap power from National grid
"	02/18/1992	3	Assembly initiates ¢28.8m Dev. Projects
"	02/19/1992	3	Ada holds rally in aid of electrification
"	"	Back	Adantia starts Dev. Project
"	"	"	PAMSCAD assistance for 10 communities
"	02/22/1992	Front	Public demand improved services
"	"	3	Assembly to complete project
"	"	8	$545m invested in water and power supplies
"	02/26/1992	Front	Rural phone system to cover 42 districts
"	03/03/1992	5	Lack of amenities hinder rural Dev.
"	"	Back	Sekyere Nsuta—Atonsu Kroye Kuo raises funds in support of the electrification project
"	03/05/1992	3	¢157m Kumasi street lighting project starts
"	03/07/1992	Back	Farmers raise funds for Dev. Projects
"	03/09/1992	3	Assemblies have enhanced Dev.
"	03/13/1992	Back	Pewosika undertakes power project
"	03/17/1992	"	Tsiame power project
NP. 1/162	03/27/1992	5	Solar power light up Rural area

Source: Created by the author

development efforts, despite a policy focus and a Ministry of Local and Rural Development that suggested the contrary.

According to a report from the Ghana Institute for Economic Affairs, decentralization was pursued as a way to tighten the grip on regional and local institutions. Because the district chief executive functioned as both chairman of the powerful executive committee at the district level and as a political appointee, the office of the DCE functioned as a mechanism of political control and did little to further the objective of decentralization.[87] Others noted that, after decentralization began, few changes emerged within the strongly centralized system of a unitary republic.[88] Some observers note that the structural adjustment process begun in the post-1992 period resulted in the politicization of state projects like electrification, while redistributive policies provided material benefit at key political moments. Daniel Green, for instance, asserts that a political business cycle was at work during the elections of 1992 and 1996, during which the NDC government publicly argued before rural audiences that government monies were better spent in the rural areas.[89]

The political machinery of rural co-optation was personally visible on a visit in 2009. In numerous rural areas along the road to the northern region, the logos/party symbols of the dominant political parties were highly visible and placed at strategic points. Such symbols remind rural constituents of the principle of "reciprocity." That is, in exchange for political support, voters in rural areas can expect to be rewarded in numerous ways—which reify patron–client relationships. Though members of parliament and district chief executives have much to worry about come election time, my findings indicate that most are unsullied by accusations of political posturing. Instead, district assemblies serve as useful conduits to gauge levels of discontent and development concerns of rural areas. In any case, rural voters across the country perpetually utter the slogan "no electricity, no power," which suggests the politically salient issue of public service/goods provision. A number of interviewees in parliament established that rural voters are vocal enough to ensure the defeat of MPs who fail to implement projects like electrification or secure dates when their community will be connected to the grid. However, Afrobarometer surveys on perceptions of accountability of both local and national representatives, and of participation and public service delivery, are telling. On the one hand, in the 2004–2005 period, 26% of rural and 24% of urban residents surveyed (out of 1197 randomly chosen) report that it is *very difficult* to obtain water, electricity and telephone services, while 29% of urban and 26% of rural report that it is *difficult*. Of those surveyed, 46% of urban and 45% of rural dwellers report they had *never given a bribe* for piped water, electricity or phone service. Yet out of housing, electricity, water supply, orphans/street children/homeless children (each ranked under government services), education ranked at the top for both urban and rural priorities—15% and 14% respectively—while only 4% of urban and 3% of rural people ranked it as an important problem the government should address. However, 63% of urban and rural respondents believed that politicians *always* made promises simply to get elected.[90]

Conclusion

Though Nkrumah and Busia attempted to connect rural development approaches and income-generating activities to electricity provision, their efforts failed to produce far-reaching outcomes for the rural poor. Instead, a structural "lock in" of choices informs the subsequent gaps and discontinuity in public service provision and through efforts to co-opt sections of society, most notably in the post-1992 period. Despite abundant hydropower and the powerful symbol of "self sufficiency and progress" that the Akosombo Dam offered, both leaders missed opportunities to articulate the country's energy values clearly. Considering the near-ubiquity of energy use and its indispensability for growth, standards of living and development, Busia's social justice approach and Nkrumah's socialist approach would likely have raised the standards of living in rural areas if vertical and horizontal linkages to rural industry were supported in development plans. Instead, the years leading up to the Fourth Republic were characterized by the neglect of electrification in rural areas and overall, even though Busia did more for electrification than Nkrumah. In current times, the failure to view and utilize electricity as a soft infrastructural input critical to public service/good for rural industry and small and medium enterprises means that potential opportunities for income generation may be squandered. Key members of parliament and officials interviewed in the MOE and EC recognize the need to develop intersectoral linkages to electrification and encourage economic activity in rural areas and, consequently, reverse the tide of rural flight. However, doing so would require a dynamic shift in the paradigm of rural development and weak district assembly system.

This chapter found that, as a component of rural development and poverty reduction strategies, electricity provision for the poor is compounded by lack of "ownership" and weak autonomy under efforts to build a "minimal" state to support decentralization. Where central government resorted to creating a system of spoils to maintain rural support, rural development projects have been incremental and discretionary. The consequences for the rural poor extend to the incremental provision of electricity and demonstrate the need for more effective vertical and horizontal linkages that combine livelihood approaches, potential income-generating activities and rural development approaches. More importantly, an exclusive reliance on donor aid, a substantial NGO presence, inadequate ownership of rural development approaches and outcomes, particularly where district assemblies are concerned, have all complicated national and local (district assembly) responses to public service delivery of key amenities like electricity. Indeed, the participatory locus for local institutions expected under political decentralization, structural adjustment and neo-liberal policies has not been borne out as envisioned. To be sure, continuing difficulties in filling positions and relocating individuals willing to live in the "hinterland" unwittingly produced gaps in the capacity of district assemblies to fulfill development and service-oriented objectives.

Under the MDGs, the plight of the poor received renewed attention, but at the same time neo-liberal policies called for a "minimal" state, which heightened political capture. Indeed, Ian Gary noted how African elites sought to tap into the NGO sector as a source of accumulation in the midst of this process. By using development projects to enhance political capital on a domestic front, DA capacity and upward mobility of the rural poor are compromised. Perhaps significantly, the conclusions of an Afrobarometer briefing paper on Popular Opinions on Local Government in Ghana (2008) found that "there is a considerable dissonance between Ghanaian understanding of the public service delivery responsibilities of local government authorities and the statutory ones."

For long-term poverty reduction and rural development to be effectively accomplished, one of the first steps towards this objective might involve a reconceptualization of electricity access and the "trusteeship" role that external actors like NGOs play. Long-term rural development and poverty reduction goals are suitable and even necessary, as are donor and NGO assistance, in democratizing transitioning countries. But the strategies implicit in current approaches unduly politicize access to public goods critical to rural development in ways that are neglected in the literature and by development partners (donors). Thus, the predisposition towards markets and efforts to integrate economies and energy systems invite us to consider how the state navigates its efforts to ensure public interest, while organizing economic life in a globalizing environment that carries unmitigated risks for the poor.[91]

Enduring service delivery challenges in an expanding economy illustrate how access to electricity is exceedingly central to the broad goals of equitable and sustainable rural development for Ghana's rural poor. Electricity represents more than a broad component of modern economies. It is not only intimately connected with the digital age and telecommunication, but to macro–micro processes that potentially connect the rural poor to small and medium enterprises that can propel them from the drudgery of rural life to an improved existence. Though Ghana can boast of substantial progress in improving rural development outcomes, it is hoped that ongoing electrification efforts eventually yield the kinds of outcomes that move disadvantaged rural communities towards a model that accrues aggregate benefits—particularly for the poor.

Notes

1. Institute for Economic Affairs, 2002, as cited in Wolde-Rufael, 204, p. 1108.
2. With almost 52% of the Ghanaian population defined as poor, public services will almost certainly remain critical in the years and perhaps decades to come.
3. USAID Comparative Assessment of Decentralization in Africa: Final Report and Summary of Findings, September 2010, p. 65.
4. See Lindsay Whitfield, "Trustees of Development from Conditionality to Governance: Poverty Reduction Strategy Papers in Ghana," *Journal of Modern African Studies* 43, no. 4 (2005): 660; Alison J. Ayers, "Demystifying Democratisation: The Global Constitution of (Neo) Liberal Polities in Africa," *Third World Quarterly* 27, no. 2 (2006): 329.
5. Institutional actors are taken here to mean district assemblies.
6. Ghana Institute for Economic Affairs, 2004, 33.
7. Ibid., 32.
8. Ibid., 32.
9. Institute for Economic Affairs—Ghana, 2004, 65.
10. Robert M. Price, *Society and Bureaucracy in Contemporary Ghana* (Berkeley: University of California Press, 1977).
11. Robert Bates (1981). *Markets and States in Tropical Africa: The Political Basis of Agricultural Policies* (Berkeley: University of California Press).
12. See D. F. Bryceson, "Agrarian Vista or Vortex: African Rural Livelihood Policies," *Review of African Political Economy* 31, no. 102 (2004), *Agendas, Past & Future* (December 2004): 621.
13. L. Hanmer, G. Pyatt, and H. White, *Poverty in Sub-Saharan Africa: What Can We Learn from the World Bank's Poverty Assessments?* (The Hague: Institute of Social Studies, 1997).

14. Bond, Patrick, *Looting Africa: The Economics of Exploitation* (London: Zed Books).
15. See Joseph Awetori Yaro, "Is Deagrarianisation Real? A Study of Livelihood Activities in Rural Northern Ghana," *Journal of Modern African Studies* 44, no. 1 (2006): 125–56. Also see D. F. Bryceson, "African Rural Labour, Income Diversification and Livelihood Approaches: A Long-Term Development Perspective," *Review of African Political Economy* 80 (1999): 171–89; D. F. Bryceson, "Agrarian Vista or Vortex: African Rural Livelihood Policies," *Review of African Political Economy* 31, no. 102 (2004), *Agendas, Past & Future* (December 2004): 617–29. Many interview participants—that is, members of parliament and even energy officials—conceded the need for creative solutions to combat the growing problem of rural flight in a bid to stem urban overcrowding.
16. See Yared Amare, *Household Resources, Strategies and Food Security in Ethiopia: A Study Amhara Households in Wogda Northern Shewa* (Addis Ababa: Department of Sociology and Social Administration and the Addis Ababa University Press, 1999), 152.
17. Ibid., 152.
18. Eboe Hutchful, "The Fall and Rise of the State in Ghana," in *The African State: Reconsiderations*, ed. Samatar Abdi Ismail and Ahmed I. Samatar (Portsmouth: Heinemann, 2002); Kwame Akonor, *Ghana and IMF Conditionality: The Unevenness of Compliance, 1983–2000* (Routledge, 2013).
19. Stein, 1997, 137.
20. Deagrarianization is defined as a long-term process of occupational adjustment, income earning reorientation, social identification and spatial relocation of rural dwellers away from strict peasant models of livelihoods (Bryceson, 1996). Depeasantization, on the other hand, is a process whereby the economic capacity and social coherence of peasantries are being progressively undermined—that is, they unravel communities and the international policy climate is directly linked to this reversal (Bryceson, 2004).
21. F. Ellis, *Rural Livelihoods and Diversity in Developing Countries* (Oxford: Oxford University Press 2000).
22. See D. Carney, Briefing, Approaches to Sustainable Livelihoods for the Rural Poor', *ODI Poverty*, January 2, 1999; A. Gordon, Non-Farm Rural Livelihoods, Policy Series 4 (Chatham, UK: Natural Resources Institute. Research, Rhodes University and Leiden: African Studies Centre Joint Working Paper 33, 1999).
23. See Deborah F. Bryceson, "African Rural Labour, Income Diversification and Livelihood Approaches: A Long-Term Development Perspective," *Review of African Political Economy* 80: 171–189. For example, Berkvens (1997) and Collier and Gunning (1997) illustrate how diversification impacted households negatively by diverting labor and capital away farming

and gains of specialization that occur through spreading risks in multiple income generating activities.

24. See Deborah Bryceson, "African Rural Labour, Income Diversification & Livelihood Approaches: A Long Term Development Perspective," *Review of African Political Economy* 26, no. 80 (1999): 174.
25. Ibid., 174.
26. Anita Spring and Barbara E. McDade, *African Entrepreneurship: Theory and Reality* (Gainesville, Florida: University Press of Florida, 1998).
27. For instance, Goran Hyden, *Religion, Politics, and the Crisis in Africa* (Indianapolis, 1986); James C. Scott, *Weapons of the Weak: Everyday Forms of Peasant Resistance* (New Haven: University Press, 1985); S. Berry, The Food Crisis and Agrarian Change in Africa: A Review Essay. *African Studies Review* 27, no. 2 (June 1984): 59–112.
28. George J. Sefa Dei, *Hardships and Survival in Rural West Africa: A Case Study of Ghanaian Community* (Dakar, Senegal: CODESRIA, 1992), 45.
29. African Media Development Initiative: Ghana Context, 2006.
30. The Canadian International Development Association (CIDA) and Japan International Cooperation Association (JICA) are a few examples among many others.
31. Gerald K. Helleiner, "Markets, Politics, and Globalization: Can the Global Economy Be Civilized?" *Global Governance* 7, no. 3 (July–September 2001): 243–63.
32. Joseph Kwadwo Tuffour, "Foreign Aid, Domestic Revenue and Economic Growth in Ghana." (2013): 31.
33. See Tim Unwin, "Beyond Budgetary Support: Pro-Poor Development Agendas for Africa," *Third World Quarterly* 25, no. 8 (2004): 1501–23; Patrick Bond, *Looting Africa: The Economics of Exploitation* (London: Zed Books, 2006); Lindsay Whitfield, "Trustees of Development from Conditionality to Governance: Poverty Reduction Strategy Papers in Ghana," *Journal of Modern African Studies* 43, no. 4 (2005): 660; Alison J. Ayers, "Demystifying Democratisation: The Global Constitution of (Neo) Liberal Polities in Africa," *Third World Quarterly* 27, no. 2 (2006): 329.
34. Jonathan Baker and Poul O. Pedersen. *The Rural-Urban Interface in Africa: Expansion and Adaptation* (Uppsala: Nordiska Afrikainstitutet in cooperation with Centre for Development Research, Copenhagen, 1992).
35. Gyimah-Boadi, symposium paper on the progress of decentralization, Center for Democracy and Development 2009, p. 7.
36. See Ofie-Aboagye, symposium paper, 2009.
37. Paul Streeten, *Empowerment, Participation and the Poor*, No. HDOCPA-2002-17 (Human Development Report Office [HDRO], United Nations Development Programme [UNDP], 2002).

38. D. Lawrence, *Reform and Decentralization of Agricultural Services: A Policy Framework* (Rome: Food and Agriculture Organization, 2001), 167.
39. In "The Politics of Decentralisation and Donor Funding in South Africa's Rural Water Sector," *Journal of Southern African Studies* 29, no. 4 (December 2003): 865.
40. F. Cheru, "Building and Supporting PRSPRs in Africa: What Has Worked Well So Far?" *Peace Research Abstracts Journal* 43, no. 3 (2006) Sage Publications.
41. Ibid.
42. See Rosemary McGee, Josh Levene, and Alexandra Hughes, *Assessing Participation in Poverty Reduction Strategy Papers: A Desk Based Synthesis of Experience in Sub-Saharan Africa* (Brighton, Sussex, England: Institute of Development Studies, 2002); H. Flack and K. Landfald, *The Poverty Reduction Strategy Process in Mozambique*, a joint NORAD/ SIDA report prepared for the Strategic Partnership for Africa (2001); B. Koudougou, *Critical Analysis of the PRSP Experience in Burkina Faso*, paper. Commissioned by the UN Economic Commission for Africa for the Second Meeting of the African Learning Group on the Poverty Strategy Papers, Brussels, 2002, 27.
43. Building and Supporting PRSPs in Africa: What Has Worked Well So Far? What Needs Changing? Source: *Third World Quarterly* 27, no. 2 (2006).
44. Tim Unwin, "Beyond Budgetary Support: Pro-Poor Development Agendas for Africa," *Third World Quarterly* 25, no. 8 (2004): 1501–23.
45. DFID, *Managing Fiduciary Risk When Providing Direct Budget Support* (London: DFID, 2002b), 118. http://62.189.42.51/DFIDstage/Pubs/files/fiduciary/pdf.
46. Akwasi P. Osei, *Ghana: Recurrence and Change in a Post-Independent African State* (New York: Peter Lang Publishing, 1999).
47. Roger Gocking, *Facing Two Ways: Ghana's Coastal Communities under Colonial Rule* (Lanham, MD: University Press of America, 1999).
48. For instance, see Alan Fowler, "Distant Obligations: Speculations on NGO Funding and the Global Market," *Review of African Political Economy* 55 (1992a): 9–29; A. Bebbington and J. Farrington, "Governments, NGOs and Agricultural Development: Perspectives on Changing Inter-Organisational Relationships," *Journal of Development Studies* 29, no. 2 (1993): 199–219; Michael Bratton, "Politics of Government-NGO Relations," *World Development* 17, no. 4 (April 1989b): 569–87.
49. Alan Fowler, "The Role of NGOs in Changing State-Society Relations: Perspectives from Eastern and Southern Africa," *Development Policy Review* 9 (1991b): 53–84.
50. A. Bebbington and J. Farrington, "Governments, NGOs and Agricultural Development: Perspectives on Changing Inter-Organisational Relationships," *Journal of Development Studies* 29, no. 2 (1993): 199–219.

51. Aloysius Denkabe, "Ghana: Country Overview," in Copestake & Wellard, *Non-Governmental Organizations and the State in Africa*, ed. Copestake and Wellard (London: Routledge, 1993): 188.
52. See Gary (1996) on the difficulties of delineating differences between local/indigenous and foreign/international NGOs and their activities. For a discussion of typology of NGOs see Bratton (1989) and Fowler (1992), which includes CBOs—community based organizations—service or intermediary NGOs, international and relief organizations—which tend to be foreign.
53. Ibid., 154.
54. See Barnes and Foley (2000); Hans Singer Wolfgang, Alec K. Cairncross and Mohinder Puri, *The Strategy of International Development: Essays in the Economics of Backwardness* (Macmillan, 1978).
55. K. Peprah, "Rural Electrification: And Economic Trigger in the Dormaa District of Ghana," *Ghana Journal of Development Studies* 5, no. 1 (2008): 128.
56. Prevailing arguments in studies such as Foley's (1990) and even among some members of parliament argue that the relationship is spurious. However, the contention here is that though other inputs and factors are needed—like the intersectoral linkages that Peprah (2008) alludes to—electrification is more than a functionality, as acknowledged by 18 interview participants from institutions ranging from Parliament to the Ministry of Energy to the Ministry of Local and Rural Development. Given the preponderance of articles about energy in many of the country's newspapers, electrification remains not only a hot-button subject but also a politicized one. Moreover, Anwobor's (2005) finding in his study of GA districts—both GA west and GA east—that electrification is not and cannot bring about "desired socioeconomic development in rural areas" is questionable, given the testimony of a former district chief executive and current district assembly member that electrification has indeed improved the livelihood of residents and that local residents often approach the assembly for the soonest dates available for grid setup. This is closer to the view of Foley (1990), who notes that "rural electrification on its own does not cause development: but where the necessary conditions are present, it has a major impact on the form that development takes; and can also provide a stimulus to economic activity especially in the service sector."
57. See Daniel Yergin and Martin Joseph Hillenbrand, *Global Insecurity: A Strategy for Energy and Economic Renewal*, Atlantic Institute for International Affairs (Boston: Houghton Mifflin, 1982); John R. Moroney and Flory Dieck-Assad, *Energy and Sustainable Development in Mexico* (College Station: Texas A & M University Press, 2005).
58. Personal communication, 2009.

59. Adu Boahen, *Ghana: Evolution and Change in the Nineteenth and Twentieth Centuries* (London: Longman Group Limited, 1975); Akwasi P. Osei, *Ghana: Recurrence and Change in a Post-Independent African State* (New York: Peter Lang Publishing, 1999).
60. Kevin Shillington, *Ghana and the Rawlings Factor* (New York: St. Martin's Press, 1992), 6.
61. Gwendolyn Mikell, "Peasant Politicisation and Economic Recuperation in Ghana: Local and National Dilemmas," *The Journal of Modern African Studies* 27, no. 3 (1989): 456.
62. See Adu Boahen (1975); Akwasi P. Osei (1999).
63. Stephen Haggard, *Pathways from the Periphery: The Politics of Growth in the Newly Industrializing Countries* (Ithaca, NY: Cornell University Press, 1990).
64. See Naomi Chazan et al., in *Politics and Society in Contemporary Africa* (London: Macmillan, 1988).
65. One can argue that the stressing of electrification as a political issue created a precedent that Rawlings followed when he initiated plans for regime transition in 1989 and announced plans for district assembly elections in 1988.
66. See Naomi Chazan, *An Anatomy of Ghanaian Politics: Managing Political Recession, 1969–1982* (Boulder: Westview Press, 1983).
67. Gwendolyn Mikell, "Peasant Politicisation and Economic Recuperation in Ghana: Local and National Dilemmas," *The Journal of Modern African Studies* 27, no. 3 (1989): 456.
68. See Paul D. Lumsden, "Towards Ghana's Third Republic," *Canadian Journal of African Studies* 13, no. 3 (1980): 471–77; Richard Jeffries, "Rawlings and the Political Economy of Underdevelopment in Ghana," *African Affairs* 81, no. 324 (July 1982): 307–17.
69. See Eboe Hutchful, "The Fall and Rise of the State in Ghana," in *The African State: Reconsiderations*, ed. Samatar Abdi Ismail and Ahmed I. Samatar (Portsmouth, NH: Heinemann, 2002); Green, Daniel in Leonardo A. Villalon and Phillip A. Huxtable, eds., *Ghana: Structural Adjustment and State Reformation: The African State at a Critical Juncture* (Boulder, CO: Lynne Rienner Publishers, 1998). Donald Rothchild and Naomi Chazan, eds., *The Precarious Balance: State and Society in Africa* (Boulder: Westview Press, 1988).
70. See Peter Lewis, "Economic Reform and Political Transition in Africa: The Quest for a Politics of Development," *World Politics* 49, no. 1 (1996): 92–129.
71. Gwendolyn Mikell, "Peasant Politicisation and Economic Recuperation in Ghana: Local and National Dilemmas," *The Journal of Modern African Studies* 27, no. 3 (1989).

72. For more, see his edited work in *Ghana: One Decade of the Liberal State* (London: Zed Books).
73. Naomi Chazan, "Liberalization, Governance, and Political Space in Ghana," *Governance and Politics in Africa* (1992): 121–42.
74. Dan Robotham, "The Ghana Problem," *Labor, Capital & Society* 21, no. 1 (April 1988): 12–35; Nii K. Bentsi-Enchill, "Steps at Grassroots," *West Africa*, August 3, 1987.
75. This is probably valid until the post-1992 period, when Rawlings' NDC party reversed the trend towards urban bias by pandering to the rural areas where most of the population resided, much to the chagrin of urban populations. In fact, in the final tally of votes in the 1992 and 1996 elections, Rawlings and the NDC were able to garner most of the rural vote, with a smaller percentage of urban residents voting for him.
76. Chatterjee Lata Aryeetey-Attoh, "Regional Inequalities in Ghana: Assessment and Policy Issues," *Tijdschrift voor Economische en Sociale Geografie* 79, no. 1 (1988): 31.
77. Berket Kebede, Dube Ikhupuleng, and O. Kalumiana, *Energy Services for the Urban Poor in Africa: Issues and Policy Implications*, Africa Energy Policy Research Network (London; New York: Zed Books, 2004), 3.
78. Charles M. Becker, Andrew Marshall Hamer, and Andrew R. Morrison, *Beyond Urban Bias in Africa: Urbanization in an Era of Structural Adjustment* (Portsmouth, NH: Heinemann; London: J. Currey, 1994).
79. R. Gyampo, *Chieftaincy and Rural Development in Ghana*. Department of Political Science, University of Ghana-at Legon, Thesis, 1997.
80. Randolph Quaye, *Underdevelopment and Health Care in Africa: The Ghanaian Experience* (Lewiston: Mellen University Press, 1996).
81. Anonymous, personal communication, 2009.
82. Anonymous, personal communication, 2009.
83. Karl Quaye Botchway, "Paradox of Empowerment: Reflections on a Case Study from Northern Ghana," *World Development* 29, no. 1 (January 2001): 135–53.
84. Kojo Osei F. Busia, Dissertation: *Structural Adjustment, Decentralization, and Agricultural and Rural Development in Ghana, 1982–1992* (1995).
85. Daniel Green (1995?) cites the World Bank's (1991) observations that "in 1987–1988, the PNDC government established a redistributive pattern of raising rural incomes with ever ever-higher cocoas producer prices while increasing its own revenue via increased petrol prices paid primarily by urban consumers" (p. 578). Green notes that the government used this early policy to solidify its hold on power, using the Assembly system by allocating some 117 seats in the 260-seat consultative Assembly, which then drew up the Fourth Republic's constitution. This strategy later helped in securing important policies beneficial to rural areas, such as the District Assembly Common Fund alluded to in an earlier chapter.

86. Afua Banful, Dissertation: *Essays on the Political Economy of Public Goods Provision in Developing Countries* (Harvard University, 2008).
87. Institute for Economic Affairs, 2004, 47.
88. Gyimah-Boadi Emmanuel, *Ghana under PNDC Rule* (Senegal: Codesria, 1993).
89. See Daniel Green, "The Politics of Adjustment," *Review of African Political Economy* 22, no. 66 (December 1995): 577–85.
90. Round 3, Afrobarometer Survey in Ghana, 2005—compiled by Edem Selormey, Joseph Asunka and Daniel Armah-Attoh.
91. See K. Dubash Navroz, "Revisiting Electricity Reform: The Case for a Sustainable Development Approach," *Utility Policy* 11 (2003): 148.

CHAPTER 5

The Numbers Game: Quantifying Access and Regional Differentiation in Electricity Provision in the Fourth Republic

Rural electricity access signifies more than simply securing electric poles and putting communities on the grid. It entails equity in pricing, affordability, and regularity in provision for the entire population. An increase from 66% several years ago to the current access rate of 80.51% in this West African nation is undoubtedly significant for a continent where almost 600 million people lack electricity. However, this figure, though admirable, does not capture the nuances of what I term a "numbers game" or the fluidity of the meaning of "access." The puzzle I explore is that of how to reconcile an electricity access rate unmatched by most of sub-Saharan Africa, except for South Africa, with an overwhelming number of Ghanaians (some 75%, according to an Afrobarometer survey last conducted in 2014) who rate government performance in electricity delivery as dismal.[1] This chapter contextualizes the dichotomy of national success in electricity outcomes and regional differentiation and uneven access from data calculated six years ago. Despite the remarkable increase in electricity access in the figures noted above, my argument, which has been updated to reflect recent changes in access, is nonetheless the same. I argue that the heightened saliency of electricity provision is evident in the regional differentiation and a "numbers game" that correlates with voting outcomes. Consequently, this chapter finds that the regions with the higher rates of electricity access are, in fact, electoral "swing" regions.[2] Using electrification data obtained from the MOE after 2008 (an election year), along with national access rates for the country's ten regions,

N. Sackeyfio, *Energy Politics and Rural Development in Sub-Saharan Africa*, https://doi.org/10.1007/978-3-319-60122-9_5

I outline the results of those findings from 2011 to explain patterns of regional variation.

The purpose of this chapter is twofold: firstly, to discuss patterns of regional differentiation in access rates and what this means in the context of the rural poor, and secondly, to unpack the nature of this study's quantitative findings, which offer puzzling but paradoxical evidence of both success and disparities. This chapter will demonstrate that differences between observed and expected (official) electricity rates are considerable. Of remarkable significance is that the Greater Accra region reveals surprising disparities. If we consider that the region represents the most developed part of Ghana, this finding dispels the notion of widespread access for the rural poor who reside in the outskirts of the region. As it were, regression results point to disparities between *observed* and *expected* rates of electricity provision. Likewise, I attribute these unexpected results to social, economic, and demographic factors, outlined in this study, which support the notion of regional differentiation, and not the convergence in electricity outcomes that original MOE documents suggest.

In the section that follows, I trace key historical moments in the development of electricity provision, to provide a political context for incongruent provision. The second section builds on the first to discuss how voting alignments inform regional differentiation and, arguably, public goods access. Subsequent sections discuss the quantitative findings and research implications of this study, including the relationship between poverty, electrification, and income generation, and offer conclusions.

Electrification in Early Post-Independence Ghana

Since the post-independence period beginning in the 1960s, the history of electrification in Ghana has been uneven. In spite of efforts by the country's first president, Kwame Nkrumah, to use the Akosombo Dam as an impetus for industrial development and rural electrification, the political fallout from negative environmental effects, economic consequences of Volta resettlement efforts, and ambiguous benefits to rural communities complicated future responses to electrification gaps.[3] Emmanuel Kwaku Acheampong's analysis of the eco-social history of the Anlo-speaking peoples—part of an Ewe national grouping located between the Volta and Mono rivers—is instructive.[4] The political impact of coastal erosion, which shaped Anlo-Ewe expectations about political inclusion and exclusion, was also influenced by frequent regime change in the post-independence era. Indeed, this development resulted in a lack of continuity in environmental policy, as new governments attempted old experiments that failed to halt coastal erosion. Acheampong's analysis also considers the development of harbors and dams, as well as the ways in which political authority shaped environmental and demographic processes and, arguably, regional differentiation in electric energy outcomes.

The Akosombo Dam was described as a panacea for the country's insufficient power supply, even though the World Bank suggested that the power project's lifespan would be a mere 60 years.[5] Built by Henry Kaiser's American aluminum company, the Akosombo Dam became a reality with the support of Kwame Nkrumah, as the government of Ghana established in a Volta River Project statement in 1961. It was the largest single infrastructure project in Ghana at the time, and one which the Nkrumah government lacked sufficient revenue to finance. However, after an elaborate negotiation by the government, coupled with the intervention of President Eisenhower of the United States, the Kaiser Aluminum Company agreed to underwrite part of the Volta River Project on the condition that it be permitted, in the form of a consortium with Reynolds Aluminum, to utilize about two-thirds of the electrical power generated by the project for smelting aluminum in Ghana. Although preparatory reports and ambitious plans in the mid-1950s aimed to usher in industrialization through the subsequent completion of the Volta River Project and Akosombo Dam, the vision of large-scale industrial transformation fell short of expectations. Indeed, the enthusiasm of a young nation to become industrialized within a relatively short time—within Nkrumah's tenure—generated its own problems, since human and material resources were overestimated by the Convention People's Party (CPP) government.[6]

Consequently, the promise of hydropower as a fulcrum for economic and industrial development proved elusive. The failure of early post-independence leaders to articulate an electric energy framework conducive to the country's electrification needs, along with a populist impulse, delayed the reemergence of electric energy concerns until the last decade of the twentieth century. Whether due to economic malaise, ruinous economic policies, or the precipitous decline in the price of cocoa—a major export—Ghana's first 25 years after independence were marked by negative economic growth, which some attributed to a causal factor of low demand for, and utilization of, electricity. Nonetheless, electricity was available primarily in urban, commercial areas, with the bulk of the country's rural population relying exclusively on wood fuels or biomass as a primary source of energy for cooking, heating, and lighting.

This is unfortunate, given that, as one member of parliament explains, "Nkrumah's tenure was one that we might term an empire state—it had a lot of money and at the same time the country had the VRA—by Kaiser, the US—which gave [sic] Nkrumah the opportunity to provide [sic] rural electricity under the colonial government."[7] After his ousting and a brief interim period, during which the military or National Liberation Army governed, the country's second president, K.A. Busia, proved more successful in his attempts to provide access to rural areas. As part of his plans to push rural development, he charted a path for infrastructural intervention that emphasized roads and electricity. Moreover, a member of parliament suggested, in 2009, that "Busia appreciated a lot more the essence of rural development. He gave Ghana the first minister of rural development and put emphasis on rural development." It is remarkable then that, while Nkrumah billed himself as the "champion of hydropower development," Busia proved much more successful in providing electricity to rural townships, perhaps as a consequence of political exigencies that were necessitated by an adoption of liberal-oriented policies.

As this study finds, although the country's first and second presidents—Kwame Nkrumah and K.A. Busia (1969–1972)—both articulated extensive plans for rural electrification, few benefits materialized from their efforts. I find that incongruent energy values and diminished political capital account for the difference in access under the country's first and second presidents. During Nkrumah's tenure from 1957–1966, political discontent with the pace of economic and political change and ensuing social cleavages led to a politics of confrontation.[8] It was not uncommon for individuals, groups, and localities to vie for representation and control over various structures of government, which began after a decisive break with the Danquah/Busia camp—two leading intellectuals and founders of the United Gold Coast Convention (UGCC). Subsequently, Kwame Nkrumah's CPP and Busia's Progressive People's Party came to reflect ideological and personal struggles for power that arguably spilled over into public goods provision. In any case, further political upheavals, several coups d'état, and a lack of institutional continuity produced glaring gaps in access, with few attempts to electrify the countryside fully until the early 1990s. It was only until then that renewed efforts to utilize the country's hydropower sources for electricity resumed in earnest.

To contextualize fully the politics of rural preference, where electricity provision and other forms of public good access are concerned, requires careful scrutiny of voter alignments since the post-independence period.

With a political sphere that centers on the country's two dominant political parties—the National Patriotic Party and the National Democratic Congress—Lindsay Whitfield argues that "elections are competitive because of the de facto two party system, in which both the NDC and NPP serve as credible oppositions. The parties mobilize voters and political elites around two political traditions,"[9] reinvented in the fold of partnership between J.B. Danquah and Busia, contenders for post-independence leadership, and Nkrumah's CPP.[10] Minion K. Morrison, concurring with Whitfield, observes that "by 1956, clear partisan lines had developed, known as the Nkrumah and Danquah–Busia axes: the one populist and state interventionist and the other liberal-mercantilist with its own tinge of interventionism."[11] Nkrumah and his supporters preferred political mobilization, populism, and state intervention, while the NDC leadership, led by Jerry J. Rawlings in the post-1992 period, appeared to reflect some sentiments of the former.[12] In similar fashion, the Rawlings regime utilized a rural strategy that included heavy infrastructural development adopted by succeeding administrations.[13] Indeed, one can argue that the NDC reflects a populist working class and is heavily dependent on rural constituencies.[14] As Paul Nugent has noted,

> in the two previous elections, the NDC played a full hand very astutely. It was aware that it was not especially popular in the cities, where structural adjustment had produced the greatest pain, but it also knew that the elections would be won and lost in the countryside. Hence, the NDC concentrated its efforts there, and made a special pitch to the Northern, Upper East, and Upper West Regions, which had been historically marginalized.[15]

The full compass of party competition and regional strongholds for both parties is expertly captured by Lindsay Whitfield.[16] Indeed, parliamentary seats won for each party in the 1996, 2000, 2004, and 2008 elections show remarkable trends. In the 2000 elections, which the NPP won, the Greater Accra, Eastern, Brong–Ahafo, and Ashanti regions were strongholds for the NPP. However, for the NDC, the Volta, Northern, Upper West, and Upper Eastern regions were featured as strongholds for the party. Perhaps as a nod to ethnicity, the Volta region has typically supported the NDC, because Rawlings, who essentially established the party, hails from the Ewe ethnic group situated in that region. However, while President Atta Mills (2008–2012) a member of the NDC, hails from the Central region, an area of support for the NDC party, it has become a swing region. In the 2004 elections, the NPP's and NDC's strongholds remained the same. A number of fascinating observations are apparent, particularly since the 2008 election. Whitfield notes,

> In the 2000 elections, the central, western and Brong–Ahafo regions functioned as swing regions since elections have been close there and because these regions determined who won in past elections. It was the NDC's poor performance in the Central and Western regions that cost it the 2004 election. Similarly, the party's dramatic turnaround in the Central and Greater Accra regions in 2008 forced the NPP to a presidential runoff and ultimately won Atta Mills the presidency. There were also very close races in the Western and Brong–Ahafo regions, with NDC catching up but NPP still in the lead…The Greater Accra became a swing region in the 2008 election and probably cost the NPP the election given that it is a region with the highest number of voters. In sum, the presidential outcome in 2008 was determined by Central, Western and Greater Accra regions.[17]

The losses of the NPP party are illuminating for two reasons. Firstly, it had not fulfilled promises made to urbanites in the 2000 election; secondly, in 2006 and 2007, the country faced a series of power supply problems that resulted in power rationing. More significantly, the NPP made several new investments in energy, but it was too early for voters to see the benefits of those actions, and utility prices continued to rise.[18] This is perhaps the most glaring instance of *unevenness* in electricity provision and the questionable success of the country's decentralized electricity initiatives. If constituents in the Greater Accra region, with the highest number of voters and urban residents, expressed concerns about improvements in electric energy production, as Whitfield suggests, it is reasonable to assume that there may not be a convergence towards uniform access as new MOE figures suggest, despite notable success for the country overall. Even an impressive improvement in access across the country's ten regions does not square with protests and calls to action by the previous administration of John Dramani Mahama (2012–2017), which was plagued with criticism and complaints about *dumsor*, the local term for a perpetual "lights on, lights off" conundrum. Consequently, the data findings and article headlines listed in the Appendix substantiate *uneven* access in Ghana's administrative regions. In Table 5.1 below, rates of access for all ten regions are tabulated using various indicators that will be discussed.

In the section that follows, I highlight the quantitative findings of this study, which reveal that, in spite of "official" or observed rates of electrification

Table 5.1 Electricity rates for Ghana's ten regions, 2008

Region	*Access rate (%)*
Greater Accra	95.77
Ashanti	80.07
Central	70.09
Brong–Ahafo	62.53
Eastern	61.56
Western	59.34
Volta	58.35
Northern	43.62
Upper West	31.95
Upper East	30.34
National Average	66.49

Source: Parliament library of Ghana

now at an increased rate of 80.51%, the situation is more complex than we might assume. After measuring against several economic indicators, a number of observations become conspicuously apparent for the national accessibility rates from six years ago. Table 5.1 lists percentages of access for all ten regions obtained from the MOE. At first glance, the Upper East, Upper West, and Northern regions are the only regions with remarkably low access rates, and the figures for all ten regions indicate an overall or national access rate of 66% in 2008, which is quite significant. After comparing the regions with the highest rates of access with electoral outcomes (that is, how each region voted—either NPP or NDC) since 2000, it appears that the Greater Accra Region, where 80% of the population have electricity, the Central Region with a rate of 70%, and the Eastern Region with a rate of 61.5%, have been swing regions. There may be no statistical correlation between the percentage of access and electoral outcomes, but the connection appears significant nonetheless.

Table 5.2 shows the raw electrification rates for each of the ten regions, while the electrification rates for Ghana's regions are plotted on Fig. 5.1.

After reading numerous newspaper articles in the course of my research trips to Ghana over the past decade, I became curious about conflicting reports of widespread access in my conversations with energy officials and in the newspaper headlines that frequently suggested otherwise. My own experiences of outages suggest persistent disparities which, as I observed, depended on locale. *This also supports the notion of unevenness and differentiation in access.* Even within the capital city of Accra, access has tended to vary. In the more privileged areas of Accra—for example, in Eastern

Table 5.2 National accessibility rates of electricity in Ghana, 2016

Region	*Access rate (%)*
Greater Accra	96.43
Ashanti	90.48
Central	84.32
Volta	79.09
Eastern	78.56
Western	78.12
Brong-Ahafo	75.77
Upper West	71.62
Northern	54.53
Upper East	51.65
National Average	80.51

Source: Report from Sixth Session of Sixth Parliament of the Fourth Republic, 2016

Legon or Osu—residents receive better access than, for instance, areas like Kokomlele, Dansoman, or Amanfro—all outskirts of Accra, where some family members live (to name just a few). It is also significant that the use of generators is prevalent. It is for these reasons that I sought to quantify these observations using electrification rates tabulated by the MOE for each of the ten regions in 2011. I should mention that these figures were initially difficult to obtain, and I only received them through a research assistant with personal connections to then Deputy Minister of Energy several years ago—who has since been replaced with the incoming administration of the current president, Nana Akufo Ado.

This study unequivocally acknowledges the successful transformation in electricity provision and access. However, it questions the extent to which the rural poor have benefitted, since an overall access or national electrification percentage of 80.51% obscures the numbers of rural constituents who lack or have limited access to electricity. It has sought to determine and deconstruct the consequences of a lifeline rate policy intended to make access possible for those who cannot afford it. If electricity distribution varies for a city like Accra, what of outlying rural counterparts? What does decentralized public service electricity through the current rural electrification and self-help schemes mean for the rural poor? While neither the data here nor MOE documents offers a breakdown of access rates for urban versus rural areas, the variation across regions strongly suggests patterns of regional differentiation, and

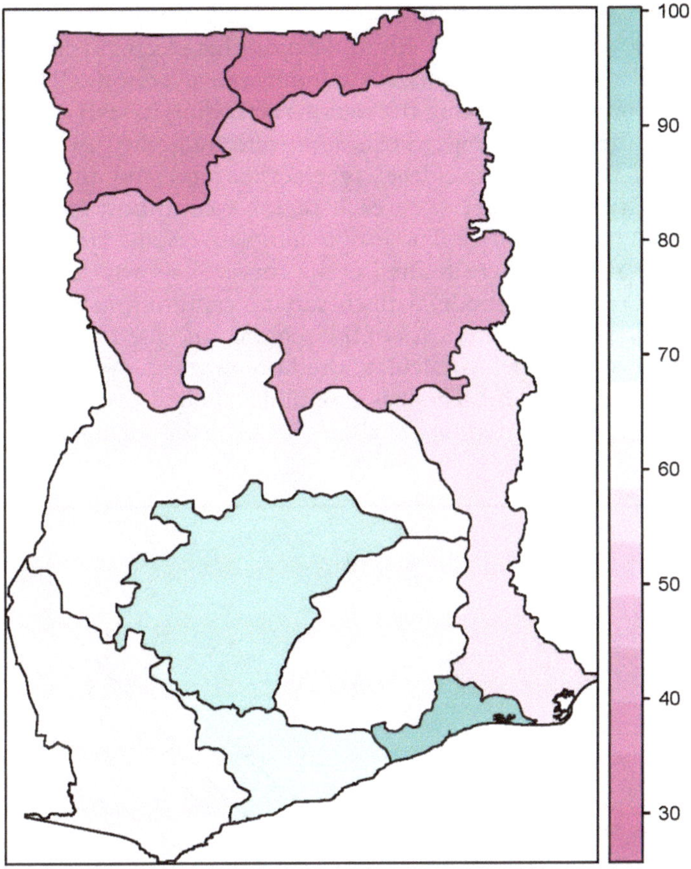

Fig. 5.1 Electrification rates for Ghana's regions (mapped)
Source: Created by the author

not necessarily a convergence toward widespread access. There is also a persistent divergence in definitions of "success." Consequently, after receiving "official rates" of electrification for each region, I decided to test the actual distribution to understand the nature of disparate access more accurately, given the disconnect between the MOE's optimism and public perceptions reflected in Ghanaian media, newspapers, and my personal observation of frequent disruptions and load shedding in 2007 and 2008. If the electrification rates were distributed evenly across all ten regions, the

Lorenz curve would follow that line,[19] but here we see that the Lorenz curve is below the line of equality, indicating that electricity is indeed not distributed evenly across Ghana's administrative regions. The Lorenz curve is computed by ranking the regions according to level of electrification (taken here to be the electrification rate multiplied by the population), then the cumulative level of electrification and the cumulative amount that is populative (i.e., each region's contribution to the total population) are calculated. These two cumulative sums are then plotted against one another to create the Lorenz curve, as shown in Fig. 5.2.

I fitted a regression model with co-variates capturing social, economic, and demographic characteristics of the regions, and used the fitted values of the regression model to calculate the Lorenz curve. (See Table 5.3 for the regression variables.) This has several advantages over using the raw data. Firstly, using a fitted model allows for probabilistic inference on the

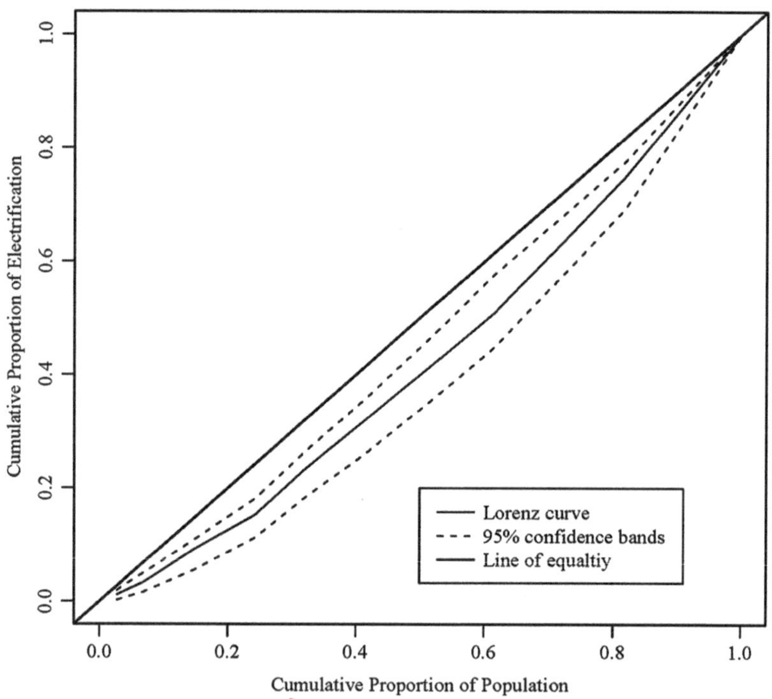

Fig. 5.2 Lorenz curve
Source: Created by the author

Table 5.3 Regression variables

	elect	*pop*	*area*	*purban*	*pagric*	*pindust*	*incpercap*	*inchh*	*pwageinc*
elect	0	0	0	0	0	0	0	0	0
pop	0.861851	0	0	0	0	0	0	0	0
area	−0.28296	−0.0338	0	0	0	0	0	0	0
purban	0.914692	0.780583	−0.50044	0	0	0	0	0	0
pagric	−0.84699	−0.74266	0.631796	−0.91646	0	0	0	0	0
pindust	0.869	0.962633	−0.26228	0.87209	−0.87144	0	0	0	0
incpercap	0.917217	0.739065	−0.07241	0.775803	−0.59324	0.692637	0	0	0
Inch	0.720368	0.657615	0.303572	0.533455	−0.33685	0.562593	0.868654	0	0
pwageinc	0.823141	0.650126	−0.51809	0.953559	−0.88714	0.785225	0.686421	0.516542	0

Source: Created by the author

Lorenz curve, as outlined in the next paragraph, and also the discrete nature of our spatial data may inject artificial concentration into the raw data. Since the Lorenz curve is below the line of equality, this indicates evidence of unequal distribution. However, I should note that these quantities are also subject to random variation, and, so as to further substantiate evidence that the distribution is not equal, I calculated 95% confidence bands by simulating 1000 draws from the regression model, calculating the Lorenz curve for each of the draws, and then evaluated the quintile function at 0.025 and 97.5, to produce a 95% confidence band around the Lorenz curve. The total area of the confidence band is also below the line of equality, indicating that, at the 0.05 level, the Lorenz curve is below the line of equality, which consequently proves unequal distribution. This also refutes assertions by prominent members of parliament and officials in the MOE, whom I interviewed, that electricity access is not politicized.

In Fig. 5.3, we can see observed versus expected rates of electrification. After using a regression model in juxtaposition to the data, we can calculate the expected rate and compare it with the observed rate based on figures from the MOE. The significance of this plot is that it demonstrates regions with higher, lower, or equal electrification rates in relation to social, economic, and demographic characteristics of the regions, which were tabulated. These indicators include population, percentage of urban residents in each region, percentage of people engaged in agriculture and industry, mean annual income, and percentage of in-migrants. The difference between the observed and expected rate of electrification is particularly significant for the Greater Accra region, which represents the most urbanized region of the country and site of the country's capital. I find this outcome surprising, given the official MOE rate of 95.77%. Frequent newspaper articles in the *Daily Guide*, the *Daily Graphic*, and the *Daily Searchlight*, among others, which highlight intermittent outages even for wealthy sections of Accra (for example, in East Legon), are substantiated by this revelation. I recognize that the Greater Accra region contains rural areas, which could explain irregularities depicted in the map. Nevertheless, I suggest that the political factors of rural capture and sequenced provision are explanatory variables that account for these findings. Additionally, the Volta and Upper Western regions appear to be the largest beneficiaries of electricity, a surprising and rather unexpected observation. Beyond my data acquired in 2010, I find that the welfare gains often assumed to be present where fiscal decentralization is underway are questionable, particularly for the

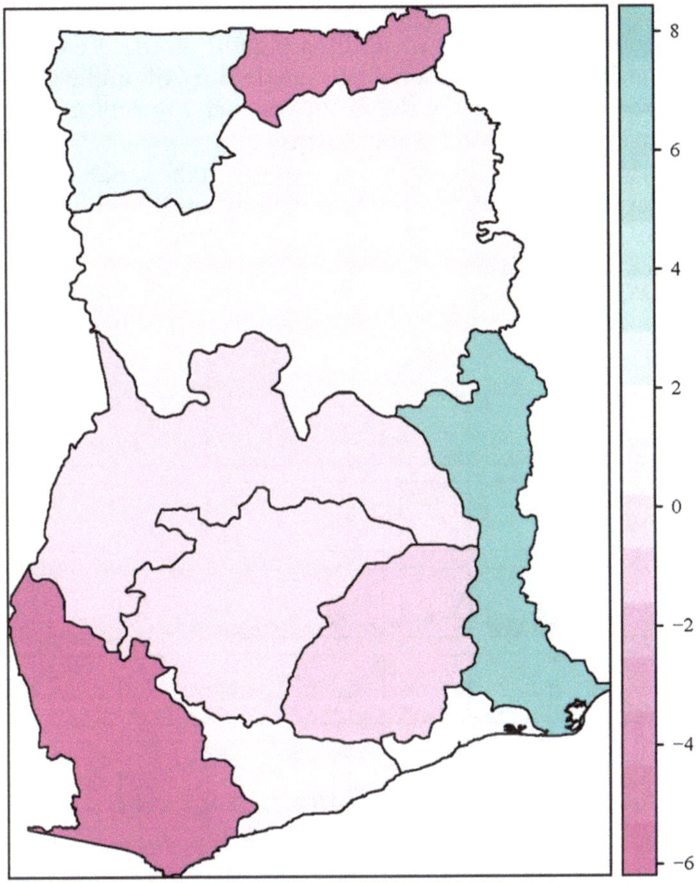

Fig. 5.3 Difference between observed and expected electrification rates
Source: Created by the author

rural poor. In an age when quantity rather than quality matters, the prioritization of public goods provision of electricity to the rural populace has more to do with the political incentives that elections generate and less to do with quality. Juxtaposed to the phenomenon of *dumsor*, a persistent energy crisis over the past few years, the substantial increase in electricity access across all ten regions (see Table 5.2) is symptomatic of the politics undergirding the presumed success inherent in an overall

80.51% access rate. Complaints about availability and the "lights off, lights on" enigma correlates with Min's suggestion that "Elections generate political incentives that privilege the delivery of public goods projects, more so than improving the quality of such projects. One reason is that improving quality is hard and expensive."[20]

The scatterplot matrix in Fig. 5.4 represents all the variables used in the dataset. Here, we can explore the interrelationships between the variables used by looking at the rows and columns corresponding to given variables to visualize the relationships.

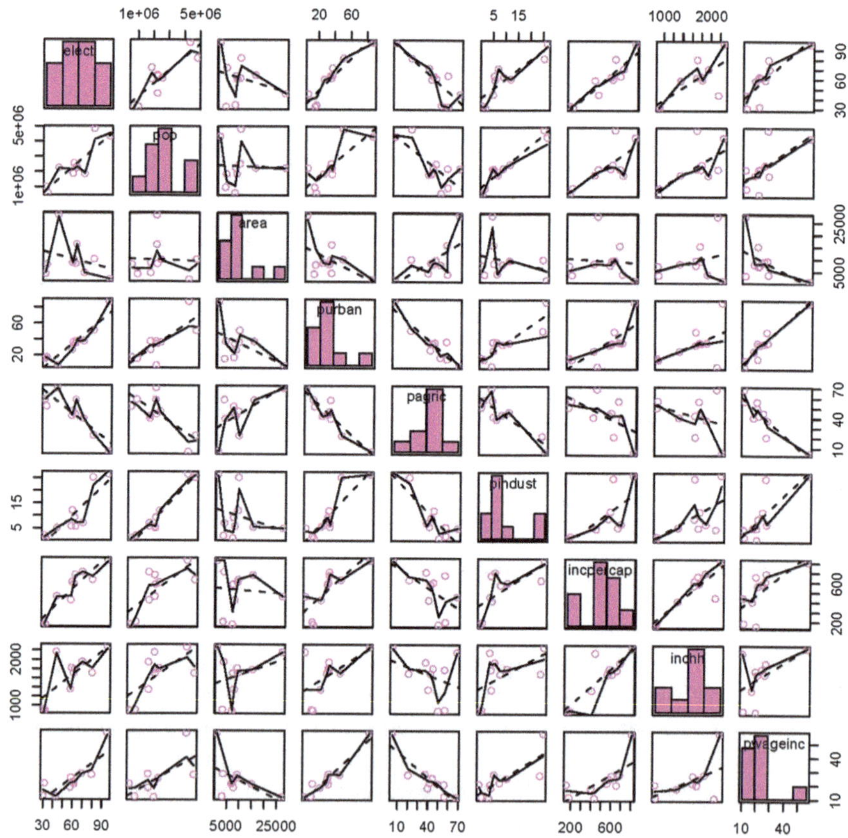

Fig. 5.4 Scatterplot matrix
Source: Created by the author

The regression model shown in Table 5.4 indicates a sample of the variables used to calculate the Lorenz curve and the observed versus expected map.

Table 5.5 summarizes the spatial correlation of electrification rates across Ghana's regions. The first analysis of raw electrification rates depict substantial spatial correlation. The second analysis depicts the residuals of the regression analysis, with no evidence of spatial correlation. Thus, I conclude that the observed correlation in electrification is due to social, economic, and demographic factors. Note that this is referring to the *correlation* between regions and not the rate of electrification itself, which nonetheless illustrates how these results can exacerbate regional inequalities. In short, electricity access is not only incongruent, but actual rates offer a picture of persistent disparities, even when historically marginalized regions like the Northern and, to a lesser extent, the Upper Eastern regions are accounted for. In tandem with newspaper articles obtained from the Office of Public Records and National Archives, the independent variables of "political influence and a political business cycle" provide evidence of

Table 5.4 Regression results

Regression Results

Term	*Coefficient*	*Standard Error*	*t*	*p-value*
(Intercept)	2.07E+01	4.46E+00	4.64	0.00354
Population	6.44E-06	1.72E-06	3.747	0.00954
Per Capita In	5.66E-02	1.06E-02	5.349	0.00175
Area	−6.20E-04	2.05E-04	−3.018	0.02345

Source: Created by the author

Signif. codes: 0 '***' 0.001 '**' 0.01 '*' 0.05 '.' 0.1 ' '1
Residual standard error: 4.552 on 6 degrees of freedom
Multiple R-squared Adjusted R-squared: 0.9499
F-statistic: 57.87 on 3 and 6 DF, p-value: 8.053e-05

Table 5.5 Moran's I

Moran's I	*Data*	*Residual*
Observed	0.5017777	−0.0829278
Expected	−0.1111111	−0.1111111
p-value	0.00151288	0.876195

Source: Created by the author

uneven provision. For virtually every election year,[21] beginning in 1992,[22] and continuing in 1996, 2000, 2004, and 2008, electricity projects were featured regularly in the newspapers, as noted in an appendix.

Implications of Research

The implications of this research are considerable. Not only is electrification multifaceted and complex, but the precise nature of economic linkages, productive uses of electric energy, and the relationships with demographic and economic indicators and actual impact will require further research. However, as one small step, this study represents an attempt to correct current and prevailing misconceptions about the nature of electricity access as public service delivery under decentralization. Secondly, there is an emerging consensus in policy circles that expanding energy delivery without adequate attention to productive uses or vertical and horizontal linkages required for income generation yields little by way of socioeconomic development.[23]

Under conditions of political transition, the simultaneous pursuit of democratization and decentralization is likely to yield precarious outcomes for public service delivery of goods when governments are donor-dependent,[24] which can inadvertently encourage a "project-based culture" that undermines the agency of district assemblies. It comes as little surprise that donor dependency and long-term-oriented poverty reduction strategy papers invariably bolstered "gradualism," as in the 30-year plan for electricity provision and the poverty reduction framework that emerged in the 1990s. Afua Banful argued that political tendencies to allocate resources in district-friendly areas declined over time, but it is possible that an incremental, community-by-community culture reconstituted the visibility of co-optation.

Poverty, Electrification, and Income Generation: A Valid Relationship or a Spurious One?

With the bulk of the country's poor in rural areas, high levels of poverty in Ghana and other sub-Saharan African countries are reflected in energy-consumption patterns.[25] Indeed, there appears to be a correlation between GNP per capita and energy use per capita.[26] Yet efforts to reach economic growth targets without sufficient energy supplies remain inadequately addressed in national policy frameworks. The nature of African institutions and the problems faced in generating outcomes that encourage development are well known. But the ways in which decentralization and minimalist government can structure service delivery of public goods, backward and forward linkages like information disclosure, water, paved roads, income-generating activities, skills, and manpower, as well as appropriate institutions to help rural citizens usher in development, are at best only partially understood. As Dr. Kwaku A. Danso of the Ghana Leadership Union remarked, "One may justifiably ask the Deputy Minister of Communication, what the heck does he mean by 'all communities will be connected to the national grid' (by 2011)? Does the young Deputy Minister know what this means, and can he break down the number of districts in Ghana that do not have electricity, explain the component steps and procedures and cost to generate electricity and deliver to communities?"[27] These questions highlight the increasing qualms of the public expressed in the Ghanaian newspapers like the *New Crusade Guide*, the *Daily Searchlight*, the *Daily Graphic*, and others. Many of these stories are startling in light of the progress that the MOE claims it has ostensibly made in provision.

While debates about the relationship between electrification and income generation are far from settled, rural communities in Ghana rightly view electricity as a critical amenity of modern life. Some suggest a weak relationship with productive uses of electricity (PUEs), but others argue that the degree to which this energy source reduces labor intensity or physical labor is considerable. As one interviewee noted, consistent with practically every other interview:

> Electrification has changed rural lifestyles in Ghana generally. For the few individuals who are engaged in non-farm work (and depend directly on electricity for their work), say operating drinking bars, corn-mills, garri and palm oil/palm kernel mills, selling iced water, video centers, tailoring, etc., I will say, their incomes have improved.[28]

Another noted that electrification was related to the larger scheme of development in a couple of ways, saying that "if you go to a rural area, drinking, mills and other economic activities help the development of community centers . . . it's really a catalyst for development."[29]

Conclusion

In sum, Ghana's development goals, including electrification targets, and the current capacity of the country's power sector to generate, transmit, and distribute power satisfactorily, are promising, despite requiring reevaluation. As a larger issue, Ghana has attempted to enter a globalizing world through market liberalization, with uneven consequences for various groups in society.[30] Meanwhile, these policy reforms do not appear to have had a uniformly beneficial effect on the poor and other vulnerable groups.[31] The success of various electrification schemes, including decentralized initiatives, gives cause for optimism and praise, given the dismal rates and quality of access in much of sub-Saharan Africa. The observed results and the overall percentage for the nation represent success and imply that much of the rural populace has access, and this is certainly indisputable. However, electricity flow versus notions of a remarkable increase in electricity access rates since the 2012 and 2016 elections point to a persistent dichotomy in interpretation. Consequently, it is reasonable to conclude that, given the correlation between swing regions in the recent elections and regions with the highest rates of access (which were calculated using data compiled in February 2010, after the election of 2008), concerns about patterns of regional differentiation are, indeed, valid. As a continued point of contention owing to periodic blackouts, severe electricity crises over the past several years point to a political environment or new infrastructural space that is ripe for electioneering and as a tool for courting new voters. Furthermore, this observation invites us to consider how the politics of interpretation frames public perceptions of access, at least in newspaper headlines, and the notable dichotomy between the former and overall patterns of success in structuring public discourse with regard to service delivery.

Appendix

While some newspaper article headlines noted below feature problems with power provision or power cuts, they also indicate the saliency of electricity provision. NP designates newspaper, NP1 refers to the *Daily Graphic,* while NP4, refers to the *Ghanaian Times.*

Document reference 1996	*Document date*	*Document page*	*Document description*
NP1/178	March 26	Back	ECG to extend power to 42 towns
NP1/179	April 25	Page 7	Bawdie, Enchi to get electricity
NP1/179	June 28	Back	115 communities to benefit from power project
NP1/180	August 10	Back	Agona Nyakrom power project commissioned

(*continued*)

(continued)

Document reference 1996	*Document date*	*Document page*	*Document description*
1996			
NP4/130	January 5	Back	Ohawu power project commission
NP4/130	January 15	Page 9	Atadanwomase spends ¢16.7m on project
NP4/130	January 16	Page 9	Fomena pools funds for electricity
NP4/130	January 20	Back	Church backs Agona Nsaba´s project
NP4/130	January 24	Back	41 Dormaa communities to get power
NP4/130	January 31	Page 9	Wusuta embark ¢287m for electricity
NP4/130	February 12	Back	4 Assin communities to benefit from ¢50m power project
NP4/130	Feb 23	Page 6	Tongo North Assembly extends power to communities
NP4/130	March 5	Page 9	Afedume works towards ¢120m power project
NP4/130	Mach 18	Page 3	5 East mamprusi communities to enjoy electricity
NP4/130	March 19	Page 3	Loan agreement for E.R. power project before House
NP4/130	March 21	Back	Bui Hydro – electric dam, a firm reality
NP4/130	March 26	Page 3	ECG, Atlas sign power pack
NP4/130	April 10	Page 9	Logba Tota Spends ¢40m on projects
NP4/130	April 10	Back	GHPC gets $326M for Tano power project
NP4/130	April 20	Page 7	Ehi purchases 90 poles for power project
NP4/130	April 26	Page 7	Abira completed phase 3 power project
NP4/131	May 8	Back	Manhean appeals for power
NP4/131	May 10	Back	Menji power project commissioned
NP4/131	May 21	Page 7	Atesikrom bags ¢5m for power project
NP4/131	June 28	Front	3 rivers identified for hydro-power projects
NP4/131	June 28	Front	VRA awards contract for power to 3 regions
NP4/131	July 18	Page 9	2 companies bid for VRA projects
NP4/131	July 24	Back	100 power poles for Asante Akyem communities
NP4/131	August 10	Back	¢20m power poles for 28 west Gomoa communities
NP4/131	August 19	Back	¢61 bn. Released for power project in W.R
NP4/131	August 22	Back	Japan provides $4.7m for electrification project
NP4/131	August 29	Back	¢562m voted for power for Asuogyaman communities
NP4/132	September 4	Page 7	Assembly assists Agona Nkum on power project
NP4/132	Sept. 10	Back	Akim Akroso erects 215 poles for power
NP4/132	Sept. 14	Pg. 9	New Fluorescent launched
NP4/132	Sept. 14	Back	Studies on streams for power begin
NP4/132	Sept. 24	Back	7 Northern Regional district capitals to enjoy power
NP4/132	Oct. 1	Back	VRA, US company to manage thermal plant
NP4/132	Oct. 7	Back	President commissions Bole power project
NP4/132	Oct. 11	Back	3 Adaklo communities bal ¢10.1m for power project
NP4/132	Oct. 18	Back	New Edubease power project commissioned

(*continued*)

(continued)

Document reference 1996	*Document date*	*Document page*	*Document description*
NP4/132	Oct. 21	Back	¢168m Kwabre, power project commissioned
NP4/132	Oct. 22	Back	President commissions ¢120m Manso Hawanta power project
NP4/132	Oct. 25	Back	Jejeti power project commissioned
NP4/132	Oct. 26	Back	President commissions ¢900m Adeiso power project
NP4/132	Oct. 30	Back	Akrofu power project at stand still
NP4/132	Oct. 31	Back	17 Ajumako-Enyan-Esiam communities to enjoy power
NP4/132	Nov. 4	Back	Nkroful power project commissioned
NP4/132	Nov. 8	Pg. 3	Ajumako to enjoy power in 1997
NP4/132	Nov. 9	Back	Breman Asikuma power project commissioned
NP4/132	Nov. 11	Back	Komenda power project commissioned
NP4/132	Nov. 16	Back	Dzodze connected to the National and
NP4/132	Nov. 18	Back	Kraboa Coaltar buys poles for power
NP4/132	Nov. 21	Front	President commissions ¢1.5 bn Shai electricity project
NP4/132	Nov. 22	Back	504 communities to enjoy power in 997
NP4/132	Nov. 23	Back	Ayensuako receives ¢20m electric poles
NP4/132	Dec. 2	Back	President commissions power project at Odoben
NP4/132	Dec. 5	Back	Breman-Beedum bals ¢1.6m for power project
NP4/132	Dec. 6	Back	Techimantia gets power
NP4/132	Dec.13	Back	Government provides 105 districts with power
NP4/132	Dec. 16	Back	60 power poles for 2 W.R communities
NP4/132	Dec. 16	Back	Boama raises ¢3.5m in aid of power
NP4/132	Dec. 18	Front	16 hydro power cites identified
NP4/132	Dec. 18	Back	Turbines for thermal plant delivered
NP4/132	Dec. 20	Back	Oda Kotoamso to finance power project with farm cash
1998			
NP4/136	Jan. 2	Back	University of Ghana solar street light commissioned
NP4/136	Jan. 3	Back	Nsuta opens ¢10.2m on power project
NP4/136	Jan. 14	Back	1,400 communities to enjoy power
NP4/136	Jan. 16	Front	Power for remaining 14 district capitals
NP4/136	Jan. 17	Back	Thermal Plant begins operation
NP4/136	Jan. 19	Front	VRA orders out in power consumption
NP4/136	Jan. 22	Pg. 7	Abaam embarks on power project
NP4/136	Jan. 24	Pg. 3	Special dispensation for Tema Industries
NP4/136	Feb. 2	Front	Electricity tariffs out
NP4/136	Feb. 3	Back	Kpoeta raises ¢6m for power project
NP4/136	Feb. 7	Front	Power crisis, Cote D'ivoire to bail Ghana out
NP4/136	Feb. 14	Back	VRA to construct Bui Dam
NP4/136	Feb. 16	Front	¢7m power cables stolen at Apam
NP4/136	Feb. 19	Back	VRA to re-appraise Bui Dam Project

(*continued*)

(continued)

Document reference 1996	*Document date*	*Document page*	*Document description*
NP4/136	Feb. 23	Front	Volta Lake at lowest level ever
NP4/136	Feb. 23	Front	Akosombo Dam to shut down if
NP4/136	Feb. 23	Front	Use 4 solar energy to be encouraged
NP4/136	Mar 7	Back	¢8.7m ECG wires stolen
NP4/136	Mar 10	Front	ECG re-designs power supply
NP4/136	Mar 12	Back	VRA signs energy pact
NP4/136	Mar 14	Back	Government out with power supply action plan
NP4/136	Mar 20	Front	ECG forced to cut more power
NP4/136	Mar 24	Back	US to fund power barges in W.K.
NP4/136	April 7	Front	Emergency power plant for Harbour
NP4/136	April 14	Front	Utilities commission angry with ECG
NP4/136	April 17	Pg. 9	ECG: Billing system has been the same
NP4/136	April 23	Front	No energy crisis in future
NP4/136	April 23	Back	Developers expose to solar energy
NP4/136	April 26	Pg. 5	26 more towns to get power
NP4/136	April 27	Front	Rural power programmes not cause for energy crisis
NP4/136	April 27	Pg. 3	Mines Ministry signs pact for 70 mega watts
NP4/136	April 27	Back	Solar energy project for Mamprusi district
NP4/137	May 4	Back	Likpe-Kururantum Dam project
NP4/137	May 14	Back	Rainfall stabilized Dam's level for 3 days
NP4/137	May 23	Back	15 Ajumako communities enjoy power now
NP4/137	May 25	Back	US firm to help produce more power
NP4/137	May 28	Back	Tema Metropolitan Assembly votes ¢599.8m for street lights
NP4/137	June 2	Back	Kpassa pays ¢12m for solar energy
NP4/137	June 4	Pg. 9	2 communities accuse ECG of bad deal
NP4/137	June 5	Back	Government secures $10m for power project in Upper East
NP4/137	June 6	Back	"Kofi Pare" raises ¢5.4m for school electricity
NP4/137	June 12	Back	¢300 Tanofield power project commences
NP4/137	June 13	Pg. 7	Wusuta acquires 160 poles for power
NP4/137	June 13	Back	GNPC to supply Tebrebe Goldfield with power
NP4/137	June 19	Back	¢6.1m power plant for Mfantsiman Assembly
NP4/137	June 19	Back	13 communities to enjoy solar energy
NP4/137	June 24	Pg. 3	VRA, ECG apply for tariff increase
NP4/137	July 3	Pg. 7	Agona Rural Bank gives towards power project
NP4/137	July 3	Back	Krachi opts for VRA as power
NP4/137	July 11	Front	Energy crisis to cost nation ¢200m
NP4/137	July13	Front	Akosombo still empty
NP4/137	July 17	Front	US energy team in to help solve power crisis
NP4/137	July 18	Back	VRA, US firm sign pact to develop power
NP4/137	July 25	Pg. 9	Ghanaians to pay more for power

(*continued*)

(continued)

Document reference 1996	*Document date*	*Document page*	*Document description*
NP4/137	July 25	Pg. 9	¢1.8m for Asuafa power
NP4/137	Aug. 5	Front	Power cuts are over for Industries
NP4/137	Aug. 19	Front	How Burkina Faso Dam affects Volta Lake
NP4/137	Aug. 19	Back	VRA, ECG urge to remove waste
NP4/137	Aug. 25	Back	Mining firm helps 6 communities on power project
NP4/137	Aug. 28	Front	Ghana-Czech in joint power talks
NP4/138	Sept. 2	Front	Power tariffs up
NP4/138	Sept. 9	Pg. 9	7 arrested for illegal re-connection of power
NP4/138	Sept. 10	Back	Czech shows interest in Bui Dam
NP4/138	Sept. 10	Back	Kraraba bags ¢1.4m for street lights
NP4/138	Sept. 16	Pg. 9	Power supply to nation is now regular – ECG
NP4/138	Oct. 14	Back	Bolga Assembly spends ¢150m on power poles
NP4/138	Oct. 17	Back	VRA opens bid for solar sub-station
NP4/138	Nov. 19	Pg. 9	Renewable energy sector development under discussion
NP4/138	Nov. 20	Pg. 3	Government to encourage private interest in power sector
NP4/138	Nov. 21	Back	GNPC focuses on power from natural gas
NP4/138	Nov. 28	Back	Bonsu embarks on ¢24m power project
2000			
NP4/143	Jan. 12	Front	More power from Takoradi
NP4/143	Mar 10	Front	AGI, TUC seek ways for reliable electricity supply
NP4/143	Mar 30	Pg. 9	VRA to supply power to 2 Burkina Faso towns
NP4/144	May 6	Pg. 13	Kome communities protest about
NP4/144	May 9	Pg. 9	IFC invests $41m in Kipevu power project
NP4/144	June 30	Pg. 3	ECG owes VRA ¢265m
NP4/145	July 1	Pg. 13	W. Africa power grid suggested
NP4/145	July 8	Pg. 13	Twedie street lights under rehabilitation
NP4/145	Aug. 11	Pg. 3	66 VR. Communities to get power
NP4/145	Aug. 26	Pg. 12	Sissala Assembly votes ¢260m for power projects
NP4/145	Sept. 9	Pg.12	8 Gomoa West communities to get power
NP4/145	Sept. 11	Pg.10	Electricity company losses ¢200 bn in 6 months
NP4/145	Sept. 18	Pg. 9	New Fluorescent launched
NP4/145	Sept. 20	Pg. 3	Bolga Police retrieves stolen power roles
NP4/146	Oct. 23	Pg. 12	Jawra Assembly spends ¢255m on power
NP4/146	Nov. 2	Pg. 3	Customers owe ECG ¢270 bn
NP4/146	Nov. 4	Front	Veep commissions Amanfrom power project
NP4/146	Nov. 14	Pg. 3	President inaugurates Takoradi Thermal power project today
NP4/146	Nov. 15	Front	Takoradi Thermal power commissioned
NP4/146	Nov. 23	Pg. 13	500,000 communities enjoy electricity under SHEP
NP4/146	Dec. 4	Pg. 3	Thieves stealing installed power poles at Ajumako

(*continued*)

(continued)

Document reference 1996	*Document date*	*Document page*	*Document description*
NP4/146	Dec. 6	Pg. 3	President commissions Ridge Hospital Extension Project
NP4/146			
2004			
NP4/161	Jan. 30	Front	Volta communities get ¢27 bn power project
NP4/161	Feb. 11	Pg. 13	Electricity (ECG) to improve revenue collection
NP4/161	Feb. 12	Pg. 10	German Envoy hands over solar electricity
NP4/161	Feb. 19	Pg. 6	How productive is the concept of productive use of electricity
NP4/161	Feb. 23	Front	Power goes to Nyinahin area
NP4/162	March 4	Back	Bush fires destroy 72 electricity poles
NP4/162	March 6	Pg. 15	204 communities join power grid
NP4/162	March 9	Pg. 3	Lawra communities soon to join power grid
NP4/162	April 22	Back	Bomaa receives street bulbs power cuts
NP4/163	May 3	Pg. 4	Abelemkpe protests against power cuts
NP4/163	May 11	Pg. 3	1,069 communities to get power this year
NP4/163	May 14	Front	Electricity meters produced locally
NP4/163	May 24	Pg. 4	Frankadua gets ¢1.6 bn electrification project
NP4/163	June 9	Front	Thermal project gets $60m support
NP4/163	June 19	Pg. 3	Who maintains streetlights?
NP4/164	July 15	Pg. 13	VRA provides electricity for settlement towns
NP4/164	Aug. 18	Pg. 4	KMA to produce power from landfill site
NP4/165	Sept. 6	Pg. 14	Central Region customers owe ECG ¢30 bn
NP4/165	Oct. 9	Pg. 14	New standard labels for electrical appliances
NP4/165	Oct. 12	Pg. 3	Legon to enforce ban on electrical appliances
NP4/165	Oct. 30	Pg. 9	Energy is crucial to nation's development
NP4/166	Nov. 9	Pg. 3	Solar power for 3 Dangbe schools
NP4/166	Nov. 11	Pg. 4	¢2 bn to improve power supply to C.R. towns
NP4/166	Dec. 4	Pg. 4	Special system to check power usage on campuses
NP4/166	Dec. 20	Pg. 7	Renewable energy use in Ghana when do we start?
2008			
NP4/197	Jan 15	Pg. 13	Kosoa streetlight damaged
NP4/197	Jan 19	Pg. 31	ECG pledges uninterrupted power supply
NP4/197	Jan 23	Pg. 19	6m energy vaving bulbs distributed
NP4/198	Feb 5	Pg. 4	2 new energy products launched
NP4/198	Feb 5	Pg. 28	Conserve energy and pay less
NP4/198	Feb 16	back	Motorway lights not functioning
NP4/198	Feb 20	Pg. 12	Review ECG reliability status
NP4/198	Feb 21	Pg. 22	45 communities in Upper West communities to be connected to national electricity grid
NP4/199	Mar 4	Pg. 4	Osagyefo to barge to begin giving power soon
NP4/199	Mar 5	Pg. 23	ECG insists on pre-paid meter policy

(*continued*)

(continued)

Document reference 1996	*Document date*	*Document page*	*Document description*
NP4/199	Mar 25	Pg. 17	Agreement for Bui power project land signed
NP4/199	Mar 27	Pg. 25	Akraman gets electricity
NP4/200	April 9	Front	Motorway lighting project suspended
NP4/200	April 10	Pg. 25	KMA'S" waste-to-energy project to commence
NP4/200	April 17	Back	Kosoa streetlights develop faults
NP4/200	April 19	Front	Kpong power project begins
NP4/200	April 23	Back	VRA explains power outages
NP4/200	April 23	Back	Motorway lighting project resumes
NP4/201	May 2	Pg. 16	Thermal plant, must not affect environment
NP4/201	May 14	Back	Traffic lights to be repaired nationwide
NP4/201	May 21	Pg. 22	New electricity transformer to boost business at Hohoe
NP4/201	May 21	Pg. 23	GT. Donates electric poles to T' poly
NP4/202	June 25	Pg. 26	High voltage electricity consumers to pay more
NP4/204	August 19	Pg. 22	Chirano Gold Mine connects electricity to 2 communities
NP4/204	Aug 25	Pg. 28	Energy supply critical to achieve middle – income status
NP4/204	Aug 30	Pg. 17	Govt. moves to reduce power cost for the poor
NP4/204	Aug 30	Pg. 19	8 communities in Amansie East to get electricity
NP4/205	Sept 1	Pg. 7	Ghana lauds India for supporting energy sector
NP4/205	Sept 1	Pg. 16	Govt. advised to expedite process for Atomic Energy
NP4/205	Sept 1	Pg. 19	ECG replaces stolen cables in mpraeso
NP4/205	Sept 13	Pg. 19	MP inaugurates street light project in Kaleo
NP4/205	Sept 15	Front	Maintaining street lights: we can't cope
NP4/205	Sept 18	Pg. 26	Sugarcane can supply electricity
NP4/205	Sept. 22	Pg. 26	4,000 megawatt power pledge is no mere talk
NP4/205	Sept 25	Pg. 7	Church funds power project at Hungua
NP4/206	Oct. 3	Pg. 34	Construction of Bui Dam commences this month
NP4/206	Oct. 16	Pg. 22	Electrification of Twifo Hemang communities almost completed
NP4/206	Oct. 18	Pg. 3	Nuclear power policy advocated
NP4/206	Oct. 23	Pg. 7	New body to handle power transmission
NP4/206	Oct. 23	Pg. 27	Juale, Pwalugo power project
NP4/206	Oct. 31	Pg. 4	ECG needs $1 bn to expand operations
NP4/207	Nov. 1	Pg. 17	Energy managers update knowledge
NP4/208	Dec. 2	Pg. 10	VRA assures of constant power
NP4/208	Dec. 4	Pg. 2	Phase 2 Bui Project begins
NP4/208	Dec. 8	Pg. 11	Power follows at Mo
NP4/208	Dec. 9	Back	Thermal Plant for Kumasi
NP4/208	Dec. 17	Pg. 3	ECG beings local shedding

(*continued*)

(continued)

Document reference 1996	*Document date*	*Document page*	*Document description*
2008			
NP1/270	Jan 4	Back	Street lights for Begoro
NP1/270	Jan. 8	Back	Electricity for 500 communities
NP1/270	Jan. 21	Pg. 53	ECG assures of power supply
NP1/270	Jan. 23	Pg. 29	ECG assures Kumasi of stable power supply
NP1/270	Jan. 24	Pg. 28	Bushfires destroy power poles
NP1/270	Jan. 31	Pg. 20	Bushfires burn power poles
NP1/270	Jan. 31	Pg. 28	West Akyem retrieves incandescent electric bulbs
NP1/271	Feb. 4	Pg. 14	Pursue other sources of energy
NP1/271	Feb. 7	Pg. 34	Two solar products launched
NP1/271	Feb. 7	Pg. 36	700 wooden electric poles to be replaced in V. R.
NP1/271	Feb. 7	Pg.43	Group to protest electricity tariff hike
NP1/271	Feb. 18	Pg.47	5 communities to link to national electricity and
NP1/271	Feb. 29	Pg. 29	Tamale residents worried about frequent power cuts
NP1/271	Feb. 29	Pg. 31	Private sector worried over poor utility services
NP1/272	Mar. 4	Pg. 24	More power from Osagyefo barge soon
NP1/272	Mar 7	Pg. 29	No frequent power outages in Tamale
NP1/272	Mar 10	Pg. 11	Solar powered street lighting system launched
NP1/272	Mar 14	Pg. 20	ECG spends ¢30.000 to replace conductors
NP1/272	Mar 20	Pg. 49	Govt. acquires land for Bui Dam project
NP1/273	April 1	Pg. 21	2 projects inaugurated at Akraman
NP1/273	April 2	Pg. 20	Work on Osagyefo barge progresses
NP1/273	April 3	Pg. 23	Possible solutions to Ghana's energy problem
NP1/273	April 3	Pg23	Wasting solar power and God's time
NP1/273	April 11	Pg. 29	ECG to replace stolen conductors in cape coast
NP1/273	April 14	Pg. 20	Regulate used electrical appliances imports
NP1/273	April 14	Pg. 24	Ghanaian invents power generating equipment
NP1/273	April 19	Front	Private power project ready to kick off
NP1/273	April 22	Front	No load shedding
NP1/273	April 22	Pg. 25	VRA explains intermittent power outages
NP1/274	May 6	Pg. 15	Africa's energy problems
NP1/274	May 6	Middle	Two to draw law on renewable energy
NP1/274	May 6	Pg. 31	Govt. to improve access to power supply
NP1/274	May 7	Back	Govt. finances solar systems for rural areas
NP1/274	May 12	Pg. 32	Streetlights for cape coast
NP1/274	May 21	Pg. 30	GT. Support T' – poly lighting project
NP1/274	May 21	Pg. 31	VRA, ECG deny local shedding
NP1/274	May 27	Front	Bui project progressing
NP1/274	May 29	Pg. 29	ECG replaces old meters
NP1/274	May 30	Pg. 24	"Let's tap all energy potential
NP1/274	May 30	Pg. 29	"Restore Tamale streetlights"
NP1/274	May 31	PG 23	85 communities in W.R. to get electricity

(*continued*)

(continued)

Document reference 1996	*Document date*	*Document page*	*Document description*
NP1/275	June 12	Pg. 28	Wa East communities to get electricity
NP1/275	June 18	Pg. 24	Interruption of power
NP1/275	June 19	32	Cuba to support energy sector
NP1/275	June 19	Pg. 54	Kasoa residents to use ECG pre-paid meters
NP1/275	June 23	Pg. 19	Veep secures ¢360m project to boost electricity
NP1/275	June 25	Pg. 29	Emergency load shedding in twin – city
NP1/276	July 2	Front	Power plant for valco
NP1/276	July 9	Pg. 20	6 communities to enjoy electricity
NP1/276	July 9	Back	More communities to enjoy electricity
NP1/276	July 9	Back	Sunon Asogli power plant course to meet deadline
NP1/276	July 10	Back	Energy commission yet to license 5 power plant
NP1/276	July 15	Pg. 24	Use energy bulbs to save power consumption
NP1/276	July 15	Back	Communities at Bui Dam project site resettled
NP1/276	July 17	Back	30 waterfalls to save Akosombo identified
NP1/276	July 23	Back	Hydro studies on 3 rivers updated
NP1/276	July 25	Pg. 29	Rehabilitation of Tamale traffic lights begin
NP1/276	July 26	Back	More communities connected to grid
NP1/276	July 29	Back	MOU (memorandum of understanding) signed on for hydro – projects
NP1/277	Aug 8	Pg. 21	H Thermal insulated buildings put up at Bui
NP1/277	Aug 11	Front	China approves $562m for Bui project
NP1/277	Aug 15	Pg. 24	Provide meters for compound houses
NP1/277	Aug 22	Pg. 26	GREL donates electric poles to 4 communities
NP1/277	Aug 27	Back	Bagre Dam spillage will feed Volta Lake
NP1/277	Aug 28	Pg. 35	SHEP 4 kicks off in Western Region
NP1/277	Aug 28	Pg. 50	Ghana has potential to harness wind power
NP1/277	Aug 29	Back	Hasten passage of Nuclear Energy Bill
NP1/277	Aug 29	Back	Breakthrough in local power generation
NP1/277	Aug. 30	Pg. 3	Water company extends power to Busumase
NP1/278	Sept. 6	Pg. 15	Ghana, Switzerland sign pact on power extension plan
NP1/278	Sept. 16	Back	GAEC (Ghana Atomic Energy Commission prepares for nuclear plant)
NP1/278	Sept. 19	Pg. 31	ECG incurs ¢9m loss
NP1/278	Sept. 25	Pg. 29	Street lighting project begins in Sekondi/Takoradi
NP1/278	Sept. 27	Pg. 18	Minister tours energy power project in Tema
NP1/278	Sept. 27	Pg. 22	Work progresses on Bui Hydroelectric power project
NP1/279	Oct. 4	Pg. 23	Akyem Eshiem, Bantama now enjoy power
NP1/279	Oct. 20	Pg. 40	Work on Bui Power project progresses
NP1/279	Oct. 21	Pg. 24	Ghana needs more power
NP1/280	Nov. 5	Pg. 21	Street light for Akyem Swedru Achiase
NP1/280	Nov. 5	Back	Electricity project for 31 communities inaugurated
NP1/281	Dec. 2	Pg. 13	VRA, ECG assure stable power supply
NP1/281	Dec. 4	Front	Bui Project in 2nd phase

Notes

1. See http://afrobarometer.org/countries/ghana-1 in conjunction with the Center for Democratic Development (CDD) Ghana (team leader for the project, Daniel Armah Attoh). Accessed April 12, 2017.
2. I draw from analyses of electoral outcomes in the Fourth Republic from Kevin S. Fridy, "The Elephant, Umbrella, and Quarrelling Cocks: Disaggregating Partisanship in Ghana's Fourth Republic," *African Affairs* 106, no. 423 (April 2007): 281–305; Minion K. C. Morrison, "Political Parties in Ghana through Four Republics: A Path to Democratic Consolidation," *Comparative Politics* 36, no. 4 (July 2004): 421–42; Lindsay Whitfield, "Trustees of Development from Conditionality to Governance: Poverty Reduction Strategy Papers in Ghana," *Journal of Modern African Studies* 43, no. 4 (2005): 660.
3. David Hart, *The Volta River Project: A Case Study in Politics and Technology* (Edinburgh: Edinburgh University Press, 1980).
4. Emmanuel Kwaku Akyeampong, *Between the Sea and the Lagoon: An Eco-Social History of the Anlo of Southeastern Ghana c. 1850 to Recent Times* (Athens: Ohio University Press, 2001).
5. Kwamina Barnes, *Economics of Volta River Project* (Accra, Ghana: The State Publishing Corporation, 1966).
6. Dan Bright Dzorgbo, *Ghana in Search of Development: The Challenge of Governance, Economic Management and Institution Building* (Aldershot: Ashgate Press, 2001), 152.
7. Member of Parliament, personal communication, July 2009.
8. Mike Oquaye, *Politics in Ghana, 1982–1992: Rawlings, Revolution, and Populist Democracy* (Accra, Ghana: Tornado Publications, 2004).
9. Lindsay Whitfield, "'Change for a Better Ghana': Party Competition, Institutionalization and Alternation in Ghana's 2008 Elections," *African Affairs* 108, no. 433 (2009): 623.
10. For more on the electoral landscape in the Fourth Republic, see Staffan I. Lindberg and Minion K. C. Morrison, "Exploring Voter Alignments in Africa: Core and Swing Voters in Ghana," *Journal of Modern African Studies* 43, no. 4 (December 2005): 565–68; Minion K. C. Morrison, "Political Parties in Ghana through Four Republics: A Path to Democratic Consolidation," *Comparative Politics* 36, no. 4 (July 2004): 421–42; Fridy, "Elephant, Umbrella, and Quarrelling Cocks." It should be noted that Rawlings never outwardly declared his support for Nkrumah's policies—only hinted at it.
11. See Morrison, "Political Parties in Ghana."
12. Lindberg and Morrison, "Exploring Voter Alignments in Africa," 577.
13. Ibid.

14. NPP party supporters, however, have tended to hail from the business, commercial, and urban interests and elites, making for a rural/urban class divide.
15. Paul Nugent, "Winners, Losers and Also Rans: Money, Moral Authority, and Voting Patterns in the Ghana 2000 elections," *African Affairs* 100, no. 400 (2001): 405–28.
16. According to Whitfield, "Some regions are considered strongholds for each party because they contain large numbers of core voters and there is not much competition." Whitfield, "'Change for a Better Ghana,'" 623.
17. Ibid., 634.
18. Ibid., 635–36.
19. The Lorenz curve can also measure income inequality.
20. Brian Min, *Power and the Vote: Elections and Electricity in the Developing World* (Cambridge University Press, 2015), 9.
21. There is one exception: electricity articles appear for 1998, a year marked by power cuts, electricity rationing, and an ongoing energy crisis from the year before.
22. Newspaper articles for the 1992 period and election year are featured elsewhere, in tandem with featured stories on rural development.
23. Muyeye Chambwera and Henk Folmer, "Fuel Switching in Harare: An Almost Ideal Demand System Approach," *Energy Policy* 35, no. 4 (2007): 2538; Charles Kirubi, Arne Jacobson, Daniel M. Kammen, and Andrew Mills. "Community-Based Electric Micro-Grids Can Contribute to Rural Development: Evidence from Kenya," *World Development* 37, no. 7 (2009): 1208–21; A.B Sebitosi and P. Pillay, "Energy Services in Sub-Saharan Africa: How Conducive Is the Environment?" *Energy Policy* 33, no. 16 (November 2005): 2044–51.
24. A country that derives at least half of its national budget from external aid is considered donor-dependent.
25. Stephen Karekezi, "Poverty and Energy in Africa—A Brief Review," *Energy Policy* 30, nos. 11 and 12 (September 2002): 915.
26. Ibid., 916.
27. See *The New Crusade Guide* 2, no. 200, December 30, 2010.
28. Anonymous, personal communication, 2009.
29. Ibid.
30. See Attoh Aryeetey and Lata Chatterjee, "Regional Inequalities in Ghana: Assessment and Policy Issues, *Tijdschriftvoor Economische en Sociale Geografie* 79, no. 1 (1988): 31–38.
31. Maurizio Bussolo and Jeffery I. Round, *Globalisation and Poverty: Channels and Policy Responses* (London and New York: Routledge, 2006), 143.

CHAPTER 6

The Politics of Energy in Comparative Perspective: Nigeria and South Africa

The massive potential for electric energy supplied by dams, natural gas, and thermal plants, including renewable sources of energy, does not match the predicament faced by hundreds of millions of Africans since independence from colonial rule in the latter half of the twentieth century. Over a decade ago, a continent of almost 800 million contained just 2% of rural Africans with access to electricity.[1] Since then, that figure has changed little. Sub-Saharan Africa reflects a 30.5% electrification rate, with 81% who rely on biomass fuels or firewood for cooking and heating.[2] In 2009, almost 600 million Africans had no access to electricity, and by 2030 this figure is expected to rise to about 652 million out of a population that numbers over a billion.[3] For a comparison with other regions, roughly 50% of the population in South Asia and more than 80% in Latin America have access to electricity; if current trends continue, fewer than 40% of African countries will reach universal access to electricity by 2050.[4] For a continent that boasts of some of the fastest-growing economies in the world, these figures stand in stark contrast to a persistent electric energy malaise. Moreover, a critical challenge the continent faces is the use of very expensive fuels to produce electricity; as it stands, a number of African countries lack access to competitively priced fuels such as oil and gas, while Africa has underdeveloped intraregional transport and logistics infrastructure.[5] Electric energy access, generation, and transmission capacities vary across the continent, but a common denominator unites them: weak institutions, infrastructural challenges that include maintenance, along with persistent gaps in access at a higher ratio of rural to urban residents.

N. Sackeyfio, *Energy Politics and Rural Development in Sub-Saharan Africa*, https://doi.org/10.1007/978-3-319-60122-9_6

This chapter broadly covers the variation in power sector delivery across the two countries with the largest economies in sub-Saharan Africa, to provide an overview of the wider problems of electricity provision across much of the continent. The selection of both countries stems from the following: firstly, South Africa represents both success and uneven outcomes in energy provision. With one of the highest rates of electricity access and an energy sector that is arguably the most developed on the continent, it nonetheless struggles to provide equitable access to its poor—both urban and rural. The availability of data also accounts for the selection of Nigeria and South Africa. In addition, the appeal of both cases here lies in the varied ways that a "lights on, lights off" scenario is largely taken for granted in development perspectives. There is an important paradox as well. South Africa has arguably the largest economy in sub-Saharan Africa and enjoys a comparative advantage in infrastructural development, marked by close ties among the mining, energy, finance, and manufacturing sectors.[6] Nigeria remains a regional power in West Africa and is often the arbiter of disputes and conflicts in its backyard. However, the country has struggled to provide electricity in thriving cities like Lagos and Abuja, which are sites for industry and commerce, as well as across its 36 states. Hydropower accounts for two-thirds of total electricity production in sub-Saharan Africa, excluding South Africa,[7] but the continent's regional diversity in energy sources is concentrated in three distinct regions, with North Africa mostly reliant on oil and gas, followed by South Africa, which depends on coal and, to a lesser extent, renewable energy, and the rest of sub-Saharan Africa, which is heavily dependent on biomass.[8]

This chapter focuses on the models of energy provision in both countries and the continent overall, on possible sources of sustainable and renewable energy, with an examination of Nigeria's and South Africa's energy sectors and power sector reforms. The analysis that follows examines the implications for rural communities in terms of pricing structures, alongside the potential impact of regional power pools. The chapter explores the potential for sustainable energy development. However, the impact of decentralization is beyond the scope of the present study, as it would involve a far more complicated institutional terrain than space permits. I argue that an inability to navigate short-term versus long-term political challenges associated with market-oriented reforms also explains the reluctance to embrace market-oriented power sector reforms fully, despite variations in energy use. I also argue that improved levels of access to electricity have yet to emerge in either state, owing to path-dependent outcomes rooted in technical capacity challenges, maintenance of utilities, modernized energy infrastructure in terms of transmission and generation capacity, as well as providing a critical exploration of renewable energy amid a problematic framework touted in prevailing neo-liberal-centered energy development discourse. The chapter questions irregular access in two of the largest economies on the continent—virtual hegemons—and simply asks, "What is to be done?"

There are compelling reasons to draw links between electricity and market economies—it has become so integrated with capitalist production that it is effectively "essential to the market"; all forms of contemporary industrial, manufacturing, and service activities require electricity to operate.[9] Unfortunately, electricity remains confined more or less to the energy-intensive subsector of commercial and industrial enterprises and high-income households, to the exclusion of rural communities and the poor. With electrical power built to serve the mining industry and to transport minerals and agricultural goods, Africans enjoyed only minuscule electricity access across the continent, even in the latter decades of the twentieth century. Electric power rationing, or "load shedding," is a regular way of life in sub-Saharan Africa. In the past two decades, however, many countries across the African continent have commissioned hydroelectric projects in an effort to expand electric power to their citizens.

Across the continent, infrastructural development of national grids have languished in disrepair for many decades. Institutional weakness—in the form of preference formation and poor technical capacity—combined with revenue shortfalls, lack of investment, and uneven prioritization in the efforts to combat energy poverty largely account for poor provision. However, South Africa and Botswana are exceptions, with a longstanding trajectory of coal-fired plants that produce most of these two countries' electricity. Ironically, Eskom, South Africa's public utility, has the largest, if not the strongest, capacity for generation and expansion through nuclear power and renewable energies, yet the unsustainable use of coal and, arguably, climate change imperil that country's energy sector and, by extension, its economy, in the long term.[10] The political will, it might be said, extends only to the strongest voices, those with access to the state: politicians and instrumental actors in government. Historically, an urban bias, owing in part to public administrative policies bequeathed by colonial administrations, poor planning by post-colonial governments and, in South Africa's case, white-minority rule during apartheid, reinforced the presence of a disengaged rural class. Consequently, permeating much of the continent are separate worlds of access, where the possibility of electricity provision is remote.

See the Afrobarometer survey, which highlights the vagaries of connectivity or access that reveals considerable disparities. As Afrobarometer summary findings note, "Neither access nor connection guarantees lights, as even in some countries where most households are connected, very few have electricity that works "most of the time" or "always." The most striking example is Nigeria, where 96% of respondents are connected, but only 18% of those connections work more than about half the time" (Fig. 6.1).[11]

It is said that sustainable development, or the ability to usher in developmental interventions for the present generation without impeding the development prospects of future generations, is one of the most pivotal challenges of the twenty-first century. Rural energy needs in both countries and across sub-Saharan Africa are vital. Renewable energy is increasingly touted as a source of future energy, with wind and solar power most commonly cited as attractive sources for electricity delivery. The latter is a source of cheap and abundant energy for communities whose connection to the national grid may not be economical due to their remote physical location from the nearest grid connection point.[12] Of critical import is a now-ubiquitous regime that structures development plans in many countries in both the developed world and the global south. Just two years ago, the United Nations celebrated a year dedicated to sustainable development, in a bid to raise the profile of a planet and global economy imperiled by climate change—mainly due to warming oceans, rising CO_2 levels, and a melting Arctic zone. The concern for sustainable development in relation to nonrenewable resources and natural resource depletion is nothing new—the first glimmers of scholarship on it emerged in the latter half of the twentieth century.

Energy development since the nineteenth century has stemmed largely from hydrocarbons—oil, gas, coal. But, for a nonreplenishable resource, the persistent use and inherent addiction of a global economy to oil is now accompanied by a growing chorus about the catastrophe likely to beset the globe and, perhaps most acutely, developing countries—in particular, cities with coastlines—along with the risk of food-security challenges that looms large. On a continent reported to contain impressive endowments of renewable energy, Nigeria and South Africa, two of the states examined here, are potentially well placed to reap the benefits of solar, wind, and biomass. In any case, environmental degradation, unstable oil prices in international markets, and intractable conflict in the Niger Delta region, where the bulk of Nigeria's petro-resources are located, have all made the choice of renewable energy all but inevitable.[13] Solar power's abundance renders it the most promising for renewable energy

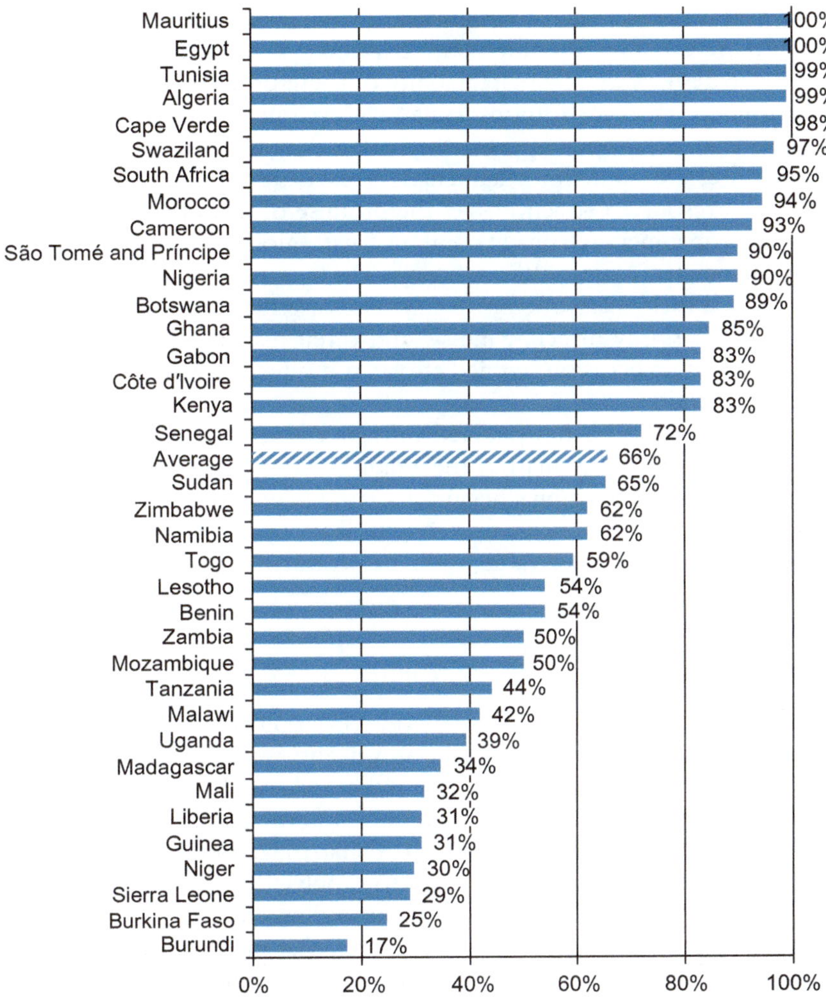

Fig. 6.1 Afrobarometer survey of access to the electric grid, 36 countries
Source: Afrobarometer Round 6 New data from 36 African countries, Dispatch No. 75, 14 March 2016

resources in Nigeria.[14] Energy radiated from the sun equals about 1083 million tons of oil per day,[15] which is the equivalent of roughly 4000 times the current daily crude oil production and 13,000 times the natural gas production.[16]

As a global power and economic giant, China is increasingly at the forefront of hydropower development, but there is a great deal of debate about the desirability and sustainability of these projects, given rapacious governments, weak institutions, runaway development, and environmental pollution. Hydropower projects proffered by Chinese contractors, as critics note, are sometimes launched in exchange for lucrative mining rights and resource extraction. Yet the promise of hydropower is equivocal; the environmental damage combined with global warming renders its use problematic. Dams, although purportedly a renewable source, have experienced their share of controversy. The resettlement of communities, which is necessarily difficult, messy, and often marred by compensation struggles, has on occasion stymied efforts and often increased resistance to dam construction.

While South Africa has pursued nuclear energy and Nigeria plans to adopt a nuclear energy matrix, the Fukushima catastrophe is reason for collective pause. For regional hegemons, these plans make sense. However, critics suggest that electric energy coming from hydropower and gas-fired plants has a much higher value, since its production follows the demand variation for electricity.[17]

Nigeria

For Nigeria to fulfill its aims of energy development, including renewables, an overreliance on hydrocarbons warrants careful scrutiny. To combat energy poverty and its costs to human and social capital will require political will, which is ambiguously reflected in the country's institutional energy landscape. It was not until 2014 that the adoption of a National Energy Policy signaled a commitment to supply reliable electricity to 75% of the population by 2020, along with expanding energy options for electricity generation.[18] A diversified energy mix that moves beyond the convenience of conventional electricity sources and technology and addresses the environmental impact is critical.[19] The intersection between rural electrification and social capital, on the one hand, and inequities resulting from rural neglect and constituent apathy on the other, amid the lingering impact of structural adjustment policies and the push for private sector development in renewable energy, reflects a complicated milieu.

As a country rich in crude oil and virtually a petro-giant, with the ninth largest source of natural gas reserves, the inefficient delivery of electricity, faltering grids, and decrepit energy infrastructure are a puzzle of development. In 2014, oil production stood at some 2.5 million barrels per day, making it the 13th largest producer of crude oil. Yet, a significant portion of the Nigerians, who constitute the continent's most populous state with 180 million, rely on wood fuels as a primary energy resource. Owing to this factor, massive deforestation has exacerbated environmental degradation, which puts the prospect for sustainable development in a carbon age in peril.[20] In part, underutilization of electric power plants, combined with heightened demand that appears to have outstripped supply, has meant that some 60% of Nigerians lack electricity—indeed, rural and semi-urban access is estimated at a mere 35%.[21] Meanwhile, a country rich in energy sources with power plants that operate below capacity and utilities that lack renovation and in acute need of modernization and maintenance—including better access to spare parts—is a puzzle that confounds.[22]

As a petro-state and economic power in West Africa, the country functions as an entrepreneurial hub and premier destination for resource-hungry states like China and India. With myriad investors and infrastructural development projects underway, one might be forgiven for assuming a well-functioning state-owned power or utility sector. However, over the past 50 years, variations in electricity delivery, through gas-fired, oil-fired and hydroelectric power stations, have done little to improve access.[23] The size of the Nigerian economy and the country's status as regional hegemon imply expansion and development, but the country's political economy over the past decade exposes a landscape marred by long-term instability since independence in 1960, while high levels of corruption have lowered public trust in institutions.

The National Electric Power Authority (NEPA), however, reveals an electric power entity struggling to thrive. The unstable political course of the country and its institutions since independence in 1960 has much do with NEPA's difficulties. Combined with a substantial deterioration in public infrastructure—notably electricity, fuel supply, and telecommunications—the paradox of its regional hegemony cannot be understated.[24] To understand the current electric industry in Nigeria, it is necessary to examine the institutional history of electrification before the creation of NEPA in 1972.

During the colonial period leading up to 1960, electricity generation and supply in Nigeria functioned as the primary fulcrum of the Public Works Department (PWD). After independence, that responsibility passed to the Nigerian government's Electricity Corporation of Nigeria (ECN).

The Nigeria Dams Authority (NDA) was established in 1962, shortly after the first hydroelectric power station in Kainji was built in northern Nigeria. NEPA was established by Decree 24 in 1972.[25] Like other sub-Saharan African states, Nigeria chose the sectoral model, which prioritized country ownership and operation of installed capacity, generation, control of procurements, and foreign exchange transactions.[26] The consequences of this longstanding development for large swathes of the country's population are intermittent outages and continued dependency on generators, for those who can afford them. Yet, over a decade ago, the possibility that foreign and local companies, including state governments, might take part in the generation, transmission, and distribution of electricity emerged in state discussions about electric energy policy. This meant that companies would be allowed to build, own, and operate independent electric power facilities and later transfer them to the government upon agreement. Following this declaration, ENRON Incorporated, the US power-generating giant, expressed interest in the Nigerian energy sector.[27] Ultimately short-lived owing to myriad factors, including the disintegration of ENRON itself, the minister's promise to restructure the entire energy sector and NEPA faltered after allegations of sabotage emerged. The stakes were inordinately high, given the endemic institutional malaise that enervated the system over several decades. Accordingly, the capacity of the country's three hydro and five thermal power stations dropped significantly at the inauguration of the post-military civilian government (after General Sani Abacha's death in June of 1998). As a virtual monopoly, NEPA has found itself at the center of discontent, corruption, attempted sabotage of installations, nepotism, and stolen equipment, factors that have compounded the physical and financial loss for utility company.[28] The loss of large sums of money owed by customers is also a significant and enduring problem.

Heightened demand in the continent's most prosperous country reflects supply-side dynamics that remain inefficient and costly. Lagos, a major city and commercial hub, suffers from frequent power outages. With a population in excess of 10 million, and the largest concentration of commercial and industrial establishments, Lagos consumes about half the total energy generated in the country.[29] NEPA's failure and continued distortions in pricing mechanisms, revenue collection, distribution, and generation have much to do with overall degeneration in regulatory agencies and crumbling infrastructure, despite massive oil revenues. The legacy of nondemocratic rule until 1999, when elections produced a return to civilian rule following General Sani Abacha's death, and enduring weak state capacity have meant that macro-economic instability is the norm, rather than the exception. Indeed, both fiscal and technical operations in the country's energy and other sectors of the economy exhibit the symptoms of path-dependency in reinforcing further debilitation, despite efforts to reform energy institutions.

Unfortunately for the country's citizens, and for metropolitan residents of other commercial areas like Lagos, attempts to deregulate the electricity sector brought little respite from energy poverty amid the subsequent demise of ENRON. Efforts to break NEPA's monopoly and reconfigure pricing schemes in terms of accurate billing cycles[30] and, perhaps more importantly, public incentives to encourage a political culture of trust or an agreed-upon compact that encourages payment for consumption of electricity are vital but lacking. It is a tale of continued mishaps and mounting debt, even as the country struggles to establish new power plants and facilitate partnerships, as with Ghana over the West Africa Gas Pipeline Project for the generation and transmission of natural gas for energy production. However desirable, consumer concerns about pricing structures, including those under which sections of society could shoulder the costs of privatization, are contentious, given resistance to taxation and competitive pricing mechanisms, which potentially put the poor at the mercy of markets. Misappropriation of government revenue, scarcity of public goods, and service delivery challenges, along with the lingering effects of a rapacious colonial apparatus whose taxation-without-representation policies produced a political culture of resistance to revenue acquisition, offer compelling explanations for path-dependent outcomes. Attempts by Shell and other companies at electric power generation utilizing natural gas, which Nigeria possesses in abundance, are governed by three types of private sector participation: BOO—build, own, and operate; ROT—refurbish, operate, and transfer; and LOT—lease, operate, and transfer, which Olukoju notes. They offer a critical example of electric capitalism, where international companies have major control of power grids, unparalleled bargaining leverage and, arguably, power. Nigeria currently has an installed capacity of over 8800 MW, but less than 50% is available, while independent power producers' agreements, promising (for gas-fired thermal plants) improved outcomes, gas scarcity, and lower water volumes, are blamed for power generation deficiencies.[31] All the while, the structural, technical, and political issues underlying public–private electricity delivery remain uneven and ambiguous.

South Africa

South Africa recently articulated a strategy for electricity generation until 2030 that provides measures for a diverse energy mix, and Cheryl McEwan argues that spatial processes are shaping an emerging energy transition with consequences that are likely to be dramatic.[32] One of the reasons that energy plays a pivotal role in the South African economy is owing to a mineral energy complex that is energy-dependent, as McEwan and other observers acknowledge.

Despite its inclusion as one of the BRICS (an acronym for Brazil, Russia, India, China, and South Africa, a group of emerging economies with growing geopolitical clout), a large number of households lack electricity. A General Household Survey found, in 2012, that 1.45 million, or roughly 11% of households, had no access, while some 3.6% acquired electricity illegally, with a reported 73.1% composed of informal connections via neighbors.[33] With an 85.3% electrification rate, which is higher than the world average of 80.5%, what explains this dichotomy? While its political economy reflects enduring structures of power among its financial sector, parastatals, government, and the private sector that underpin the minerals energy complex, a number of factors nonetheless make it unsustainable.[34] For one, a reliance on bountiful coal, though offering a comparative advantage in cheap energy, is nevertheless fraught with environmental setbacks amid efforts to adopt renewable energies. Its ranking as the 12th most attractive investment destination for implementation of renewable energy technologies appears ideal.[35] In the view of some observers, the Green Economy Accord is one of 12 job drivers that could help create 5 million additional jobs by 2020.[36] McEwan suggests that the South African government has attempted to leverage local, primarily rural, economic development out of a Renewable Energy Independent Power Producer Procurement Programme (REI4P), conceived as a public–private partnership that spurs an energy transition. Some critics, as she notes, point to a number of problems that include notions of community-oriented development and arbitrarily defined geographical spaces for development intervention.[37]

As the largest producer and exporter of electricity, beginning in 1988, Eskom, South Africa's state-owned electricity generating monopoly, launched its "Electricity for All" mass electrification program, which aimed to expand domestic as well as foreign supply to many of its neighbors.[38] The experiment in electrifying Soweto in the early 1980s and beyond is instructive, as it highlighted a number of problems, including funding to local black authorities responsible for local government in black townships. Payment boycotts for municipal services were deployed as a weapon of struggle, with the accompanying problem of inability to collect payment for services.[39] Despite an ambitious National Electrification Programme crafted in the post-apartheid era (1994–) that aimed to electrify rural areas and culminated in a remarkable 75% access rate 13 years later in 2007, and seemed testament to the power of democracy, a full scale pandemic soon emerged in 2008.[40] Min cogently asks what explains why the African National Congress (ANC) government's quest to provide electricity as a public good stumbles in 2008? The answer lies squarely with the role of political externalities, which shape how governments choose to deliver public goods; in effect, costly commitment to low-profit consumers in a bid to expand access—through free electricity and rate elimination—and the failure to construct new power plants, along with increased difficulties in securing coal, in the wake of a shift to small suppliers and preferential terms for black owners, are contributing factors, among others.[41] From the potential for social upheaval ensued an onslaught of protests over the past decade, also attributable to the political calculations that led to a prioritization of electricity delivery. In 2008, for example, massive discontent spurred by unprecedented blackouts weakened the legitimacy of President Thabo Mbeki, who eventually resigned.[42] The media, including newspapers and radio, helped to galvanize public opinion about the rates of electrification, the disparate process, and the role of politicians in pandering to the rural vote—especially before elections. Arguably, the expansion of political pressure against apartheid in the form of renewed resistance from the black population, combined with economic sanctions, fueled the impetus for domestic electrification, as energy officials explored new technologies, which produced a pre-payment system for electricity in South Africa.

However, lingering inequalities render energy poverty an increasingly salient socioeconomic issue. Rural access, though deemed critical, suffers from overly quantitative assessments, which, as Bram Büscher contends, produce the erroneous assumption "that when income rises rural people will automatically make the transition to more sustainable fuels (instead of biomass for example)."[43] There are reasons to believe that South Africa's policymakers view the synergy between energy policy and pro-poor development as critical.[44] Much as other states have undertaken national electrification schemes, South Africa appears to have embarked on one as an extension of efforts to reverse apartheid-era policies of exclusion. Growing levels of inequality have produced economic tensions, reflected in the xenophobia directed at African nations from black South Africans over the past few years. On a separate note, the heightened cognizance of energy as a possibly pro-poor growth instrument[45] accompanies perspectives by international financial institutions, which suggest that levels of energy consumption support or correspond to the human development index.[46] Ironically, though, this awareness of energy as a pro-poor instrument utilized by African governments stands in contrast to the market-oriented push for liberalized power sectors, on which competitive, price-driven models assume the ability of consumers to pay. Indeed, the spatial processes and identification of zones for renewable energy transition hold critical consequences. For one, McEwan suggests a kind of infrastructure space dominated by the shift to liberalization and privatization in terms of the ways in which public and private actors have acquired the power to build energy and development infrastructure—which, she notes, is a questionable development.[47]

Across much of the continent, post-independence states have preferred state ownership of electric utilities. However, in the 1990s, international public financial institutions were increasingly reluctant to finance declining public utilities trapped in a cycle of low revenue and declining quality.[48] This new political and economic impulse accompanied an expanding role for private corporations and renegotiation of the appropriate role of the state in economic activity in developing countries. Poorly functioning energy sectors inspired efforts aimed towards markets and away from state-led activity, promoted by two decades of World Bank policies.[49]

However, as part of a mosaic of externally driven, macro-economic structural adjustment programs, which called for the elimination of state-led development paradigms in favor of open and free competitive market economies, power sector reform emerged as a critical lever for economic renewal.[50] During the 1990s, international financial institutions espoused this proscription, which suggested that efficient and financially viable electric power sectors were necessary to jumpstart and sustain economic growth and development. Market-oriented reforms not only swept across developing countries, but also emerged first in European states, across member countries of the OECD. Based on the success of Chile and reforms undertaken in the UK and elsewhere, a standard model emerged and developing countries were encouraged to adopt a series of policies thought to transform poor performance, encourage competition, and attract foreign investment.

These policies were attractive for many developing countries, including African states that sought to capitalize upon sizable profits from the privatization and commercialization of the power sector. An accompanying driver of reform was private capital—sought in a bid to rehabilitate existing installations and construct new power plants.[51] Sharon Beder asserts that this policy prescription benefitted international financial institutions at the expense of local business, and always at the expense of the poor.[52] Without exception, electricity reform in developing countries came to reflect mixed outcomes, stalled reforms and uncertainty.[53]

As a natural extension of market-oriented energy sector reform, the advent of independent power producers, noted elsewhere, generated controversy, with allegations of corruption and collusion between government officials and private sector companies involved. Controversies associated with international power producers (IPPs) have been particularly acute in Kenya, Tanzania, Uganda, and Zimbabwe. However, IPP projects are understandably more common in countries with small power systems (e.g., Zimbabwe), due to inadequate generating capacity to meet demand.[54]

Sharon Beder contends that western multinational corporations have sought investment in developing countries as a source of new markets, because profit opportunities in affluent countries, especially in traditional areas such as primary industries and manufacturing, declined. For instance, in South Africa, the ANC government acceded to the IMF's call for privatization, in the hopes of attracting foreign investment—with a resulting loss of jobs for thousands. In preparation for a partial sale of Eskom, the national electricity provider, subsidies were eliminated and household bills in the poorest areas increased up to 4%, while bills for industry fell by 15%.[55] Market-driven policies in this instance are questionable, given persistent disparities in incomes and an ongoing urban–rural divide. Nevertheless, the Asian Development Bank, in 1995, advised that the electricity industries in various countries be restructured to introduce competition, reorganize utilities into corporate, commercial entities, and "allocate a greater role for the private sector," particularly foreign companies. The sustainability of this model depends on the establishment of effective and autonomous regulatory institutions, whose success depends on possessing and developing a regulatory memory.[56]

Access to energy within a political economy framework, such as Bram Büscher has outlined, cannot be understood without the recognition of an overarching framework of power that highly influences, if not outright determines, their particular characteristics.[57] Significantly, Bram Büscher and David A. MacDonald allude to the ways in which electric capitalism serves private interests and question the assumption that processes that intensify the former cannot be expected to bear fruit for marginalized populations. Calling into question the notion that open energy markets will work optimally, as Howell, Gaunt, Elias, and Alfstad suggest, Büscher contends that energy providers, their relationships to each other, and their relationship to the poor, who are to be serviced in these markets, need examination. A rational choice approach, implicit in the ubiquitous assumption that, under a capitalist framework, market-oriented energy institutions and sectors will thrive, arguably touts a fallacy. How should promoting the interest of capital fare, especially if we consider that South Africa retains one of the highest levels of inequality in the world.[58] The exclusive emphasis on economic efficiency that permeates a great deal of scholarship is at odds with concerns for equity, because they subsume the challenges that accompany market-oriented frameworks, which are inimical to fulfilling a mandate to reduce energy poverty. The lowest common denominator, then, is ultimately profit, which is difficult to reconcile with the notion of a competition-driven utility sector in emerging economies plagued by economic inequality or, at the very least, a large portion of the poor lacking basic access to amenities. A successful system of governance needs to be built on an understanding of the different functions, which define the relationship between the state, the energy industry, and users.[59]

Consequences of Power Sector Reform and Pricing Mechanisms for Rural Communities and the Poor

The partial removal of government subsidies to render electricity delivery more competitive reflects a dilemma for governments bent on the political support and survival. The provision of subsidies runs counter to the World Bank's past reform policy, and some have argued that removing subsidies would increase rural electrification by making decentralized renewable technologies more competitive.[60] However, this assumes that the cost of electricity generation from such technologies would be accessible to rural communities. As a result, there is growing recognition that targeted strategies are required to meet the challenge of universal electrification everywhere.[61] Indeed, adequate and sustained transmission of electricity to rural communities and especially the poor depends not just on the utilities themselves, or government efforts, but on autonomous regulatory institutions that can offer independent and objective assessment of challenges and solutions.

The introduction of user fees for installations and repairs, especially in relation to changing household incomes despite proration, causes low-income households in cities like Cape Town to face two choices: under-consumption, or inability to pay their electric bills.[62] Pricing schemes in South Africa are uneven, with a comparative advantage for industrial users over domestic consumers. Equitable access for rural consumers is likely to require smart and just financing, which encompasses flexible tariff structures and payment schemes that provide access to electricity services.[63] The notion that the wholesale liberalization of energy sectors, which include electric utilities, can produce uniform outcomes in terms of productivity, efficiency, and access across countries that differ so widely in their per capita incomes, endowments, economic structures, and population sizes has done more to reinforce energy poverty than combat it.[64] A study of ten countries with the most IPP activity found that private sector participation exposed countries to foreign risks higher than was recorded in the pre-reform period.[65]

The use of market-based instruments like subsidies and the elimination of taxes, which are strategic interventions, becomes critical in weakly performing states whose rural populations without access to basic amenities outnumber those with access. Although Usman, Abbasoglu, Ersoy, and Fahrioglu suggest that the effects of deregulation can be minimized by encouraging people to set up electricity co-operative societies in remote and poor communities, the precise mechanisms for doing this would require social, human, and financial capital that would vary by district and region.[66] However, such an initiative would offer the prospect of collective action by disgruntled communities, where cost-effective measures, and poor or irregular supply prevail.[67] Addressing these circumstances by utilizing mixed economic instruments and incentive-based structures can mitigate pricing mechanism constraints and poorly performing energy regimes.

There are currently four power pools in sub-Saharan Africa: the Southern African Power Pool (SAPP), established in 1995, which comprises 12 countries; the East African Power Pool (EAPP), established in 2005, with at least seven countries from the Common Market for Eastern and Southern Africa, the East African Community, and the Nile Basin Initiative (NBI); the Central African Power Pool, or *Pool Energetique d'Afrique Centrale* (PEAC), which includes 11 countries of the Economic

Community of Central African States, and was created in 2003;[68] and the West African Power Pool (WAPP), which includes 14 countries in the Economic Community of West African States. The WAPP began its efforts to boost power supply in the region in 2003.[69] It represents a power sector integration backed by several international institutions and African leaders through the New Partnership for Africa's Development (NEPAD) but, strangely enough, African ownership remains absent.[70] Institutional weakness and constraints in capacity building and regional integration may well be the culprits. However, for a continent where trade between countries is a mere 12%, political will is also likely to blame. It is anticipated that WAPP will be fully operational by 2023; however national planning and utilities were completed in 2004 with USAID funding, which also supports the institutional needs of the WAPP.[71] Nigeria's role will be pivotal and one to watch closely in the coming decade. On another note, a visible problem with these regional power plans (though they are laudable in terms of cooperation) is that neither the processes nor the criteria for the projects like hydro-dams are clear, and many of these countries have removed their energy planning from public view.[72]

Conclusion

To varying degrees, power sector institutions and subsequent reform efforts of Nigeria and South Africa highlight the endemic challenges of modern infrastructural development, particularly for the former, alongside financial constraints, preference formation and an ambiguous focus on marginalized communities. Fiscal and investment problems, compounded by low returns and poor revenue, have produced debilitating consequences, such as power shortages and uneven transmission, particularly in rural areas across both states. Expansion of access in both states, and particularly South Africa, points to the simple conclusion that electoral pressures induce democracies to prioritize the delivery of electricity, owing to valuable externalities that accrue over time, as Min contends.[73] The importance of energy infrastructure cannot be overstated. However, uneven political, economic, and ultimately path-dependent development of these post-colonial states has produced thorny issues of ownership over energy sectors, amid global developments that heightened the push for liberalization of the utility industry to foster growth by attracting private sector investment. A regulatory environment that has been characterized by heavy state interventionism is often blamed for poor energy investments in sub-Saharan Africa. Yet to embrace market-oriented reform of utilities is to commit political suicide in light of the large numbers of rural poor. Currently, there is very little indication on the part of international financial institutions that have pushed restructuring and reform to suggest cognizance on their part of these enduring, if not endemic, constraints. The myriad backward and forward linkages between electricity, as a critical input, industry, and other sectors that electric energy contributes to in thriving economies are often taken for granted in developing countries.

Electricity delivery for telecommunication and technology is a foregone conclusion. Averting piecemeal implementation—long the preference of African governments—must be reconciled with the opportunity costs for doing so. The reluctant embrace of structural adjustment policies that essentially amounted to "economic reform with political costs" is illustrative. International financial institutions like the World Bank and International Monetary Fund have yet to resolve the dissonance between political or electoral survival of regimes tasked with the pursuit of market-oriented electric energy reform and the demographic populations that are largely affected—typically the rural populace. As the chapter demonstrates, there are multiple reasons to urge caution in the wholesale adoption of market-oriented reforms of electric energy sectors. Privatization, according to conventional wisdom, would inject much-needed competition into ailing government monopolies, and new technologies would expand supply. With the exception of a handful of countries like South Africa, Mauritius, and Namibia, which embraced power sector management in the form of the sectoral model, restructuring reduced the pursuit of the former over much of the continent. Although minimally addressed in the chapter, corruption in private public utility production is a poorly understood but serious issue across sub-Saharan Africa, as is elite capture of energy benefits, which is alarmingly the norm. If this represents a growing yet oblique trend, it suggests grave consequences for rural electrification efforts and local private investment in utilities. Pivotal to a neo-liberal framework of power sectors is the near blanket acceptance of these reforms by international financial institutions rich countries in the western hemisphere. The emergence of IPPs, now in existence for over a decade and a half, appears to have placed onerous responsibilities in the hands of governments eager to accrue revenue from the sale of utility companies and transfer of generating and transmission capability. Additionally, the consequences of large hydropower projects for the environment, in terms of the social costs alluded to earlier, are as critical as ever. While Nigeria dominates the current power market, understanding the true scale of energy provision, and prevailing institutional framework amid efforts to attract investment in domestic markets—which often include a large number of the poor—is critical to address. The various power pool groupings are an important development, with implications that may be far-reaching in consequential ways, for instance, in the issue of ownership.[74] There is also the question of "ownership for whom?" Thus, stakeholder interests are deeply connected with the success of integration and outcomes for reform, and roles must be properly adjudicated. High rural-to-urban ratios and decisions over grid or nongrid transmission constraints render provision more difficult in dispersed areas. Poorly decentralized frameworks in these instances can compound the costs for rural access, making affordability gravely elusive. Moreover, the predisposition towards markets, amid efforts to integrate economies and reduce energy poverty, is an invitation to consider how the state navigates public interest and organizes economic life in a globalizing environment that carries unmitigated risks for the poor.[75] A constellation of variables that include, but are not limited to, its relative stability, institutional framework under decentralization and perhaps sheer luck explains Ghana's electric energy matrix. But as a political experiment in progress, the success of its rural electrification program and self-help electrification scheme has as much to do with the politics of rural preference as it has with a participatory locus that is increasingly cognizant of holding its politicians accountable. In sum, electricity remains an indelible component for creating an industrialized society. While many countries in sub-Saharan Africa are far from this reality, one can only hope for a reversal of the present course to produce rural-centric measures that harness green economics to accrue aggregate benefits.

Notes

1. See Itai Madamombe, "Energy Key to Africa's Prosperity," *Africa Renewal* 8, no. 4 (2005): 6–8. See also Anton Eberhard, Vivien Foster, Cecilia Briceño-Garmendia, Fatimata Ouedraogo, Daniel Camos, and Maria Shkaratan, "Underpowered: The State of the Power Sector in Sub-Saharan Africa," *World Bank Background Paper* 6 (2008). Retrieved from http://documents.worldbank.org.
2. Dumisani Chirambo, "Addressing the Renewable Energy Financing Gap in Africa to Promote Universal Access: Integrated Renewable Energy Financing in Malawi," *Renewable and Sustainable Energy Reviews* 62 (2016): 793–803.

3. Manuel Welsch, Morgan Bazilian, Mark Howells, Deepak Divan, David Elzinga, Goran Strbac, Lawrence Jones, et al., "Smart and Just Grids for Sub-Saharan Africa: Exploring Options," *Renewable and Sustainable Energy Reviews* 20 (2013): 336–52.
4. Eberhard et al., "Underpowered," 5.
5. Bruno G. Pollet, Iain Staffell, and Kerry-Ann Adamson, *The Energy Landscape in the Republic of South Africa* (Cham, Switzerland: Springer International Publishing, 2016), 3–12.
6. See Sören Scholvin, "South Africa's Energy Policy: Constrained by Nature and Path Dependency," *Journal of Southern African Studies* 40, no. 1 (2014): 185–202.
7. United States Energy Information Administration report, 2004, cited in Terri Hathaway and Lori Pottinger, "The Great Hydro-rush: The Privatisation of Africa's Rivers," in *Electric Capitalism: Recolonising Africa on the Power Grid*, ed. David A. McDonald (London: Earthscan, 2008), 152.
8. See Stephen Karekezi, "Poverty and Energy in Africa—A Brief Review," *Energy Policy* 30 (2002): 916.
9. David A. McDonald, "Electric Capitalism: Conceptualising Electricity and Capital Accumulation in (South) Africa," in *Electric Capitalism*, ed. McDonald, 4.
10. See Scholvin, "South Africa's Energy Policy," 185.
11. Afrobarometer Round 6 New data from 36 African countries, Dispatch No. 75, March 14, 2016, 3. Accessed May 11, 2017: http://afrobarometer.org/sites/default/files/press-release/round-6-releases/ab_r6_pr5_Electrification_in_Africa_ENG.pdf.
12. Mohamed Shaaban and J. O. Petinrin, "Renewable Energy Potentials in Nigeria: Meeting Rural Energy Needs," *Renewable and Sustainable Energy Reviews* 29 (2014): 76.
13. O. Awogbemi and C. A. Komolafe, "Potential for Sustainable Renewable Energy Development in Nigeria," *The Pacific Journal of Science and Technology* 12, no. 1 (2011): 161–69.
14. P. A. Ilenikhena and Li N. Ezemonye, *Solar Energy Applications in Nigeria*, WEC Montreal Paper No. 135 (2010). Accessed from http://www.indiaenergycongress.in/montreal/library/pdf/135.pdf.
15. A. S. Sambo, "Renewable Energy for Rural Development: The Nigerian Perspective," *ISESCO Science and Technology Vision* 1 (2005): 12–22.
16. Koso I. Idigbe and S. O. Onohaebi, "Repositioning the Power Industry in Nigeria to Guarantee Reliability in Operations and Services," *Journal of Engineering and Applied Sciences* 4, no.2 (2009): 119–25.
17. Michael Dittmar, "Nuclear Energy: Status and Future Limitations," *Energy* 37, no. 1 (2012): 35–40.

18. Shaaban and Petinrin, "Renewable Energy Potentials."
19. Abubakar Sadiq Aliyu, Ahmad Termizi Ramli, and Muneer Aziz Saleh, "Nigeria Electricity Crisis: Power Generation Capacity Expansion and Environmental Ramifications," *Energy* 61 (November 2013): 354–67.
20. Zubairu Gatugel Usman, Serkan Abbasoglu, Neyre Tekbiyik Ersoy, and Murat Fahrioglu, "Transforming the Nigerian Power Sector for Sustainable Development," *Energy Policy* 87 (2015): 429.
21. Aliyu et al., "Nigeria Electricity Crisis," 356; Musiliu O. Oseni, "Improving Households' Access to Electricity and Energy Consumption Pattern in Nigeria: Renewable Energy Alternative," *Renewable and Sustainable Energy Reviews* 16, no. 6 (2012): 993.
22. See Usman et al., "Transforming the Nigerian Power Sector," 430 for more. Musiliu O. Oseni also notes that the country's quandary is rooted in its difficulties transforming energy from its raw state to a usable form, which means that most of it must be imported. Oseni, "Improving Households' Access," 3968.
23. O. I. Okoro and E. Chikuni, "Power Sector Reforms in Nigeria: Opportunities and Challenges," *Journal of Energy in Southern Africa* 18, no. 3 (2007): 52–57.
24. Peter Lewis, "Nigeria: An End to the Permanent Transition?" *Journal of Democracy* 10, no. 1 (1999): 141–56.
25. J. Ikeme and Obas John Ebohon, "Nigeria's Electric Power Sector Reform: What Should Form the Key Objectives?" *Energy Policy* 33, no. 9 (2005): 1213–21.
26. Jacques Girod and Jacques Percebois, "Reforms in Sub-Saharan Africa's Power Industries," *Energy Policy* 26, no. 1 (1998): 21–32; John Turkson and Norbert Wohlgemuth, "Power Sector Reform and Distributed Generation in Sub-Saharan Africa," *Energy Policy 29*, no. 2 (2001): 135–45.
27. Ayodeji Olukoju, "'Never Expect Power Always': Electricity Consumers' Response to Monopoly, Corruption and Inefficient Services in Nigeria," *African Affairs* 103, no. 410 (2004): 51–71.
28. Ibid., 62.
29. Ibid., 51.
30. See Okoro and Chikuni, "Power Sector Reforms," 56.
31. Olukoju, "'Never Expect Power Always'"; Elijah Ige Ohimain, "Diversification of Nigerian Electricity Generation Sources," *Energy Sources, Part B: Economics, Planning, and Policy* 10, no. 3 (2015): 298–305.
32. McEwan, Cheryl. "Spatial Processes and Politics of Renewable Energy Transition: Land, Zones and Frictions in South Africa," *Political Geography* 56 (2017).

33. Statistics South Africa, 2012.
34. World Bank (2014). World Bank open data. http://data.worldbank.org/.
35. South African Department of Energy (DoE).
36. Pollet et al., *Energy Landscape*; Jacqueline M. Borel-Saladin and Ivan N. Turok, "The Impact of the Green Economy on Jobs in South Africa," *South African Journal of Science* 109, nos. 9–10 (2013): 1–4.
37. McEwan, Cheryl. "Spatial Processes and Politics of Renewable Energy Transition: Land, Zones and Frictions in South Africa," *Political Geography* 56 (2017): 2, 7.
38. Antonio Estache, "Infrastructure and Development: A Survey of Recent and Upcoming Issues," *Rethinking Infrastructure for Development* 2 (2008): 47.
39. Daniel Malzbender, "Domestic Electricity Provision in the Democratic South Africa," *University of Pretoria, AWIRU/CiPS* 2 (2005).
40. Brian Min. *Power and the Vote: Elections and Electricity in the Developing World* (Cambridge University Press, 2015), 7.
41. Ibid., 163.
42. Ibid., 7.
43. Bram Büscher, "Connecting Political Economies of Energy in South Africa," *Energy Policy* 37, no. 10 (2009): 3952.
44. Nicholas Ngepah, "Exploring the Impact of Energy Sources on Production, Inequality and Poverty in Simultaneous Equations Models for South Africa," *African Development Review* 23, no. 3 (2011): 335–51.
45. World Bank Report, "Proposed Fifth Poverty Reduction Support Credit" (2007).
46. See Ngepah, "Exploring the Impact of Energy Sources," 335. For more on the dynamics between income inequality and a comparison of electricity access and income levels, see Ibid., 336.
47. McEwan, Cheryl. "Spatial Processes and Politics of Renewable Energy Transition: Land, Zones and Frictions in South Africa," *Political Geography* 56 (2017): 10. On the notion of spatial processes and zones for a renewable energy transition, she builds on Easterling, Keller's concept of 'extrastatecraft'—*Extrastatecraft: The Power of Infrastructure Space* (Verso Books, 2014), 10—which is pivotal to her conclusion about infrastructure space.
48. Navroz K. Dubash, "Revisiting Electricity Reform: The Case for a Sustainable Development Approach," *Utilities Policy* 11, no. 3 (2003): 143–54.
49. See Ibid., 147.
50. From UNIDO 2000 report, cited in Njeri Wamukonya, "Power Sector Reform in Developing Countries: Mismatched Agendas," *Energy Policy* 31, no. 12 (2003): 1274.

51. John Turkson, ed., *Power Sector Reform in Sub-Saharan Africa* (New York: Macmillan, 2000); Turkson and Wohlgemuth, "Power Sector Reform," 135, 145.
52. Sharon Beder, *Power Play: The Fight for Control of the World's Electricity* (Victoria, Australia: Scribe Publications, 2003).
53. James H. Williams and Rebecca Ghanadan, "Electricity Reform in Developing and Transition Countries: A Reappraisal," *Energy* 31, no. 6 (2006): 836.
54. Stephen Karekezi and John Kimani, "Status of Power Sector Reform in Africa: Impact on the Poor," *Energy Policy* 30, nos. 11–12 (September 2002): 923–45.
55. Beder, *Power Play*, 287.
56. See Jon Stern, "Electricity and Telecommunications Regulatory Institutions in Small and Developing Countries," *Utilities Policy* 9, no. 3 (2000): 148.
57. Büscher, "Connecting Political Economies," 3951.
58. Büscher, "Connecting Political Economies"; McDonald, "Electric Capitalism." For more on this question, see Patrick Bond, *Elite Transition: From Apartheid to Neoliberalism in South Africa* (London: Pluto Press, 2014).
59. Anton A. Eberhard and Clive Van Horen, *Poverty and Power: Energy and the South African State* (London: Pluto Press, 1995), 196.
60. D. Burtraw, K. Palmer, and A. Paul, "Regional Impacts of Electricity Restructuring on Emissions of NO sub (x) and CO sub (2)," *Maryland Power Plant Research Program Report* 123 (2000).
61. See Wamukonya, "Power Sector Reform," 1281.
62. David A. McDonald, "Electric Capitalism," 8.
63. Manuel Welsch, Morgan Bazilian, Mark Howells, Deepak Divan, David Elzinga, Goran Strbac, Lawrence Jones, et al., "Smart and Just Grids for Sub-Saharan Africa: Exploring Options," *Renewable and Sustainable Energy Reviews* 20 (2013): 336–52.
64. See Dumisani Chirambo, "Addressing the Renewable Energy Financing Gap in Africa to Promote Universal Energy Access: Integrated Renewable Energy Financing in Malawi," *Renewable and Sustainable Energy Reviews* 62 (2016): 793–803.
65. Wamukonya, "Power Sector Reform."
66. Zubairu Gatugel Usman, Serkan Abbasoglu, Neyre Tekbiyik Ersoy, and Murat Fahrioglu, "Transforming the Nigerian Power Sector for Sustainable Development," *Energy Policy* 87 (2015): 429–37.
67. Marilyn Chikaodili Amobi, "Deregulating the Electricity Industry in Nigeria: Lessons from the British Reform," *Socio-economic Planning Sciences* 41, no. 4 (2007): 291.

68. Terri Hathaway and Lori Pottinger, "The Great Hydro-rush: The Privatisation of Africa's Rivers," in McDonald, ed., *Electric Capitalism*, 162.
69. UNECA 2004 report, p.158, cited in Pierre-Olivier Pineau, "How Sustainable is Policy Incoherence? A Rationalist Policy Analysis of the Cameroonian Electricity Reform," *Journal of Cleaner Production* 15, no. 2 (2007): 166–77.
70. Pierre-Olivier Pineau, "Electricity Sector Integration in West Africa," *Energy Policy* 36 (2008): 221.
71. Pineau, "How Sustainable is Policy Incoherence?," 163.
72. Ibid. This is attributable to perceptions about awareness by the general populations, which function as a hindrance to scrutiny at the national level.
73. See Brian Min. *Power and the Vote: Elections and Electricity in the Developing World* (Cambridge University Press, 2015), 167.
74. Pineau, "Electricity Sector Integration."
75. See Dubash, "Revisiting Electricity Reform," 148.

CHAPTER 7

Conclusion

How has a West African state, widely hailed as a model for stable democratic governance across much of the continent, managed to achieve an impressive rate of electrification of some 80.51%, albeit with mismatched outcomes for its rural populace, amid a clamor to end *dumsor*? Over the past several years, an identity crisis of sorts is more than embryonic. Despite the clarion call for industrialization and development envisioned by the country's first president, Kwame Nkrumah, a burnished record as a West African powerhouse is not matched by a faltering economy arguably precipitated during President John Dramani Mahama's administration (2012–2017). With a persistent electricity quagmire that continues to perplex domestic and international observers alike, political observers ask: why has a decentralized institutional framework not produced more successful outcomes for public service delivery of electricity, despite the transformation of access since the 1990s? What accounts for uneven access in Nigeria and South Africa? What possible lessons does Ghana offer Nigeria, and other sub-Saharan African states? This book has argued that a laudable access rate is attributable to the deliberate circumvention of market-driven reforms of power sectors in key swing regions of Ghana—the equivalent to states—while the definition of electricity access is highly fluid, politicized and simultaneously uneven in rural areas. This study has also argued that uneven electricity provision to rural constituents is the result of equivocal energy institutions and preferences; political patronage;

N. Sackeyfio, *Energy Politics and Rural Development in Sub-Saharan Africa*, https://doi.org/10.1007/978-3-319-60122-9_7

and unwieldy political reforms, in the form of decentralization initiatives undertaken over the past 20 years.

Key to the argument about the fits and starts of both national and rural electrification programs in Ghana is that the quest for political survival and continuity, cohesive state–societal relations, and uneven agency of civil society actors conditioned responses to energy provision, supply and demand in Ghana. Uneven benefits for the rural populace, including the poor, and political capture of local institutions via patronage by succeeding governments in power accounts for the observed success and conversely differential benefits for the rural poor. The paradox of successful and unprecedented access nationally is rooted in the partial nature/implementation of neo-liberal power sector reforms—an affront to what we observe in a number of perspectives treated in an earlier chapter. Indeed, as a conclusion to this study, governments inevitably have little choice but to circumvent market-oriented policies if they are to end energy poverty and supply electricity to all domestic consumers. In addition, the capacity for optimal provision under decentralization is only possible under an institutional rearrangement between political actors on African soil (both governmental and nongovernmental), donor states and international financial institutions to foster local agency.

The case study of Ghana offers valuable empirical observations for much of sub-Saharan Africa, where an electricity divide is virtually ubiquitous. By focusing on what many have deemed a "success story", this work systematically chronicles the contradictions of political decentralization under a market-oriented agenda of electricity sector reform. The intersection between public and neo-patrimonial outcomes in service delivery, amid attempts to inculcate a minimal state in the economy, offers a critical vector of a collision course on the horizon. Why is an important but near inconspicuous component of modern life minuscule for the rural populace, including the poor? The argument laid out in this work supports the logic that it structures their lives in critical ways. Whether economically, through access to modern goods and services, or through citizen engagement that invites a resource compact for how hydropower, thermal and other sources of energy will be harnessed, equitable access to this micro–macro component is in many ways a microcosm of a contested public–private battleground to reconstitute state authority, especially in emerging economies.

Through the primary case of Ghana, this work reveals the ways in which obscure provision for the rural poor in Ghana reinforced district assemblies as vehicles for local governance, while paradoxically strengthening central government authority under decentralization and a market-oriented agenda of energy sector reform. The latter, in particular, informs a continuing dialectic of an enduring role of the state in the economy. Furthermore, as a critical but inaccurately perceived micro-component of rural welfare and development, expanding electricity access for the rural populace, including the poor, is pivotal to increasing economic and political gains as Ghana hurtles forward in the twenty-first century.

A fundamental conclusion of this study is that, since the resumption of civilian rule in 1992, political incentives for public goods delivery of electricity provision proved critical to heightened efforts to expand access.

The first chapter accounted for why electricity efforts under Nkrumah proved less successful than under Busia. Nkrumah's attempts to adopt socialist policy without an industrial base and materialist conditions required for a Marxist approach produced dismal failures, while Busia's social-justice approach, which aimed to improve standards of living for the rural populace in particular, also yielded better but insufficient outcomes, despite hundreds more communities put on the grid. The subsequent clash between Nkrumah's heavy-handed, interventionist and, later, socialist approach and Busia's market-oriented policies inevitably produced disjointed efforts that affected the pace of industrial development going forward. Though electricity was identified as a key economic input—via the Akosombo Dam and Volta River Project—conflicting political frameworks limited the promise of hydropower. In effect, optimistic, but poorly conceptualized energy values obscured Nkrumah's efforts. As early as 1957, Ministry of Works' documents hint at the potential politicization of rural electrification schemes at independence. Rural electrification efforts took on greater precedence than under Nkrumah. However, it is to Nkrumah's credit that the institutional groundwork for electricity schemes emerged. Armed with more political capital, electricity projects commenced in a more effective manner. After his overthrow and the subsequent political upheaval, succeeding administrations had little capacity to power the country, owing to absent demand, as a VRA official in 2009 explained. On the other hand, Nkrumah squandered an opportunity to utilize political capital to connect electrification to infrastructural planning effectively and, in tandem, to provide a social compact. Amid the Akosombo dam's initial status as national symbol of self-sufficiency and promise of industrial development, public ambivalence, subsequent wrangling over dam costs and other pressing concerns reflected a tenuous era when citizens in post-colonial African states struggled to define themselves in relation to their newly found status as sovereign nations. The promise of hydropower ironically yielded little for rural populations in the nationalist period and later in the Fourth Republic, when global warming and uneven rainfall have limited electricity delivery. The role of energy values, which include the use of energy sources, urban planning, target regions, revenue for electricity grids, and how a state defines these aspects, deserves greater attention and certainly informs the political choices that early post-independent leaders faced, as well as future outcomes in electricity provision.

The second chapter established that service delivery of electricity, which took on a public goods aspect, reflected mixed "success" despite numerous advances in the transfer of various functions to district assemblies. Differential benefits of electricity access and the "presumed success" of a 80.51% access rate is a consequence of recentralization and weak district assemblies, whose responsibilities are, in many ways, thwarted by capacity and revenue shortfalls.

In support of the chapter's argument, the "center" or national government remained reluctant to cede political control to local and decentralized vehicles of government. Two contradictions became apparent: the promotion of self-help electrification projects, as evidence of the transformation of access and progressive decentralization, likely created a conflict of interest between central government hegemony in determining district initiatives and in maintaining a locus of rural co-optation.

Most significantly, the chapter illustrated how the transformation of electricity access was not matched by the reported "moderate" district assembly capacity in a rural electrification questionnaire administered to Ministry of Energy officials and other individuals from related institutions. Indeed, the noted dependency syndrome (on the district common fund) and inadequate mechanisms for independent revenue accruals suggest a strong disconnect between questionnaire responses, in which roughly half the respondents rated the capacity of DAs to meet financial and material needs as *moderate*. Even more questionable are the numbers of respondents—some 68% offered high marks for district assembly performance in recognition of self-help and rural electrification schemes. If the observations of a donor partner from the Canadian government are correct, government officials privately view district assemblies as ill equipped to delivery proper services. Notions of successful delivery of electricity are incongruent with ongoing constraints of the weak capacity of local institutions amid the push for decentralized government by western donors and international financial institutions.

Moreover, the questionnaire results discussed in this study offer a contrary perspective, which raises the question of who may be held to account for the transformation of electricity access. The numbers of towns under the National Electrification, Self Help Electrification and Rural Electrification Schemes have been considerable. In fact, the rates of access increased almost ten-fold, from several hundred communities at the turn of the 1990s to several thousand communities just three years ago. The transformation of access is indisputable. However, new alignments between the Ghanaian government, donor states, and international financial institutions have contributed to subsequent efforts of succeeding government to co-opt the rural poor through deliberately interval and targeted provision of electricity.

The third chapter established how the uneven historical development of the country's energy institutions intersected with the politics of the post-1992 period. Notably, the clamor for socioeconomic change and political legitimacy marshaled political will and incentives in pursuit of electricity delivery. The partial adoption and simultaneous circumvention of liberalized, market-oriented power sector reforms, however, informs the transformation of access, which represents a logical political choice for a regime pressed to reinvent itself. Intermittent political upheaval, along with an imbalance between energy production and the use of indigenous energy sources, such as wood and biomass, exacerbated lackluster efforts to power the country fully. Operational and technical problems led to high losses and, ironically, to power sector reforms that were consequently abandoned in favor of incremental changes. In place of reform, the continuation of piecemeal measures and electricity subsidies to economically vulnerable populations virtually ensured that sections of the rural poor could be protected by the low tariffs. Consequently, the limited adoption of market-oriented electric energy policies represents a logical strategy, despite endemic gaps in provision and access for the rural poor. The political consequences of these burdens have, in large part, driven the pursuit of otherwise inimical policies, at least in the view of donor partners and IFIs that helped to bail out the poorly performing energy sector in the country during the 1990s.

The emergence of a new conditionality of external institutional involvement (IFIs and, to a lesser extent, NGOs) described in the fourth chapter demonstrates the constraints of agency for service delivery of electricity in tandem with rural development approaches. As a result of heightened inequities of a resource and amenity that is now ensconced in a tenuous public–private good binary, public goods may redefine electricity access from communities or locales that are on the grid, due to the nature of connectivity, quality, quantity—in essence, "the lights on, lights off" conundrum that periodically generates controversy and discontent to produce a clamor for collective action. The consequences of these developments in the contemporary political period apprise political struggles between national government, donor partners and nongovernmental organizations that wield considerable influence. In some ways, a shifting dynamic of power and struggles over appropriate authority have moved into the realm of service delivery in lieu of *dumsor* in terms of whom to hold responsible. The short-term use of floating barges from countries like Turkey and a number of others speaks of the ongoing struggles to balance short-term fixes with a long-term stratagem that considers the spatial and temporal implications of energy interventions beyond conventional hydrocarbon use—especially as Ghana attempts to distinguish itself as an oil producer that escapes the resource curse other states have fallen victim to. Moving beyond the short-term solutions requires shedding a discretionary, project-by-project institutional culture shaped, in part, by donor funding, but also proclivities for timing and sequencing. One might render this a politics of "disorder", or a political tool that inadvertently reinforced disjointed suboptimal approaches to rural development and amenities like electricity, while inadvertently limiting the capacity and autonomy of decentralized institutions or district assemblies. As the chapter articulates, a weak district assembly system provided a rationalization for what some deem as the growing centralization of various departmental functions, which, in turn, facilitates political co-optation of the rural poor. My research also revealed that the actions of past and present governments to satisfy private rural interests via rural development projects worked to reinforce political instrumentalism, whereby a system of spoils via electrification projects was indispensable for maintaining rural political support. Numerous newspaper headlines indicated the emergence of rural preference and, indeed, a political business cycle that began in 1992.

Key factors explain the relationship between weak public service delivery and a resultant emergence of conditionality or "reform ownership". Although decentralized institutions, such as subnational units (Metropolitan, Municipal, and District Assemblies) are noted for self-reliant, self-sufficient norms that ostensibly encourage a participatory locus, and articulation of political preferences by rural constituents, the reconstitution of public–private domains in rural development limited pressure from constituents for development interventions squarely in their interests. Increasingly acute electricity shortages over the past two years, however, have brought into sharper focus the politics of discontent by Ghanaians from all walks of life. Given an urban preference that permeated much of the post-independence period, except for the 1980s, it is little wonder that favorable agricultural policies, which aimed to secure the support of agriculturalists in the mid-1980s, along with public goods provision of electricity in the 1990s had rural voters uttering the slogan "no electricity no power (political)."

The argument, contained in the sixth chapter, for viewing electricity provision as a public good that correlates with regional differentiation and a "numbers game" offers important insights for how high rates of access could demonstrate both success and disparities. Similarly, the inability of Nigeria and South Africa to balance short-term objectives with long-term energy-related development is symbiotic of path-dependent institutional as well as electricity woes reflected across sub-Saharan Africa. With the forecast that hundreds of millions of Africans will be mired in energy poverty amid heightened demand, regional integrative efforts through the African Union, a deliberative and intercontinental body of 54 states, is perhaps the continent's best hope for enhancing regional power pool instruments to deliver equitable electricity in the twenty-first century.

It is widely recognized that a confluence of factors contributed to substantial gaps in access to electricity for the poor, including, as some have attributed to the "subdued role of the would-be recipients". Critically, theorization has aimed to uncover the nature of the political transfer of power, authority, resources and responsibilities from national level to local level actors (decentralization). Service delivery, as a new ground for capital accumulation under the guise of reinvigorating energy infrastructure, is a microcosm of development interventions gone wrong that warrant further theorization and empirical perspectives than are currently available. In the wake of African civil society and leaders who sought new governance strategies in the tumultuous period of the 1970s and 1980s (Ndegwa, 2002), among the goals were democratization, social and economic development, and stabilization of African states (Conerelye, Easton, and Smoke, 2010). Chronic problems of governance, such as corruption, inability to deliver services at local levels, and inadequate infrastructure (Dickovich & Wunsch, 2014), informed these challenges. An inability to tackle inadequate accountability mechanisms and structures (Hiskey, 2010) and the ways they short-circuit the relationship in democracies between citizens as "principals" and government officials as their "agents" (Dickovich & Wunsch, 2014) is worth noting. Although the problem of moral hazard is ambiguous for service delivery under political decentralization, rural preference is arguably connected to endemic patronage in the country's major political parties and to the persistent problems of service delivery: in terms of roads, water, sanitation, and electricity.

Mancur Olson's observation that only a small number of people will have the incentive to pay for the costs to provide these goods, which are enjoyed by everyone, is precisely the sort of challenge faced by Ghanaians, where it is widely reported that few customers are willing to pay for intermittent service.[1] In an age of quasi-public–private goods provision, the problems of mobilizing resources to pay for utility service may explain the weak capacity of district assemblies, of which regional co-ordination institutions (RCIs) are a key component. Indeed, as Dickovich and Wunsch note, effective local governments (or subnational units) will be absent until communities can be persuaded to believe that these institutions will be accountable to them and are therefore willing to pay for the costs to sustain them.[2]

Since the post-independence period, the persistence of routines and the inadvertent "lock in" of political choices constrains institutional change in much of the continent. As a path-dependent mechanism, the inability to usher in sweeping change and thus disrupt continuity in norms, political values and processes is a critical contribution of historic institutional perspectives. Although democracy has passed the threshold for its consolidation in African states with several peaceful transfers of power since 2000, it is still a fairly nascent one by western standards. Newer democracies, as is well known, confront daunting challenges in meeting the political preferences of electorates. In the developing world, they must also meet the expectations of external actors (donors partners and governments), and international financial institutions, placing them at a further disadvantage, notwithstanding the constraints for sovereignty.

Further Contributions

This study makes important empirical insights that illuminate the twin phenomena of advances and drawbacks of public service provision of electricity in Ghana. Successful service delivery of public goods like electricity in ethnically diverse and democratizing states is not possible without co-optation and patronage. At first glance, the merits of privatization and market-oriented policies that offer domestic consumers of electricity a wider pool of independent power producers, affordable rates, and more efficient delivery appear incontrovertible. However, the promotion of policies that invite political suicide and reinforce endemic patronage is counterproductive. The failure to allow for, or create, institutional mechanisms that mitigate these circumstances accounts for the *partial* nature of electricity sector reforms in developing sub-Saharan states. The case study of Ghana illustrates that, while the benefits of electricity access are differential and uneven, the partial implementation of power sector reforms is a logical and optimal course of action for a state that must navigate the tenuous terrain of public/private spaces in service delivery, national policy and under a neo-liberal agenda or framework. This study, it is hoped, illuminates the ways in which natural resource management, citizen engagement, and the new "conditionalities" implicit in electric power sector paradigms have structured the public–private domain of domestic political authority and challenged assumptions about a seemingly inconspicuous component of economic development. By charting the contradictions of "success" and a continued electricity divide in what many recognize as a model state in sub-Saharan Africa, this study demonstrates how the vagaries of power sector reforms, political decentralization, external donor and IFI authority, as trustees of the neo-liberal agenda, continue to configure an important index of rural life and agency. These developments are significant because they reflect the indomitable foray of neo-liberal and, in many ways, illiberal reach into the lives of the rural poor, who remain marginalized, despite the political gains of empowerment, and more responsive local and national representation under decentralized institutions.

Moreover, because of its importance as a key public service, governments of LDCs have often kept energy tariffs unrealistically low for political reasons.[3] As a result, Ghana has achieved a laudable rate of electrification, but the extent to which the rural poor have benefitted, when measured against various social indicators, demonstrates ambiguous outcomes in terms of pricing, affordability and other development components or linkages that boost their livelihoods.

Perhaps significantly, the relative absence of ethnicity in structuring public service delivery is arguably connected to the fiscal constraints of subnational governments across all regions, which appear to have rendered electricity provision as a cross-cutting issue. This may explain not only why urban–rural cleavages are not as heightened as we might expect, but also the general complaints in Ghanaian newspapers and across society.

Participation, Empowerment and Collective Action

Governments will act in the public interest only if there are pressure groups behind the call for action.[4] Which factors explain the lack of agency in demanding equitable public service delivery since the dawn of the Fourth Republic by the rural poor, who comprise the bulk of the country's population?

Given the opposition to Rawlings' policies in the 1980s and a wave of popular protest movements that swept the globe, including Ghana, the muted response of rural classes since this period is surprising.

While Ghana can boast of a rich culture of resistance and indigenous civil society groups, resistance to political co-optation, particularly during political business cycles (Ghana International Economic Association interview) and collective action, has been relatively absent since the 1990s. But from the late nineteenth century, the country produced various indigenous civil society groups that exerted considerable political influence over the course of the twentieth century. During the 1980s, patterns of resistance to adjustment policies were visible and, in 1990, pressures for democratization from groups like the Movement for Freedom and Justice (MFJ), the Trades Union Congress—a powerful group—and other professional and church groups highlighted the capacity for group interests/mobilization.

On the other hand, a plethora of nongovernmental organizations that operate in Ghana frequently encourage self-reliance and a participatory locus in the communities they assist. To a considerable extent, their activities invoke the themes of participation and decentralization. However, what does this really mean in the context of outcomes for public service delivery, and how can the voices of the mobilized poor effect change, particularly where their preferences are concerned?

The Efficacy of Power Sector Reforms: A Dream Deferred?

Prevailing wisdom under neo-liberal power sector reforms holds that the injection of private capital should rehabilitate existing utilities and create a thriving electric energy sector. These policies, for instance, represented a broader political framework of reform during the 1980s and 1990s that expanded the role of private corporations and involved a renegotiation of the role of the state in economic activity. Not only are the benefits of full privatization likely to produce further inequities, but they can also debilitate access for the poor. If the "social compact" implicit in lifeline tariff policies, which make electrification possible for the rural poor possible, shifts from the state to markets in Ghana, the future role of government under such circumstances will be critical. Even though regional power-sharing arrangements aim to address this possibility, it is unclear that the rural poor would benefit.

Moreover, as countries like Ghana move closer to expanding independent electricity generation, outcomes for the rural poor will be significant. How equity in pricing and quality of access are approached in rural areas where private providers will ostensibly operate is anyone's guess. As it stands, affordability and pricing equity are beyond the concerns of electricity utilities. While hardly new, the main function of these authorities would be to act on behalf of the government in planning, organizing and financing rural electrification programs. Though laudable, it would severely undercut and undermine the role of members of parliament and their political leverage. While Ghana has mostly managed to escape electric energy conundrums facing countries like Nigeria, it still faces a number of potential pitfalls that raise further questions about the future role of the state in public and private utility production and public service delivery.

An important observation from one interview revealed that rural electrification has enhanced community participation, because of "the extent to which communities themselves have to contribute in terms of procurement of low-tension poles—even when they cannot afford it—but it is not a pro-poor programme."[5] In the economically disadvantaged north, for instance, far more communities could be connected in areas like Tamale, a metropolitan area where gross disparities remain.

If a pro-reformist argument is valid, the existence of more efficient and profitable electricity and mining sectors in developing countries should lead to improved national welfare and provide benefits to impoverished communities. Yet, the extension of privatization and market-oriented pricing policies—requisites of neo-liberal norms—have produced questionable outcomes. While state-owned utilities are partially unbundled in some African countries, including Ghana, ownership and management largely remain under state control—and understandably so.

In the process of inculcating neo-liberal reforms that minimize government involvement and privatize or devolve certain functions to local institutions, weak capacity or poorly functioning markets will likely produce pressures to redefine certain processes and goods in a "social justice lens" and cause developing states to undertake measures contrary to neo-liberal expectations. This is why electricity provision has emerged as a flashpoint for national government and for the bulk of Ghana's rural poor.

The inability to cushion vulnerable populations, amid uneven terms of trade for the small producer or enterprise, portends negative outcomes for the rural populace in Ghana and further marginalization. While markets can at least marginally lift all boats, they can also sink them, and their partial integration amidst weak institutions and economic instruments can create additional problems (Wolf, 2006). Though Ghana has resisted "blanket acceptance" of power sector reform, partial market-oriented power sector reforms are still insufficiently understood, in no small part due to gaps in data. Easterling's (2014) exploration of the ways that states navigate a new medium of power through infrastructure is a compelling reminder of the pitfalls of what he terms "extrastatecraft" by private actors.[6] Current power arrangements, including regional power pools, offer the potential to mitigate risks associated with private power production, and yet few details have emerged about the nature of these groupings. Given that an impending boom of private power producers may transform the electric energy sector, with no guarantees that service quality will necessarily improve in rural areas, regional efforts are all the more critical. However, if rural political mobilization emerges, public service amenity provision may be redefined. Such a development would speed up rates of electrification, thus enabling the country to reach its target rate ahead of a scheduled date of 2020.

With these challenges in mind, it is critical that the MOE and the EC consider new perspectives to weigh the extent of market-oriented reforms of Ghana's power sector along with the spillover effects, and backward and forward linkages for rural development. The inequities of infrastructural investments also represent an important component and are a contributing factor, along with a deficit in decision-making. As more countries in sub-Saharan Africa look to integrate their economies and power sectors via electric energy networks (i.e., the West African Power Pool and Southern African Power Pool), in tandem with donor suggestions, the potential consequences of what MacDonald calls "electric capitalism" are grave. Though power sector reforms are not unique and are part of a global shift towards privatization and globalization, the pivotal importance of the electricity sector as a driver of the economy makes these developments particularly critical.[7] On another note, politician promises of access and delivery only serve to deepen the perception that governments have the responsibility to cover this amenity in full. As a result, Ghanaians are increasingly questioning the logic of paying for electricity. Indeed, the former mayor of Accra explained to me that poor zoning laws make sabotage relatively easy. Two engineers for the NES noted that, in some areas, it was common for parts of a house to have electricity while other rooms did not. Frequent reports of partial access to electricity in one half of a neighborhood, even in urban spaces, suggest that this problem is endemic and not simply a few isolated incidents. Though public service delivery is ostensibly a hallmark of decentralization, uneven benefits, despite the transformation of access, mean that Ghana will remain embedded in a perpetual dance of interventionism and disengagement. How rural people resist the "lights on, lights out" scenario and how governments navigate the tenuous terrain of neo-liberal-oriented governance will most certainly inform the loss of authority under these arrangements. But the need to strike bargains with the rural poor as a broad section of Ghanaian society under a decentralized state is sure to determine the tapestry of Ghanaian politics and role of the state in public service delivery for years to come.

The collective futures of Africans across sub-Saharan Africa rests not on their ability to attract investment from abroad or harness externally determined growth, but on their resolve to redirect new spaces of capital accumulation, touted under the guise of infrastructural development that includes energy provision, and top-down governance to co-operative arrangements from below. Participatory movements need not end with the outcry inspired by *dumsor* or the clamor for change by ordinary Ghanaians during electricity crises, but will hopefully coalesce to produce greater engagement by rural constituents across Ghana and beyond it.

Notes

1. See James T. Dickovick, and James S. Wunsch, eds., *Decentralization in Africa: The Paradox of State Strength* (Lynne Rienner Publishers, Incorporated, 2014).
2. James T. Dickovick and James S. Wunsch, eds., *Decentralization in Africa: The Paradox of State Strength* (Lynne Rienner Publishers, Incorporated, 2014), 8.
3. See A. Gabrielle, "Policy Alternatives in Reforming Energy Utilities in Energy Utilities in Developing Countries," *Energy Policy* 32, no. 11 (2004): 1319–37.
4. See Tony Killick, *A Reaction Too Far: Economic Theory and the Role of the State in Developing Countries* (London: Overseas Development Institute, 1989).
5. Anonymous, personal communication, 2009.
6. Keller Easterling, *Extrastatecraft: The Power of Infrastructure Space* (Verso Books, 2014).
7. Wamukonya, 2003, 1279.

Index[1]

0-9, AND SYMBOLS

A

B

[1] Note: Page number followed by "n" refers to notes.

N. Sackeyfio, *Energy Politics and Rural Development in Sub-Saharan Africa*, https://doi.org/10.1007/978-3-319-60122-9

Kolibri 360 GmbH
Ferdinand-Jühlke-Straße 7
99095 Erfurt, Deutschland
produktsicherheit@kolibri360.de